The Stalin Revolution

PROBLEMS IN
EUROPEAN CIVILIZATION

Under the editorial direction of
John Ratté
Amherst College

The Stalin Revolution

Foundations of Soviet Totalitarianism

Second Edition

Edited and with an introduction by

Robert V. Daniels
University of Vermont

D. C. HEATH AND COMPANY
Lexington, Massachusetts Toronto London

CONTENTS

INTRODUCTION   vii
CONFLICT OF OPINION   xvii

I   THE SETTING

Isaac Deutscher
THE LEADER AND THE PARTY   3

Alexander Erlich
THE PROBLEM OF INDUSTRIAL DEVELOPMENT   14

Robert V. Daniels
THE STRUGGLE WITH THE RIGHT OPPOSITION   22

Raymond A. Bauer
IDEOLOGICAL REVISION   39

II   THE REVOLUTION FROM ABOVE

Joseph Stalin
THE SOCIALIST DRIVE   49

Alec Nove
ECONOMICS AND PERSONALITY   56

Manya Gordon
THE FATE OF THE WORKERS   68

M. Lewin
COLLECTIVIZATION: THE REASONS   76

Merle Fainsod
COLLECTIVIZATION: THE METHOD   95

III THE COUNTERREVOLUTION FROM ABOVE

David J. Dallin
THE RETURN OF INEQUALITY   109

George S. Counts
THE REPUDIATION OF EXPERIMENT   117

Edward J. Brown
THE MOBILIZATION OF CULTURE   128

Nikolai Bukharin
THE CRACKDOWN ON THE PARTY   138

Nikita S. Khrushchev
THE CULT OF PERSONALITY   145

IV INTERPRETATIONS AND PERSPECTIVES

James H. Billington
THE LEGACY OF RUSSIAN HISTORY   159

Rudolf Schlesinger
THE LOGIC OF THE REVOLUTION   169

Boris N. Ponomaryov
FULFILLING THE LENINIST PLAN   178

Leon Trotsky
SOVIET BONAPARTISM   189

Carl J. Friedrich and Zbigniew K. Brzezinski
THE MODEL OF TOTALITARIANISM   198

Roy A. Medvedev
THE SOCIAL BASIS OF STALINISM   213

SUGGESTIONS FOR FURTHER READING   230

INTRODUCTION

The "Stalin Revolution" refers to those years in the history of Soviet Russia in the late 1920s and 1930s when Joseph Stalin, with the iron hand of his newly established dictatorship, imposed upon the country the essential forms of economic, social, and cultural organization which have characterized Soviet Communism ever since. As much as the Revolution of 1917, the Stalin Revolution must be appreciated by anyone who hopes to understand the Soviet Union, no matter whether he is working in the framework of a special discipline of social science—political science, economics, or sociology—or whether he proceeds from a general historical or cultural standpoint. As the formative era for one of the world's great powers, the Stalin Revolution ranks as one of the most important phenomena of modern times.

The present collection of readings is intended first of all to provide a historical case study of this momentous event. Furthermore, there are problems in studying the Soviet Union in general and the Stalin Revolution in particular that draw the student quickly and deeply into exciting and controversial issues of historical opinion and judgment. For this reason the Stalin Revolution is a good topic for learning how to cope with the eternal historical problems of interpretation, bias, and conflict.

It goes without saying that any inquiry relating to the revolutionary movement of Communism, as with any of the truly dramatic events and conflicts in history, inevitably arouses powerful feelings. The student will find strong emotions not only in the material he reads, but in himself as he reads it. This reaction is natural, although it cannot go uncontrolled, for it is death to serious history if feeling gets the upper hand over explanation.

Historical explanation requires the investigator to look at human affairs with honest detachment, a quality that is often lacking in discussions of Communism, even among experts. History is above all the recognition of change in human affairs—the realization that changing or unforeseen circumstances may put people, their ideas, their actions in a very different context and alter the significance of all that is said or done. This is true of the Soviet Union no less than the rest of the world, contrary to the too frequent assumption that the basic institutions, practices, and aims of the Communist regime were fixed by the Revolution of 1917.

Since 1929 citizens of Soviet Russia have had little opportunity to discuss the meaning of changes in their own revolution. Outsiders have less excuse for ignoring the vast historical developments which have gone on within the Soviet system, and the potential for further change as well. For the historian, the challenge is not just to relate himself to a movement, pro or con, but to penetrate the history of that movement and learn where, why, and how historical changes, for better or worse, have been going on in the movement itself.

There is no lack of historical study of the Soviet Union by serious scholars in the West, whether they are specialists in one of the areas of the social sciences or humanities, or historians concerning themselves with the total flow of events in time. From their work, together with the official and unofficial documentary source material which has emanated from the Soviet Union, the student can derive an immensely detailed and fairly reliable picture of Soviet history and Soviet life year by year. What is not immediately clear, however, is the explanation, the cause, the ultimate implication, of the events and changes which students of history observe.

All schools of thought about Soviet history acknowledge the years from 1929 to 1932 as a revolutionary turning point in the development of the Communist system, though they may differ widely in their estimates of the reasons, achievements, and implications of the changes which came about during this period. Stalin's policies—the forced industrialization in the First Five-Year Plan, the elimination of all business and labor freedom, the collectivization of the peasants, the intensification of Communist Party discipline and police measures, the imposition of totalitarian controls on cultural life, and the abandonment of libertarian social experiments, all capped by the trials and purges of 1936–1938, established what are still the basic and enduring features of the Soviet regime.

A central question about the Stalin Revolution is its relation to the Communist revolution of 1917. Was the Stalin Revolution a direct continuation of Lenin's movement, the logical next step? Or was it a break away from the course of 1917, a new historical turning point, even a betrayal of the hopes of the original revolution? The answer to these questions has fundamental implications regarding the nature of Soviet Russia and of the worldwide Communist movement. Has Communism evolved according to plan, in line with the original revolutionary impetus of its founders, or has it in some respects turned onto a new path where practice contradicts theory and where a native dictatorship contradicts the international mission?

Ever since the event, the official Communist view of the Stalin Revolution has presented it as the strict application of Marxist principles. Many Western writers agree, though in the eyes of some this only meant that Russia was driven from bad to worse. Dissident Marxists like Trotsky, on the other hand, have held that Stalin's revolution was a profound betrayal of Communist principles. Other observers have taken the position that Russian circumstances, for better or worse, induced or compelled Stalin to make fundamental changes in the Communist program. No one denies that crucial changes occurred in the Stalin Revolution, but why they occurred, and what they meant for the country's history, are questions that open the door to the most diverse interpretations. Was the Stalin Revolution a fulfillment—good or bad—of the Bolshevik promise of 1917? Or was it a betrayal—cynical or practical—of the aspirations of the October Revolution?

The actual steps of the Stalin Revolution were scarcely anticipated beforehand. The initial revolutionary period of terror, civil strife, and utopian experiment—the so-called era of "War Communism"—had been terminated by Lenin's adoption of the more moderate "New Economic Policy" or "NEP" in 1921. This permitted a money economy, salary differentials, individual farming, private ownership of small business (by the so-called "Nepmen"), and considerable intellectual freedom, all on the premise that the Marxist movement would have to mark time in Russia while it waited for world revolution to come to pass. The Communist Party—ruling as a one-party dictatorship but still enjoying some freedom of controversy within its ranks—fell to disputing over all manner of policy matters, and especially over the question of Russia's future industrial development.

The stakes were raised with Lenin's death in 1924 and the question of succession to the leadership of the party and the government. Leon Trotsky, Gregory Zinoviev, and Nikolai Bukharin, the party theoretician, bid one after another for supremacy. Each in turn was defeated by the man who, as General Secretary since 1922, controlled the keys to power in the Communist Party organization—Joseph Stalin. Trotsky and Zinoviev, after belatedly combining forces, were crushed by Stalin and Bukharin in the party organizations in 1926 and 1927, and at the Fifteenth Party Congress in December 1927, the Trotskyists and Zinovievists were expelled from the Communist Party. Trotsky was exiled to Central Asia in January 1928, and in February 1929 he was deported from the USSR altogether. Meanwhile Stalin turned against the Right Opposition led by Bukharin, Alexei Rykov (Lenin's successor as prime minister), and Mikhail Tomsky (the chief of the trade unions). Stalin easily defeated this group in the fall of 1928, partly by borrowing arguments from the Trotskyists, and by the spring of 1929 he was to all intents and purposes an absolute personal dictator (even though he actually held no government post).

The rise of Stalin is recounted with compelling insight by Isaac Deutscher in his *Stalin: A Political Biography,* from which the first selection in this book is taken. Deutscher combines a Marxist appraisal of the underlying forces in Russian society with a painful awareness of Stalin's personal impact, and raises basic questions concerning both the source and the use of Stalin's power. The student should try to see how Stalin derived his power from the Communist Party organization, and then attack the question: Did this all-powerful dictator really abide by the perspective of Marxian socialism, or did he fundamentally alter the planned course of events in Russia?

Stalin's radical steps of 1929 were closely connected with the frustrating problems of economic backwardness and industrial development which Russia faced in the 1920s. Bitter controversies had been going on among the Communist leaders ever since 1921 over continuing the capitalistic concessions of the New Economic Policy or launching an ambitious governmental program of planned industrialization. These two alternatives—the "Right" policy of Bukharin and the "Left" program of Trotsky and Preobrazhensky—are assessed in the second selection in this book, from *The Soviet Industrialization Debate, 1924–1928,* by Alexander Erlich. Erlich suggests that the difficulties inherent in both the "Left" and "Right" proposals cast considerable doubt on the validity of the Marxian perspective for Russia. Did Stalin's ultimate answer—a violent break in agricultural and industrial policy—nevertheless mean that Marxism was salvaged after all? Or is it more realistic to view it as a unique new program dictated by the problems of Russian backwardness?

Another problem is the manner in which Stalin arrived at the policies of the Stalin Revolution. Was he truly the far-sighted statesman pursuing a long-range plan? Or did day-to-day political questions contribute to his policy decisions? This issue arises in the selection from my own book, *The Conscience of The Revolution: Communist Opposition in Soviet Russia,* where I describe Stalin's struggle with the Right Opposition led by Bukharin. There is reason to question whether policy differences were Stalin's reason for fighting the Bukharin group, or whether the issues were contrived as weapons of political warfare against his rivals in a power struggle.

Following his victory over the Right Opposition, Stalin intensified his dictatorial control over the country through the agencies of the secret police and the Communist Party organization. He made special efforts to impose controls on intellectual life—the writers, artists, scientists, and even Communist theorists. He directed a substantial change in the official Soviet interpretation of Marxism, described in the selection taken from the theoretical introduction to Raymond Bauer's *New Man in Soviet Psychology.* The question raised here is fundamental in understanding the relation between Marxist theory and Soviet policy: Were Stalin and his followers making a genuine effort to clarify the "activist" truth of Marxism, or were they trying to get around the theory where it appeared to balk their determination to overhaul the Russian economy by political command? Was the Stalin Revolution based on a real revival of Marxism or a cynical manipulation of the doctrine?

The two greatest policy innovations of the Stalin Revolution were the collectivization of the peasants and the Five-Year Plan of intensive industrialization. Actually, neither of these programs was original with Stalin—he borrowed them mainly from the Trotskyists, and used them in exaggerated form to discredit the Bukharinists. By the end of 1929 industrialization and collectivization were in full swing, and in his public speeches—typified by the two selections from his *Problems of Leninism,* Stalin was already congratulating himself on the victory of Marxism over Russian backwardness. According to Stalin there was only one alternative—his own—apart from surrender to the forces of capitalism. But as the judgments of such economists as Alec Nove suggest, there is reason to doubt that Stalin's high-speed program was really the most effective path to industrialization.

In his article, "Was Stalin Really Necessary?" Nove undertakes to identify the assumptions and decisions that made Stalin's revolution, his economic and political harshness, and at least some of his cruelties more or less unavoidable. He raises the question whether any determined group of rulers in Russia's economic circumstances could maintain their domestic and international power without resort to some of the methods of Stalinism.

In the course of Stalin's industrial drive, many of the Marxist ideas and practices previously subscribed to by the Soviet authorities were sacrificed in the name of industrial efficiency. This was especially striking in the case of industrial labor, where revolutionary hopes for equality and industrial self-government gave way to bureaucratic power, inequality, and impoverishment of the workers. Part of Stalin's struggle with the Right Opposition involved a fight to remove Bukharin's ally Mikhail Tomsky from the trade union leadership because he wanted the unions to represent the workers in any conflict with the state. This is recounted in the selection from Manya Gordon's history of Russian labor, *Workers Before and After Lenin.* She raises the question of what, after all, the "dictatorship of the proletariat" was supposed to mean for the proletariat itself. Stalin's policies as she describes them caused a dismal deterioration in the proletariat's conditions of working and living. Was this necessary to Stalin's industrial plans, and if so, what was the real objective of the plans?

The initiation of Stalin's forcible collectivization drive, paralleling the First Five-Year Plan, has prompted considerable questioning about the necessity as well as the cost of this radical transformation of the Soviet countryside, and the nature of the decision-making process involved. A major article by Moshe Lewin, reprinted here in abridged form, examines in detail the path by which Stalin arrived at his commitment to collectivize, with conclusions sharply at variance with the assumptions of Professor Nove, not to mention the claims by Stalin himself. The actual impact of collectivization on the peasants is exposed in the selection from Merle Fainsod's *Soviet Rule in Smolensk,* a remarkable book based on captured Soviet documents. Fainsod's material suggests that such ruthlessness was inherent in the Communist Party dictatorship, though it could perhaps be argued that the brutalizing conditions of Russian rural backwardness and old class feuds among the peasants were responsible for carrying local atrocities beyond anything the leadership intended.

What might be termed the secondary effects of Stalin's industrialization and collectivization drive were responses to the problems which the drive revealed or to the opposition which it engendered. It was in these years that Soviet society became fully totalitarian, in the sense of tight party control not only in political affairs but over all aspects of life. Autonomous economic activity came to an end with the nationalization of the small businesses of the "Nepmen," the subordination of the trade unions to the interests of production, and the elimination of individual farming. The basic social policies of the government—up to then a mixture of utopianism tempered by expediency—were deliberately revised in a conservative and disciplinarian direction. In the official view, these changes were intended to eliminate "petty-bourgeois" notions of equality and individual freedom. The sociological appraisal by David J. Dallin, contained in the selection from *The Real Soviet Russia,* suggests a contrary appraisal: to what extent did Stalin's acceptance of bureaucratic organization and inequality represent a permanent adjustment away from the revolution and toward an implicit conservatism?

Similar shifts of policy can be discerned in other fields—in Soviet education, for example, as George S. Counts maintains in the selection from *The Challenge of Soviet Education.* Counts describes the atmosphere of "progressive" educational experimentation in Russia in the 1920s, and the abrupt rejection of such experiments when Stalin's industrialization program put a premium on mass training and sheer literacy. Again, the question is whether Stalin was finally getting Soviet Russia on the correct Marxist track, or whether the requirements of political survival in industrial society compelled him to abandon the revolutionary ideal.

Most fields of intellectual life felt the heavy hand of tightened Communist Party control during the Stalin Revolution. Party dictation was particularly severe in the field of literature, as is depicted in the passages from *The Proletarian Episode in Russian Literature* by Edward Brown. The controls on literature, like other aspects of Stalin's policy, raise the question whether Stalin's intensification of the Communist dictatorship was not so great in degree as to make it different in kind as well. A particular issue in the case of literature is whether the ruling Averbakh group of the First Five-Year Plan period were purged because they resisted Stalin's crude Marxist demands, or because they themselves were too doctrinaire to adjust their notions of "proletarian literature" to the propaganda requirements of the Stalin Revolution.

The harshness of Stalin's policies was not accepted by his subordinates without dissent. Although Bukharin's Right Opposition had been defeated by 1929, similar objections to Stalin's violent methods were widespread within the Communist Party, and Bukharin and his friends remained at liberty with minor government jobs. The hopes of the anti-Stalinists rested with the Leningrad party secretary, Sergei Kirov, who appeared to have some success in 1933 and 1934 in promoting a relaxation in some of Stalin's policies. Stalin, however, was preparing to destroy all who stood in his way. He was probably responsible for the assassination of Kirov in December 1934. The Great Purge of 1936–1938 soon followed. In 1936, when his own days were numbered, Bukharin gave the outside world an account of the intrigues in the Soviet leadership and the old Communist's sense of betrayal at Stalin's hands. Excerpts appear here from the edition published anonymously in New York, the *Letter of an Old Bolshevik*. They reveal to the reader the sense of total disillusionment—whether tragic awakening or sour grapes—felt by a Communist has-been, as he viewed the aftermath of the Stalin Revolution. Historically the revelations about Stalin and the purges by First Secretary Khrushchev in 1956 came as an anti-climax, but excerpts from Khrushchev's secret speech are included here to illustrate the latter-day Soviet attempt to blame Stalin's personality for the misfortunes of his era.

The final section of this book is directed at broader evaluations and explanations of the phenomenon of Stalinism. The selection by James Billington from *The Icon and the Axe* aims to show Stalin as a consistent product of Russian tradition (even though his native nationality was Georgian). Rudolf Schlesinger, in *The Spirit of Post-War Russia,* combines a similar recognition of the Russian environment with a Marxist view of the requirements of the revolution, and proceeds to an apology for Stalin a great deal more frank than Stalin himself would admit.

Thanks to the control which the party exercised over all media of communication, it was possible for Stalin to describe every aspect of his revolution as the necessary and proper development of Marxism-Leninism and the dictatorship of the proletariat. This position is still held by the official Communist historians, including Boris Ponomayov, the chief editor of the official *History of the Communist Party of the Soviet Union.* As the selection from this volume shows, Stalin's personal role was minimized to conform with de-Stalinization, but the Communist Party got credit for faithfully implementing the Marxist ideal of socialist industry and collective agriculture. Bearing in mind that this is an official text for an audience that cannot compare it with other sources, the reader might ask himself what distortions had to be introduced to sustain the picture of Soviet history demanded by the party authorities. Does it suggest that Stalin has really been repudiated?

Not surprisingly, Stalin's principal rival, Leon Trotsky, was less hesitant to repudiate him. In the selections from *The Revolution Betrayed,* Trotsky endeavors to explain Stalin's perversion of the revolution in terms of a Marxist analysis, equating him with the dictatorships of the two Bonapartes in France. This approach is broadened in the work of Carl Friedrich and Zbigniew Brzezinski in their *Totalitarian Dictatorship and Autocracy.* The excerpts from this work raise fundamental questions about the similarity or dissimilarity of Stalinist Communism on the one hand and the Fascist and Nazi dictatorships on the other.

The concluding selection in this book represents an attempt by one of the most articulate of present-day Soviet dissenters to explain the anguishing experience his generation went through at the hands of Stalin. The excerpts from *Let History Judge* by Roy Medvedev reveal how far a critical mind, using only internally available sources, has been able to progress toward an understanding of the issues that occupy the whole of the present volume.

An overall review of the materials on the Stalin Revolution cannot fail to bring some profound problems into focus. The Stalin Revolution was an unprecedented event, calling for some particular explanation in terms of the individual, the political institutions, the economic circumstances, and the national experience. As an aspect of the history of Communism, the Stalin Revolution requires an appraisal of the truth and relevance of Marxist theory, and of the relation between theory and actual Communist behavior. Finally, outside the Communist frame of reference altogether, the reader may wish to make his own informed moral judgments about the good or evil of the Stalin Revolution, or about its necessity and its achievements. Was the Stalin Revolution in some way justified, whether from the standpoint of theoretical ideals, national power, or everyday progress, or was it an unredeemed historic crime?

Conflict of Opinion

The root difference between Stalinism and the traditional socialist outlook lay in their respective attitudes towards the role of force in the transformation of society.

ISAAC DEUTSCHER

Stalin . . . was determined to maneuver those who held to the old official policy into a position where they appeared to be deviators.

ROBERT V. DANIELS

By force of circumstances, the least theoretically minded of Bolshevik leaders seems to have become the sponsor of one of the most sophisticated and possibly the most sophistic of theories.

RAYMOND A. BAUER

Trotskyism's Menshevik "conception" that the working class is incapable of leading the great bulk of the peasantry in the cause of socialist construction is collapsing and being smashed to atoms.

JOSEPH V. STALIN

The whole-hog Stalin . . . was not necessary but the possibility of a Stalin was a necessary consequence of the effort of a minority group to keep power and to carry out a vast social-economic revolution in a very short time.

ALEC NOVE

Stalin's attitude towards labor was precisely the same as that of the early Russian capitalists towards the erstwhile serfs.

MANYA GORDON

While it is agreed that the process of industrialization was bound to involve sweeping changes in the countryside, it is, in our view, wrong to suppose that these changes could not have been effected otherwise than by collectivization as Russia experienced it.

MOSHE LEWIN

The Soviet leaders . . . became painfully aware of the general backwardness of Russia. . . . As a consequence, a new Soviet school emerged . . . which resembled in many respects the school of old Russia and would have been labeled counterrevolutionary in the earlier period, but one which in fact expresses the basic philosophy of Bolshevism far more faithfully than its predecessor.

GEORGE S. COUNTS

Stalin reasoned . . . : If the old Bolsheviks, the group constituting today the ruling caste in the country, are unfit to perform this function,
it is necessary to remove them from their posts, to create *a new ruling
caste.*

NIKOLAI BUKHARIN

The foundations of socialism had been laid in the Soviet Union. . . .
The question: "Who will beat whom?," posed by Lenin, had been settled
in favor of socialism. . . . This was an *epoch-making* victory of the
working class, working peasantry and intelligentsia of the USSR, won
under the leadership of the Communist Party.

BORIS N. PONOMARYOV ET AL.

The Stalin regime, rising above a politically atomized society, resting
upon a police and officers' corps, and allowing of no control whatever,
is obviously a variation of Bonapartism. . . .

LEON TROTSKY

Fascist and Communist dictatorships are basically alike, or at any
rate more nearly like each other than like any other system of government. . . .

CARL J. FRIEDRICH AND ZBIGNIEW BRZEZINSKI

Stalin . . . in many respects . . . can properly be called a counterrevolutionary. But he also continued to rely on the masses, which was
the chief peculiarity of Stalin's actions and the ultimate determinant
of his success.

ROY MEDVEDEV

I THE SETTING

Isaac Deutscher

THE LEADER AND THE PARTY

The lever for setting the Stalin Revolution in motion was the personal dicta-
torship which Joseph Stalin had established over the Russian Communist
Party. One of the best-known accounts of Stalin's rise to power is the work
of Isaac Deutscher (1907–1967), a native of Poland and a one-time Commu-
nist and Trotskyist, who later made his home in England and devoted him-
self to historical and political writing on the Soviet Union. Deutscher tries
to show how Stalin combined organizational loyalty and shrewd maneuver
to clear the path for his own supreme power.

Few important developments in history are so inconspicuous and
seem so inconsequential to their contemporaries as did the amazing
accumulation of power in the hands of Stalin, which took place while
Lenin was still alive. Two years after the end of the civil war Russian society already lived under Stalin's virtual rule, without being
aware of the ruler's name. More strangely still, he was voted and
moved into all his positions of power by his rivals. There was to be
an abundance of somber drama in his later fight against these rivals.
But the fight began only after he had firmly gripped all the levers of
power and after his opponents, awakening to his role, had tried to
move him from his dominant position. But then they found him im-
movable. . . .

. . . The day-to-day management of the party belonged to Stalin.
The Politbureau discussed high policy. Another body, which was,
like the Politbureau, elected by the Central Committee, the Organization Bureau (Orgbureau), was in charge of the party's personnel,
which it was free to call up, direct to work, and distribute throughout
the army and the civil service according to the demands of the civil
war. From the beginning of 1919 Stalin was the only permanent
liaison officer between the Politbureau and the Orgbureau. He ensured the unity of policy and organization; that is, he marshalled
the forces of the party according to the Politbureau's directives. Like
none of his colleagues, he was immersed in the party's daily drudg-
ery and in all its kitchen cabals.

From *Stalin: A Political Biography* by Isaac Deutscher, pp. 228, 231–233, 235–236,
256–257, 273–275, 294–296, 314–317, 343–344. Copyright 1949 by Oxford University
Press. Reprinted by permission.

At this stage his power was already formidable. Still more was to accrue to him from his appointment, on 3 April 1922, to the post of General Secretary of the Central Committee. The Eleventh Congress of the party had just elected a new and enlarged Central Committee and again modified the statutes. The leading bodies of the party were now top-heavy; and a new office, that of the General Secretary, was created, which was to coordinate the work of their many growing and overlapping branches. It was on that occasion, Trotsky alleges, that Lenin aired, in the inner circle of his associates, his misgivings about Stalin's candidature: "This cook can only serve peppery dishes." But his doubts were, at any rate, not grave; and he himself in the end sponsored the candidature of the "cook." Molotov and Kuibyshev were appointed Stalin's assistants, the former having already been one of the secretaries of the party. The appointment was reported in the Russian press without any ado, as a minor event in the inner life of the party.

Soon afterwards a latent dualism of authority began to develop at the very top of the party. The seven men who now formed the Politbureau (in addition to the previous five,[1] Zinoviev and Tomsky had recently been elected) represented, as it were, the brain and the spirit of Bolshevism. In the offices of the General Secretariat resided the more material power of management and direction. In name the General Secretariat was subordinate to the illustrious and exalted Politbureau. But the dependence of the Politbureau on the secretariat became so great that without that prop the Politbureau looked more and more like a body awkwardly suspended in a void. The secretariat prepared the agenda for each session of the Politbureau. It supplied the documentation on every point under debate. It transmitted the Politbureau's decisions to the lower grades. It was in daily contact with the many thousands of party functionaries in the capital and the provinces. It was responsible for their appointments, promotions, and demotions. It could, up to a point, prejudice the views of the Politbureau on any issue before it came up for debate. It could twist the practical execution of the Politbureau's decisions, according to the tastes of the General Secretary. Similar bodies exist in any governmental machinery but rarely acquire independent

[1] Lenin, Trotsky, Stalin, Kamenev, and Rykov.—Ed.

authority. What usually prevents them from transgressing their terms of reference is some diffusion of power through the whole system of government, effective control over them, and, sometimes, the integrity of officials. The overcentralization of power in the Bolshevik leadership, the lack of effective control, and, last but not least, the personal ambitions of the General Secretary, all made for the extraordinary weight that the General Secretariat began to carry barely a few months after it had been set up. . . .

Stalin was in a sense less dependent on Lenin than were his colleagues; his intellectual needs were more limited than theirs. He was interested in the practical use of the Leninist gadgets, not in the Leninist laboratory of thought. His own behavior was now dictated by the moods, needs, and pressures of the vast political machine that he had come to control. His political philosophy boiled down to securing the dominance of that machine by the handiest and most convenient means. In an avowedly dictatorial regime, repression often is the handiest and most convenient method of action. The Politbureau may have been thrown into disarray by Lenin's disappearance; the General Secretariat was not. On the contrary, since it had no longer to account for what it did to the vigilant and astute supervisor, it acted with greater firmness and self-confidence. . . . The General Secretary knew how to justify each act of repression against malcontent Bolsheviks in the light of the party statutes as they had, on Lenin's initiative and with Trotsky's support, been amended by the Tenth and Eleventh congresses. He was careful to explain every step he made as an inevitable consequence of decisions previously adopted by common consent. He packed the offices with his friends, henchmen, and followers, the men of Baku and Tsaritsyn.[2] Dismissed malcontents complained to the Politbureau, where Trotsky took up their cases. In reply, Stalin referred to the commonly agreed division of responsibilities: the Politbureau was to pass decisions on matters of high policy; the General Secretariat and the Orgbureau were in charge of the party's personnel. The Politbureau was only bored with Trotsky's carping criticisms. . . .

---

[2] A reference to the prerevolutionary Bolshevik organization in the city of Baku, and to the fighting at Tsaritsyn (later Stalingrad, now Volgograd) during the Russian Civil War.—Ed.

To be able to marshal its forces, the personnel department kept solid files with the most detailed records of the party's "key-men." The party had now, after the first purges, about 400,000 ordinary members and about 20,000 officials. So far the personnel department had compiled the records of the upper and medium layers, including 1,300 managers of industry. The investigation, Stalin disclosed, was still on. The files were compiled with special attention to every member's professional skill and specialization, political reliability, and moral bearings. Every blemish in a member's record was duly registered. "It is necessary to study every worker through and through," said Stalin, "in every detail." "Otherwise policy loses sense and becomes meaningless gesticulation." Since the personnel department had to meet or help in meeting any demand for officials, it had spread a network of branches throughout the country. It had the power to order members to change their occupation and place of residence at the shortest notice, to shift from the capital to the wilderness of Siberia or to an embassy abroad, in order to carry out any assignment. An assignment, even an honorable one, might be a pretext for the punishment of a somewhat restive member. Few persons, whatever their merits, could have been quite sure that if their politics displeased the General Secretariat, some *faux pas* committed by them in the past would not now be publicly held out against them. But, so far, this had not become common practice.

The General Secretary was also responsible for appointments of provincial party leaders. He spoke about this with specious sadness. It was time, he told the congress, that provincial organizations elected their secretaries, instead of getting them appointed from above. Unfortunately, the lack of qualified men was so acute that local branches were all the time pestering the General Secretariat to send them people from the center. "It is very difficult to train party leaders. This requires five, ten, or even more years. It is much easier to conquer this or that country with the help of Comrade Budienny's cavalry than to train two or three leaders from the rank and file." He defended the provincial committees that had so often been attacked and ridiculed in the newspapers. He spoke for the whole phalanx of his secretaries; and he excused even their squabbling and intriguing, which had their good as well as their bad sides, because they helped in the crystallization of "coherent nuclei of leaders." In other words, the provincial committees were miniature replicas of the Politbureau with their own little triumvirates and duumvirates and their groups of oppositionists. . . .

. . . It had always been admitted that history might repeat itself; and that a Directory[3] or a single usurper might once again climb to power on the back of the revolution. It was taken for granted that the Russian usurper would, like his French prototype, be a personality possessed of brilliance and legendary fame won in battles. The mask of Bonaparte seemed to fit Trotsky only too well. Indeed, it might have fitted any personality with the exception of Stalin. In this lay part of his strength.

The very thing which under different circumstances would have been a liability in a man aspiring to power, his obscurity, was his important asset. The party had been brought up to distrust "bourgeois individualism" and to strive for collectivism. None of its leaders looked as immune from the former and as expressive of the latter as Stalin. What was striking in the General Secretary was that there was nothing striking about him. His almost impersonal personality seemed to be the ideal vehicle for the anonymous forces of class and party. His bearing seemed of the utmost modesty. He was more accessible to the average official or party man than the other leaders. He studiously cultivated his contacts with the people who in one way or another made and unmade reputations, provincial secretaries, popular satirical writers, and foreign visitors. Himself taciturn, he was unsurpassed at the art of patiently listening to others. Sometimes he would be seen in a corner of a staircase pulling at his pipe and listening immovably, for an hour or two, to an agitated interlocutor and breaking his silence only to ask a few questions. This was one of his qualities that seemed to indicate a lack of any egotism. The interviewer, glad of the opportunity to get his troubles off his chest, rarely reflected on the fact that Stalin had not revealed his mind in the conversation. For Stalin, to quote his secretary, "did not confide his innermost thoughts to anybody. Only very rarely did he share his ideas and impressions with his closest associates. He possessed

[3] Refers to the Directory in revolutionary France from 1795 to 1799, representing a step backward for the revolution.—Ed.

in a high degree the gift for silence, and in this respect he was unique in a country where everybody talked far too much."

His private life, too, was beyond reproach or suspicion. "This passionate politician [says Bazhanov] has no other vices. He loves neither money, nor pleasure, neither sport, nor women. Women, apart from his own wife, do not exist for him." In the middle of the civil war he married for the second time. His wife, Nadezhda Allilu-yeva, the daughter of the workman in whose home Lenin hid in the July days of 1917, was twenty years younger than himself. She had been one of Lenin's secretaries after the revolution and went to Tsaritsyn in 1919. There the love between the commissar and the Communist girl began. Now they had a small lodging in what used to be the servants' quarters in the Kremlin; and Nadezhda Alliluyeva was earnestly studying at a technical college in Moscow. The air of plain-ness and even austerity about the General Secretary's private life commended him to the puritanically minded party, which was just beginning to grow apprehensive at the first signs of corruption and loose life in the Kremlin.

Nor did Stalin at that time impress people as being more intolerant than befitted a Bolshevik leader. He was, as we have seen, less vicious in his attacks on the opposition than the other triumvirs. In his speeches there was usually the tone of a good-natured and sooth-ing, if facile, optimism, which harmonized well with the party's grow-ing complacency. In the Politbureau, when matters of high policy were under debate, he never seemed to impose his views on his colleagues. He carefully followed the course of the debate to see which way the wind was blowing and invariably voted with the major-ity, unless he had assured his majority beforehand. He was therefore always agreeable to the majority. To party audiences he appeared as a man without personal grudge and rancor, as a detached Leninist, a guardian of the doctrine who criticized others only for the sake of the cause. . . .

In 1929, five years after Lenin's death, Soviet Russia embarked upon her second revolution, which was directed solely and exclu-sively by Stalin. In its scope and immediate impact upon the life of some 160 million people the second revolution was even more sweep-ing and radical than the first. It resulted in Russia's rapid industrialization; it compelled more than 100 million peasants to abandon their small, primitive holdings and to set up collective farms; it ruthlessly tore the primeval wooden plow from the hands of the *muzhik* [peasant] and forced him to grasp the wheel of a modern tractor; it drove tens of millions of illiterate people to school and made them learn to read and write; and spiritually it detached European Russia from Europe and brought Asiatic Russia nearer to Europe. The rewards of that revolution were astounding; but so was its cost: the complete loss, by a whole generation, of spiritual and political freedom. It takes a great effort of the imagination to gauge the enormousness and the complexity of that upheaval for which hardly any historical precedent can be found. Even if all allowance is made for the different scales of human affairs in different ages, the greatest reformers in Russian history, Ivan the Terrible and Peter the Great, and the great reformers of other nations too, seem to be dwarfed by the giant form of the General Secretary.

And yet the giant's robe hangs somewhat loosely upon Stalin's figure. There is a baffling disproportion between the magnitude of the second revolution and the stature of its maker, a disproportion which was not noticeable in the revolution of 1917. There the leaders seem to be equal to the great events; here the events seem to reflect their greatness upon the leader. Lenin and Trotsky foresaw their revolution and prepared it many years before it materialized. Their own ideas fertilized the soil of Russia for the harvest of 1917. Not so with Stalin. The ideas of the second revolution were not his. He neither foresaw it nor prepared for it. Yet he, and in a sense he alone, accomplished it. He was at first almost whipped into the vast undertaking by immediate dangers. He started it gropingly, and despite his own fears. Then, carried on by the force of his own doings, he walked the giant's causeway, almost without halt or rest. Behind him were tramping the myriads of weary and bleeding Russian feet, a whole generation in search of socialism in one country. His figure seemed to grow to mythical dimensions. Seen at close quarters, it was still the figure of a man of very ordinary stature and of middling thoughts. Only his fists and feet contrasted with his real stature—they were the fists and the feet of a giant.

. . . Since then Stalin's Communist opponents have repeatedly described him as the leader of an antirevolutionary reaction, while most anti-Communists have seen and still see the haunting specter of communism embodied in his person. Yet, among the Bolshevik leaders of the twenties, he was primarily the man of the golden mean. He instinctively abhorred the extreme viewpoints which then competed for the party's recognition. His peculiar job was to produce the formulas in which the opposed extremes seemed reconciled. To the mass of hesitating members of the party his words sounded like common sense itself. They accepted his leadership in the hope that the party would be reliably steered along the "middle of the road" and that "safety first" would be the guiding principle. It might be said that he appeared as the Baldwin or the Chamberlain,[4] the Harding or the Hoover of Bolshevism, if the mere association of those names with Bolshevism did not sound too incongruous.

It was neither Stalin's fault nor his merit that he never succeeded in sticking to the middle of any road; and that he was constantly compelled to abandon "safety" for the most dangerous of ventures. Revolutions are as a rule intolerant of golden means and "common sense." Those who in a revolution try to tread the middle of the road usually find the earth cleaving under their feet. Stalin was repeatedly compelled to make sudden and inordinately violent jumps now to this now to that extreme of the road. . . .

. . . The defeat of each successive opposition violently narrowed the margins within which the free expression of opinion was possible. The leaders of each opposition could not get for themselves more elbow room than that to which they themselves, in coalition with Stalin, had reduced their adversaries. After each showdown, actions hitherto regarded as unimpeachable were classed as unpardonable. . . . Only specific offenses against discipline, clandestine printings, and unauthorized street demonstrations, offences into which Stalin had provoked his adversaries, could justify reprisals against the opposition in 1927. Less than a year later a whispered conversation between a member of the Politbureau and a repentant leader of the opposition, the conversation between Bukharin and Kamenev, was already a grave offence, for which Bukharin tearfully begged pardon from the Politbureau. The alternative to submission was an ostracism

---

[4] References to the British Conservative prime ministers of the 1920s and 1930s.—Ed.

doubly unbearable; for it was pronounced against the "offender" not by a class enemy but by his associate in the revolution, and it left the "offender" incapable even of crying in the wilderness. . . .

After Stalin had finally removed Trotsky from the Russian scene, he hastened to rout the leaders of the right wing. Rykov was deposed from the premiership of the Soviet government, in which he had succeeded Lenin. Tomsky was ousted from the leadership of the trade unions, on the ground that he had used his influence to turn the unions against industrialization. Bukharin was dismissed from the leadership of the Communist International, where he had replaced Zinoviev, as well as from the Politbureau. Before the year 1929 was out, Bukharin, Rykov, and Tomsky repudiated their own views and thus bought a few years of spurious breathing space.

Stalin's ascendancy was now complete. The contest for power was at its end. All his rivals had been eliminated. None of the members of the Politbureau would dream of challenging his authority. In the last days of the year Moscow celebrated his fiftieth birthday as if it had been a great historic event. From every corner of Russia tributes were addressed to the Leader. His virtues were praised, immoderately and crudely, by every party secretary in the country. The walls of Moscow were covered with his huge portraits. His statues and busts of all possible sizes filled the squares, the halls of public buildings, and the windows of every shop down to the humblest barber's shop. "Stalin is the Lenin of today," the propagandists shouted themselves hoarse. Some of the older people recalled Lenin's fiftieth birthday. It had been a small and modest occasion, which Lenin reluctantly attended only to remonstrate with his admirers for their growing fondness for pomp and ceremony. The new Stalinist cult was now visibly merging with the old Leninist cult, and overshadowing it. When, on ceremonial occasions, Stalin appeared at the top of the Lenin mausoleum in the Red Square, Lenin's colossal tomb appeared to be only the pedestal for his successor. . . .

It is easy to see how far Stalin drifted away from what had hitherto been the main stream of socialist and Marxist thought. What his socialism had in common with the new society, as it had been imagined by socialists of nearly all shades, was public ownership of the means of production and planning. It differed in the degradation

to which it subjected some sections of the community and also in the recrudescence of glaring social inequalities amid the poverty which the revolution inherited from the past. But the root difference between Stalinism and the traditional socialist outlook lay in their respective attitudes towards the role of force in the transformation of society.

Marxism was, as it were, the illegitimate and rebellious offspring of nineteenth-century liberalism. Bitterly opposed to its parent, it had many a feature in common with it. The prophets of *laisser faire* had deprecated political force, holding that it could play no progressive role in social life. In opposition to liberalism, Marxists stressed those historic instances and situations in which—as in the English and French revolutions, the American War of Independence and the Civil War—force did assist in the progress of nations and classes. But they also held that the limits within which political force could effect changes in the outlook of society were narrow. They held that the fortunes of peoples were shaped primarily by basic economic and social processes; and that, compared with these, force could play only a subordinate role. Much as the Marxist and the Liberal ideals of society differed from one another, both trends shared, in different degrees, the optimism about the future of modern civilization, so characteristic of the nineteenth century. Each of the two trends assumed that the progress of modern society tended more or less spontaneously towards the attainment of its ideal. Marx and Engels expressed their common view in the famous phrase that force is the midwife of every old society pregnant with a new one. The midwife merely helps the baby to leave the mother's womb when the time for that has come. She can do no more. Stalin's view on the role of political force, reflected in his deeds rather than his words, oozes the atmosphere of twentieth-century totalitarianism. Stalin might have paraphrased the old Marxian aphorism: force is no longer the midwife—force is the mother of the new society.

FIGURE 1. Red Square in November 1930—the thirteenth anniversary of the Communist Revolution (*New York Public Library Picture Collection*).

Alexander Erlich

THE PROBLEM OF INDUSTRIAL DEVELOPMENT

Alexander Erlich (b. 1912) is professor of economics at Columbia University and a specialist on the history of Soviet economic doctrines. Polish born, he was the son of Henryk Erlich, a noted leader of the Jewish Socialist Bund, executed by the Russians in 1941. Professor Erlich nevertheless writes with remarkable objectivity about the efforts of various Communist schools of thought—Left, Right, and Stalinist Center—to find a successful path to socialism which would surmount the difficulties of the backward Russian environment. He finds in the end that economic realities made the best ideals f the revolution a tragic impossibility.

The years 1924–1928 witnessed a remarkable debate in the Soviet Union. Its major participants were leading Communist theoreticians and eminent nonparty economists; the keenly interested audience included everyone who was politically and intellectually articulate in Soviet society. The debate ranged far and wide from issues concerning the theory of value to day-to-day political minutiae. At its center, overshadowing all the rest, loomed the problem of the appropriate speed and pattern for the prospective economic development of the country. . . .

. . The successes of the NEP carried the Soviet economy beyond the range in which immediate survival was at stake, and enhanced the state's power to influence the course of events not merely by desisting from wrong-headed interference. But the jolts of imbalances and the steadily approaching ceilings for smooth increases indicated clearly that recovery was drawing to a close and that an enlargement of the capacity for growth was necessary. In Soviet parlance, the transition from "restoration" to "reconstruction" was impending. The perspective of protracted isolation within a hostile and much more powerful world, finally, made it imperative for the country to rely in this expansion upon its own resources, to a much greater extent

Reprinted by permission of the author and publishers from Alexander Erlich, *The Soviet Industrialization Debate, 1924–1928* (Cambridge, Mass.: Harvard University Press, 1960), pp. xv, xvii, xx–xxi, 31–32, 34–34, 56–59, 79, 88–89, 164–165, 180–182. Copyright 1960 by the President and Fellows of Harvard College.

than had been true of tsarist Russia, or than had been hoped for in those heady years when the frontiers of the revolution seemed to lie on the Rhine. . . .

. . . The Soviet economic advance since 1928 has been one of the dominant facts of our time: there are few equally monumental truisms one can utter these days. The broad outlines of the pattern which emerged at the very beginning of the process have since then become familiar: a rate of investment set at a level which has few, if any, equals in the development of capitalist economies over a comparably long stretch of time; the overriding priority of producers' goods over consumers' goods in terms of the relative amount and quality of resources allotted to them; the change in terms of trade against agriculture, carried to unusual lengths for a country meeting the bulk of its food requirements from its own production. The results are history. According to the virtually unanimous view of Western students, the expansion of the Soviet industrial capacity has proceeded at a rate which is, by any meaningful standard of comparison, unprecedented. It is equally uncontroversial that this formidable drive, which has propelled the Soviet Union into the position of one of the two superpowers of the world, has entailed not only untold sacrifices in the welfare of the Soviet population but also grave risks for its rulers. Lags in low priority areas have resulted every now and then in major bottlenecks; convulsive shakeups and persistent all-pervading stresses and strains have cut into the efficiency of the huge investment efforts and have weakened the stability of the economy. Indeed, there is every indication that the whole system was more than once on the verge of explosion during its initial years.

What were the alternatives open to the Soviet economy at the end of the twenties? To what degree were Soviet leaders aware of their nature and potentialities? Did the actual course of events follow a design laid down well in advance or was it, to a significant extent, an improvised response to circumstances? These questions are central to the understanding and appraisal of the Soviet experience in accelerated industrialization. . . .

. . . Evgeni A. Preobrazhensky, who had been Bukharin's comrade-in-arms in the latter's Left Communist period . . . , was . . . the chief economic theorist of the renascent Left Opposition, led by Trotsky.

It was not surprising that the challenge to the "ideology of the
restoration period" came from this side. The left-wing Communists
wanted to solve the harrowing problems of a socialist regime in a
backward Russia, faced with advanced capitalist countries, by aiming
at a resumption of all-out revolutionary action in the West and at the
rapid growth of the industrial proletariat at home. The less chance
the first part of the blueprint had in the immediate future, the stronger
was the emphasis put on the second. The time had come, it was
felt, to turn the tables against the "private sector," first of all against
the peasantry which had imposed upon the Soviet regime the retreat
toward the "mixed economy" of the NEP and which was certain to
bring about a full-scale restoration of capitalism unless drastically
reduced in its social and economic weight. The task consisted in
stating the case not in terms of wishful thinking or nostalgic longing
for the "heroic period of the Russian Revolution" but in the language
of present-day realities and necessities. . . .

. . . [As Preobrazhensky saw it,] the impact of revolutionary change
had upset the precarious equilibrium of the Russian economy not
only from the side of supply but also from that of demand. The share
of industrial labor in national income had increased: "Our present
wages are determined to a lesser extent than before the war by the
value of labor power and in the future will be even less determined by
it." Of still greater portent, however, was the transformation in the
status of the peasantry. In tsarist Russia a large portion of the income
originating in peasant agriculture was absorbed by payments to the
government and landlords. In order to get the money for the fulfillment of these obligations, the peasant had to sell a corresponding
part of his produce without buying anything in return. This had a
twofold effect. On the one hand, a relatively large marketable surplus
of agricultural goods was provided; on the other, the claims of the
great majority of the population upon industrial output were reduced
by the sum total of these "forced sales." The amount deducted from
peasant income was undoubtedly respent in the main. This reex-
penditure, however, absorbed a smaller share of domestic output
than a corresponding amount of peasant spending would have done;
a large part of it (together with a sizeable fraction of industrial
profits) went abroad either to service the foreign debt or as payment
for imported luxury consumption goods, while its physical counterpart

was exported. The October Revolution put an end to the old system. Rent payments were wiped out and agricultural taxes amounted in 1924–1925 to less than one-third of the total peasant obligations before the war. The unstabilizing effects of this upheaval were momentous:

> Out of a given amount of the marketable output . . . a much smaller amount than before the war is going for forced sales; this means that the effective demand of the peasantry for industrial commodities and for the products of interpeasant exchange must correspondingly increase. . . . [Consequently] the stabilization of the relation between the total volume of the industrial and of the agricultural marketable output at the level of their prewar proportions implies a drastic disturbance in the equilibrium between the effective demand of the village and the marketable output of the town.

The conclusion was clear—productive capacity had to increase over and above the prewar level in order to catch up with the increased effective demand. The failure to accomplish this would result in a recurrence of the goods famine a few years hence, just as the failure to make sufficient provision for capital maintenance in the past made inevitable the present goods famine. . . .

. . . While the large addition to the existing stock of capital could be expected to have most salutary effects on the supply situation in the future, the investment which was necessary for producing this addition was bound to make things worse for the time being. Preobrazhensky, in fact, said this quite explicitly when he stated that "a discontinuous reconstruction of fixed capital involves a shift of so much means of production toward the production of means of production, which will yield output only after a few years, that thereby the increase of the consumption funds of the society will be stopped." He did not, however, add the inevitable conclusion that the amount of consumption goods per employed worker would decline.

In such a situation an uncontrolled economy could not avoid a wage-price spiral; but neither would the "workers' state" acting in accordance with Preobrazhensky's directives be able to keep the wages down in order to prevent an inflation. The shift of the main burden of the sacrifice to the nonindustrial population was the remaining alternative. This was what Preobrazhensky actually proposed to do by his policy of "primitive socialist accumulation." But it was he who had insisted that the increase in the peasants' ability to spend out of given income was the strongest single stimulant to "nonautonomous" investment; more importantly, no one stated more forcefully than he the ever-present danger of a peasants' strike in view of the lag in industrial supply. Such a danger could materialize during the "discontinuous reconstruction" when peasants were expected to give up more of their produce than before, while not getting correspondingly more in return (or more likely getting less). Preobrazhensky's celebrated directive: "Take from the petty bourgeois producers more than capitalism did [but] out of a [proportionally] still larger income," could hardly hold at this particular juncture. The "petty bourgeois producers" could respond to the attempt at an increased squeeze by withdrawing from the market, thus killing the industrial expansion by cutting off the supplies of food and, indirectly, of the foreign capital goods bought from the proceeds of agricultural exports. Or else, by forcing the state to capitulate, they could impose an increase in food prices and let the inflation start from this side. The cure would prove deadlier than the disease; this was, in effect, the point Preobrazhensky's opponents were making.

Preobrazhensky struggled vainly for a way out of this dilemma. . . .
. . . He concluded that

> the sum total of these contradictions shows how strongly our development toward socialism is confronted with the necessity of ending our socialist isolation, not only for political but also for economic reasons, and of leaning for support in the future on the material resources of other socialist countries.

At worst, this amounted to an admission that all attempts to find a solution within the limits of the isolated Soviet economy would be merely squaring the circle. At best, this was a desperate effort to obtain tomorrow's stability at the expense of enormously increased tensions today, without knowing too well how to withstand them.

It was not difficult for Preobrazhensky's opponents to prove that the "superindustrialist" way was leading to an impasse. To show a flaw in his reasoning was quite a different matter. Indeed, the main argument seemed ominously foolproof. The high rate of growth appeared as a vital necessity and at the same time as a threat. Granted the underlying assumptions, it was the case of a choice between mortal sickness and virtually certain death on the operating table.

. . . "Our economy," Bukharin declared, "exists for the consumer, and not the consumer for the economy." He praised this "new economy" which "differs from the old by taking as its guiding principle the needs of the masses and not the profit you are earning on Monday and Tuesday without thinking of what will happen on Thursday and Friday"; and he felt certain that the policy of keeping industrial prices down would force the plant managers to lower costs. At the same time, however, a new note crept into his pronouncements. He recognized that the Soviet economy was now facing a transition from the "period of restoration" to the "period of reconstruction." This assignment whose fulfillment "depends primarily upon our success in acquiring and applying capital . . . for the expansion of the basis of production, for the construction or the laying down of the new enterprises, to a considerable extent on a new technical basis" constituted "the task of greatest difficulty." . . .

. . . Bukharin and Rykov . . . were, no doubt, firmly convinced that the "American way" of combining a high rate of investment with a steady rise of the consumption levels of the urban and agricultural population could be emulated under the very different conditions of the Soviet economy of the twenties. The sum total of the policies outlined above, they felt, would be instrumental in bringing this about. But while the resolutions of the Fifteenth Congress spoke in ringing tones of confidence, their spiritual godfathers did not attempt to hide that the situation was bound to be touch and go for quite a while. True, they continued to insist that "we cannot and we must not choose the path of development at which the tasks of keeping up the highest possible tempo and of maintaining the moving equilibrium of the whole economic system exclude each other." But the significance of this statement was considerably reduced by the frank admission that "there is no guaranty" against "temporary imbalance" as long as there are no adequate reserves of raw materials, foodstuffs, finished goods, gold, etc. The building-up of such safety margins would be possible only by slowing down the tempo of capital construction—a policy which was now ruled out. It was therefore only logical for Rykov to declare that "if we want to develop heavy industry out of our own resources, and we must do it, we will have to retrench ourselves somewhat for a time." The "temporary excesses of demand over supply" were now accepted as well-nigh inevitable. The crucial task was to prevent them from reaching a level of "general economic crisis." The leaders of the Trotskyite Opposition would find here little to disagree with. True, the left wingers were still setting the "tempos" higher and were ready to rely in the main on the drastic levies imposed on the peasantry while the Bukharin-Rykov group preferred the methods of "repressed inflation." But these differences, important as they were, could not alter the fundamental fact that the former "harmonists" and the proponents of "primitive socialist accumulation" were by now solidly on the horns of the same dilemma, and none of them found this a comfortable position.

. . . Toward the end of the great debate the two main groups were much closer to each other than at its beginning: Bukharin and his followers admitted explicitly the inevitability of discontinuous growth, while Preobrazhensky became increasingly outspoken about the risks involved in such policy. It would not be unnatural to expect, under such circumstances, an attempt to work toward some middle ground.

Actual developments did not follow this path. The resolutions on economic policy adopted by the Fifteenth Congress of the CPSU could indeed be interpreted as a step toward a synthesis between the older right-wing and left-wing conceptions. However, this change of attitude had its corollary not in a rapprochement between the majority and the Opposition, but in the crushing of the latter by force. All the leaders of the left wing, including Trotsky and Preobrazhensky, were expelled from the party. But this turn of events, however stunning, paled into insignificance in comparison with what came later. The "synthesis" went overboard within less than two years, and the new policy line which superseded it swung to extremes which the most ardent "superindustrializers" of the suppressed left wing had never imagined. The First Five Year Plan proclaimed as its objective an expansion in investment goods-output to the level which would make the fixed capital of the economy double within five years—a rate of growth unparalleled in history. And while according to the professed intentions this expansion was to be accompanied by a marked increase in per capita consumption, in the process of actual fulfillment the first part of the program was pushed through unwaveringly at the expense of the second. . . .

. . . The rapid-fire industrialization and the sweeping collectivization were not merely devices of economic policy, but means of extending the direct control of the totalitarian state over the largest possible number within the shortest time. Yet the way in which this extension was brought about had, from the viewpoint of the "controllers," a high value of its own. The lightning speed of the drive pulverized the will to resist. It whipped into enthusiastic action millions of young people yearning for heroic adventure. Last but not least, it succeeded in producing among many former stalwarts of the various intraparty oppositions the feeling that what had occurred was too far-reaching to be reversed without wrecking the whole social setup born of the revolution and that the thing to do under the circumstances was not to "rock the boat" but to close ranks in order to minimize the risks involved in the adopted policies.

It was this unique blend of creeping fear, exhilaration of battle, and *la-patrie-en-danger* psychosis that provided the intellectual climate for Stalin's "revolution from above." In such a climate there was no room for the ideas and concepts which have been presented on the pages of this study. We have seen the men who had defended them to be far apart in their initial blueprints, and even more—in the political premises on which these blueprints were based. But all of them—Left, Right, or Center—operated under the assumption that in the sphere of economic policy there are resistances of material which call not for a smashing knockout blow but for some kind of coexistence of heterogeneous socioeconomic setups for a long time to come, with the result of an uneasy compromise shifting only gradually in the desired direction. They were more than once swayed in their reasoning by the emotions of political battle, in which quarter was neither asked nor given. Yet their basic ideas, as different from the occasional twists in their argument, reflected not the "ideological" juggling of facts and theoretical concepts but a genuine effort to come to grips with complex and intractable realities and to make the eventual solutions stand up against criticism. True, most of the participants in the great debate had been intellectually

formed in the ranks of the Bolshevik old guard, which represented in
the prerevolutionary period the authoritarian wing of Russian Marxism. But none of them succeeded any more than Lenin himself did
in carrying through to its Stalinist perfection the basic attitudes
toward man and society inherent in the elitist conception—the refusal to tolerate spheres of social life not fully manipulable from
above, seeing weakness if not outright betrayal behind any diversity
in thought and action, and the determination to use every means in
order to stamp it out. It was the failure of Bukharin, Preobrazhensky,
and others to live up to this totalitarian code that sealed their fate.
All of them perished in the purges of the thirties.

Robert V. Daniels

THE STRUGGLE WITH THE RIGHT OPPOSITION

*Stalin's struggle with the Right Opposition of Bukharin, Rykov, and Tomsky
was the immediate prelude to the "Stalin Revolution" and the actual occasion for many of the new steps Stalin took. This episode has been studied
in detail by the editor of the present collection of readings, as part of a
history of all the Communist opposition factions from the revolution to the
triumph of Stalin. Much of the most revealing material on which this account
is based, particularly the discussions at party meetings, comes from unpublished reports and minutes included among the papers which Trotsky
brought out of Russia. These materials are now in the Trotsky Archive at
Harvard University.*

For all its affirmation of the virtue and necessity of monolithic unity,
the Bolshevik Party could not yet dispense with the function provided
by an opposition. Stalin and Bukharin had hardly finished congratulating themselves on their triumphant victory over the Trotskyists

Reprinted by permission of the publishers from Robert V. Daniels, *The Conscience
of the Revolution: Communist Opposition in Soviet Russia* (Cambridge, Mass.:
Harvard University Press, 1960), pp. 322–324, 327–332, 337, 339–341, 348–352, 358–
360. Copyright 1960 by the President and Fellows of Harvard College.

when a new party split began. In a matter of months, Stalin's senior associates in the Politburo—Bukharin, Rykov, and Tomsky—found themselves the victims of precisely the same political tactics whose use against the Left they had so vigorously applauded such a short time before.

The Right Opposition led by these three men was quite different in character from the previous Trotskyist movement. The Left oppositionists had exhibited a certain continuity of ideological tradition over a considerable span of years, and their disagreements with the Leninist leadership were substantially grounded in deep-seated intellectual and social differences. By contrast, the Right Opposition was a phenomenon of the moment, emerging on the political scene with little forewarning. The Right Opposition had no background as a deviation, for the simple reason that before its appearance as an opposition it had been, both as a group of men and as a program, an indistinguishable part of the party leadership itself. In the form of its origin the Right Opposition thus closely resembled the Left Communists of 1918. Each group represented the previously prevailing line of the party from which the leading individual in the party suddenly swerved. In both instances the split thus produced was deep, and the manner in which the party crisis would be resolved was not immediately apparent. . . .

The pronouncements of the Fifteenth Congress were sufficiently vague to allow a variety of interpretations, as would soon become apparent. Indications are that the Stalinists still had no definite idea of the policy changes which they were soon to make, nor of the immediate economic and political problems which would force this shift. As usual in Soviet politics, the departure from the NEP and the new cleavage in the party were precipitated when expedients had to be devised to meet a sudden crisis.

The problem was a familiar one—the peasantry and the food supply. Even before the sessions of the Fifteenth Party Congress had been completed with the formal expulsion of the whole Left Opposition, the party leadership began to express alarm about grain procurement. Two directives issued from the Central Committee to local party organizations, warning of a decline in the collections of grain from the peasants. These were followed in January 1928 by an order threatening disciplinary action against local party leaders if they failed to remedy the situation. By February the entire party was agitated over the suddenly looming grain crisis. . . .

Despite the growing misgivings of many party figures, Stalin proceeded toward the statement of a basically new agricultural policy, though he disclaimed innovation by speaking of "implementing the decisions of the Fifteenth Congress." In a talk to a gathering of Communist scholars late in May, Stalin made public his new approach: "The solution lies in the transition from individual peasant farming to collective, common farming." He did make a gesture in the direction of improving individual farming while it lasted, but the toughness of his new orientation was reaffirmed in his comment on industry:

> Should we, perhaps, as a measure of greater "caution," retard the development of heavy industry and make light industry, which produces chiefly for the peasant market, the basis of our industry as a whole? Not under any circumstances! That would be suicidal; it would mean undermining our whole industry, including light industry. It would mean the abandonment of the slogan of the industrialization of our country, and the transformation of our country into an appendage of the capitalist system of economy.

Here Stalin announced what was to become the main theme of the economic discussions and controversies of the ensuing year. He had opted for the high-tempo industrialization which had just been condemned along with the Left Opposition, and he went even further with his refusal to recognize any limits either on the country's need for heavy industry or on its capacity for building it.

Bukharin's first response to the new stress on collectivization was a panegyric on the "cultural revolution," which would put an end to "the contrast of city and country," but soon he removed his rose-colored glasses. By the first of June, Bukharin had privately attacked Stalin as the representative of a "Trotskyist danger," and he soon became the leading spokesman for a determined though still behind-the-scenes faction committed to the defeat of Stalin's line on agriculture. . . .

By the time of the July meeting of the Central Committee, rumors of dissension in the highest councils of the party were rife. Trotsky took note of "the existing breach between the apparatus and the right wing," although the make-up of the latter was not entirely clear to him. Stalin apparently contemplated some kind of drastic action, though he may not yet have been sure of its precise direction.

Among Stalin's potential supporters and critics the lines had not definitely formed. Molotov spoke on June 30 with weighty caution, stressing the burden of backwardness in Russian agriculture and warning against excessive reliance on planning alone. At the same meeting, Uglanov [party secretary for the Moscow Province], who was about to take the Moscow organization into the Right Opposition, expressed precisely the opposite, optimistic, view of planning. Earlier, Kaganovich [at the time party secretary for the Ukraine] had supposedly wavered. Kalinin [chief of state], Voroshilov [commissar of defense], Andreyev, Ordzhonikidze, and the deputy GPU[1] chief, Yagoda, among others, were rumored to be sympathetic toward Stalin's opponents. They were reportedly afraid to act or restrained by threats of blackmail by Stalin. Voroshilov, for example, apparently feared the exposure of his sin of patriotic fervor which prompted him to volunteer for the tsarist army during World War I.

The Central Committee assembled for its regular meeting in Moscow on July 4. Again the focus of its deliberations was the peasant problem, which was the subject of a climactic debate on July 9 and 10. Reports were delivered by Kalinin, Molotov, and Mikoyan [commissar of trade], dealing respectively with state farms, collective farms, and grain collections; they spoke in relatively moderate terms, with emphasis on maintaining the tie with the middle peasant. The principal resolution, proposed by Mikoyan, was a compromise document which stressed the need for raising the productivity of individual peasant farming, underscored the temporary nature of the extraordinary measures, and even admitted the necessity of raising the price of grain to correspond with the price of other agricultural products. It was, in fact, essentially Bukharin's resolution, "stolen from my declaration," as he put it.

---

[1] GPU or OGPU: The "Chief Political Administration" or "United Chief Political Administration," the political police (originally the "Cheka" or "Extraordinary Commission to Combat Counter-Revolution"; later the "NKVD" or "People's Commissariat of Internal Affairs"; now the "KGB" or "Committee of State Security"). —Ed.

Mikoyan's presentation was the signal for a series of right-wing comments, by Osinsky, Andreyev, A. I. Stetsky, and Sokolnikov,[2] that the agricultural situation was still serious and that further concessions to the middle peasants (especially price increases) were imperative. Uglanov and Rykov followed with warnings about the general state of popular discontent and the danger of allowing the extraordinary measures to become an accepted system. Kaganovich entered the argument to protest that the extraordinary measures had been criticized too much, and that it was equally wrong to rely wholly on price policy. Some of his remarks were the harshest heard at the plenum: "The kulak's[3] struggle with us will be cruel. . . . We must prepare for this. We must quicken the pace of the grain collection campaign." Rykov replied emotionally to Kaganovich, "It would be wrong to make a distinction between the extraordinary measures and 'excesses.' 'Excesses' sometimes include criminal or semicriminal offenses committed by individual persons in the process of collecting grain. This is altogether wrong. A crime is a crime. A whole series of 'excesses' was an organic part of the entire system of grain collections which we resorted to in January." Kaganovich, according to Rykov, was an apologist for violence as an end in itself: "The whole meaning of Kaganovich's speech reduces to the defense of extraordinary measures as such for any time and under any conditions." Kaganovich was "cut to pieces," in Sokolnikov's estimation.

Stalin took part in the discussion with a major speech on July 9. His point of departure was the Osinsky-Sokolnikov price-raising proposal, which he denounced as "putting the brakes on the industrialization of the country." By concentrating his fire against the most extreme representatives of the right-wing view (whom Rykov himself repudiated), Stalin endeavored to identify their heresy with all the opposition to his own view. The substance of Stalin's speech was to give the NEP a new meaning—it was not a retreat but an offensive, in which vigorous measures against the kulaks and the collectivization of the rest of the peasants had an appropriate place. Thus, in his usual fashion, Stalin was able to indulge himself in a new policy and

[2] At the time deputy chairman of the State Planning Commission; formerly a Zinovievist.—Ed.
[3] "Kulak": a prosperous individual peasant, from the Russian word for "fist," implying "tight-fisted."—Ed.

still profess orthodox adherence to past authority. He anticipated objections to accelerated collectivization by classing them with opposition to the collectivist goal per se: "Those who fail to understand that, or who do not want to admit it, are not Marxists or Leninists, but peasant philosophers, looking backward instead of forward."

Stalin took pains to distinguish his new policy from the Trotskyist program, with which many people had naturally associated it. In fact he was moving rapidly toward the Left position and was soon to go far beyond it with the initiation of violent, rapid, and wholesale collectivization of the peasants. Trotsky took note of a rightist hope that a fear of conceding the correctness of the Left would inhibit the Stalinists in changing their policy. But Stalin again evidenced that doctrinal adroitness which belies the impression that he was clumsy and unlettered in matters of theory. His interest in theory was, to be sure, primarily a weapon to use against his enemies, but he wielded it with dexterity. As Bukharin confided to Kamenev, "Stalin . . . is an unprincipled intriguer who subordinates everything to the preservation of his power. He changes his theories according to whom he needs to get rid of at any given moment."

Stalin's problem in the summer of 1928 was to borrow the leftist policy of increased pressure on the peasants without appearing to adhere to the Trotskyist heresy. At the same time he was determined to maneuver those who held to the old official policy into a position where they appeared to be deviators. Bukharin complained, "He maneuvers in such a way as to make us stand as the schismatics." Stalin's strategy for accomplishing these simultaneous feats of political sleight of hand was his usual redefinition of old party clichés, with the support of appropriately culled quotations from Lenin, to make accepted ideas mean something quite different. At the same time his firm adherence to the authoritative pronouncements of the party would be loudly proclaimed, and anyone who ventured to suggest divergence in the actual application of such pronouncements would immediately find himself charged with an un-Leninist attitude. So it was with those who complained that the actual trend of peasant policy was violating the spirit of the NEP. They were dismissed as a "kulak deviation."

On July 10, as recriminations between the factions at the Central Committee plenum grew increasingly bitter, Bukharin rose to make the major statement of his case. He was in deadly earnest, throughout frequent clownish heckling by the Stalinists, and sincerely alarmed over the security of the Soviet state, which he feared was threatened by a mass uprising under the leadership of the kulaks. "To undertake the slightest campaign in the country," he warned, "means to mobilize against us to an ever greater degree the kulak element, the petty bourgeoisie . . . the middle bourgeoisie . . . etc. The reserves of these forces remain very great, and the slightest vacillation on the question in the ranks of our party will have a disproportionately great political significance."

The grain crisis, Bukharin explained, was a reflection of the country's basic economic weakness: reserves were seriously lacking, and it was proving impossible to advance simultaneously in agriculture, industry, and consumer satisfaction. "Give us your panacea," interjected Voroshilov, who was at pains to demonstrate by his repeated heckling of Bukharin that he sided firmly with the Stalinists.

"I don't want to give you a panacea, and please don't you make fun of me," replied Bukharin, stung by the remark but apparently unable to grasp the factional vindictiveness of his critics. He went on to criticize Stalin for suggesting that industrial development inevitably implied a threat to the worker-peasant alliance: this was a Trotskyist notion. It was wrong to attack reliance on price measures as capitalistic: prices were the decisive means whereby the government could regulate the individual peasants. Poor planning and incorrect pricing were responsible for the crisis that required such special measures. The extraordinary measures had tended to become a system of War Communism; their economic value was questionable and their political effect was indisputably bad. At all costs the allegiance of the middle peasants had to be kept, and this meant that their individual farms should be allowed to prosper more. The offensive against the kulaks could be continued, but only in the form of exploiting their productive capacity through taxation; the kulaks would be no threat as long as the middle peasants did not decide to follow them. Conciliation of the peasants was the key to the future—"We must in no case allow a threat to the smychka."[4]

The compromise resolution on the grain collections was passed

---

[4] Smychka: the supposed "bond" or alliance between the workers and the peasants. —Ed.

unanimously by the Central Committee after the close of debate on July 10. It gave many people the impression that the issues between the Stalinists and the Rykov-Bukharin group had been completely settled. The shifting balance was subtly revealed, however, where the resolution condemned the rightists' principal complaint that the extraordinary measures were becoming an established policy: "Interpretations of these measures as organic consequences of the decisions of the Fifteenth Congress . . . testify only to the fact that at certain levels of the party an alien ideology has had influence." The rightist leaders discovered that their position was crumbling, as a number of the people on whom they thought they could count—including Voroshilov, Kalinin, and Kuibyshev [at the time chairman of the Supreme Economic Council]—lined up on Stalin's side. Stalin's attitude on July 11, the last day of the session, was correspondingly tougher. The general secretary was confidently unyielding about suggestions for further leniency toward the peasantry.

Stalin's opponents now decided to act. It is not hard to imagine how their feelings took form—after enthusiastic collaboration with a strong and resourceful comrade, the growing discord, the verbal altercation when unleashed tempers turned uneasy friends into vengeful enemies, the nursing of grudges and the restrained growling in public encounters, and finally the horrifying realization that the old associate was a power-hungry intriguer who now held most of the cards and would stop at nothing in his determination to destroy them. While reports flew about that the Right was planning to depose Stalin, Bukharin took the risky step of establishing contact with former members of the Left Opposition. Sokolnikov arranged a meeting between Bukharin and Kamenev. For some reason Bukharin had come to fear a rapprochement between Stalin and the Zinoviev-Kamenev group, and he hastened to seek out the old oppositionists to be his own allies on the ground that they had a common cause to make.

On the morning of July 11, Sokolnikov and Bukharin slipped into Kamenev's Moscow apartment without ringing, and Bukharin, in a desperate mood, at once revealed his fears:

Stalin's line is ruinous for the whole revolution. It can make us collapse. . . . The differences between us and Stalin are many times more serious than all our former differences with you. Rykov, Tomsky, and I agree on

FIGURE 2. Stalin and the Right Opposition.

Joseph Stalin in 1936 (*N.Y. Public Library Picture Collection*).

Valerian Kuibyshev (*N.Y. Public Library Picture Collection*).

Nikolai Bukharin in 1931 (*Sovfoto*).

Sergei Kirov in 1932 (*Sovfoto*).

*formulating the situation thus: "It would be much better if Zinoviev and
Kamenev were in the Politburo instead of Stalin."... I have not spoken
with Stalin for several weeks.... Our arguing with him reached the point
of saying, "You lie!" He has made concessions now, so that [later] he
can cut our throats.*

In the comments which he appended to the record of the talk, Kamenev observed, "Stalin knows only one method . . . to plant a knife
in your back."

*   *   *

The scene of the organizational struggle between Stalin and the
Right was Moscow. The party machine in the Moscow province was
the only major organizational force at the disposal of the rightists
and accordingly was of strategic significance. In contrast to the
spontaneous and relatively democratic surge of Opposition sentiment
among the Moscow Communists in 1923 and earlier, the 1928 Moscow
Opposition was an apparatus affair, on the order of Zinoviev's Leningrad Opposition of 1925. Uglanov's Moscow Opposition was no more
a democratic protest movement than was Stalin's central party machine. Uglanov was a typical organization man, installed in the key
Moscow post in 1924 and rewarded for his loyalty to the general
secretary by elevation to the Politburo as a candidate member in 1925.

The fact that a man such as Uglanov should have thrown his lot in
with the Bukharin group indicates that the issues between Stalin and
the Right had driven a deep wedge into the ranks of the party officialdom. While the motive of personal political advantage cannot be
ruled out, Uglanov's stand during and after the July Plenum of the
Central Committee leaves no doubt that he was genuinely concerned
over economic policy and that he took the Bukharinist alarm to heart.
Like the other rightist leaders, he linked the success of the Communist Party with the well-being of the country and recoiled before the
social conflict which Stalin's aggressive line portended. . . .

The central party leadership . . . proceeded to deal with the Opposition in Moscow with the usual organizational measures. Under
the convenient pretext provided by the current campaigns for "self-
criticism" and "intraparty democracy," and utilizing the scheduled
elections for new bureaus or directing committees for all party cells,
the Stalinists by-passed the Moscow leadership in order to apply
pressure and seek supporters in the district organizations nominally

under the jurisdiction of the Moscow Committee. "It is true" the Central Committee announced, "that some members of the Moscow Committee and the leaders of some districts have recently shown a certain inconsistency and vacillation in the struggle against the Right deviations from the Leninist line by tolerating a conciliatory attitude toward these deviations which is inacceptable to the Bolshevik Party. This has aroused the dissatisfaction of a certain section of the active membership of the Moscow organization who wished to correct these mistakes." Here were the tactics employed so effectively against the Zinovievists in Leningrad in January 1926. They demonstrated the top leadership's ability to go outside the normal lines of bureaucratic authority and make use of democratic forms in order to buttress central control over the middle echelons.

Soon there were subtle indications of the effect of central pressure. Some of the Moscow district organizations, passing resolutions about the Comintern Congress, began to express the new central line against "petty-bourgeois opportunism" in the Russian party itself. Other Moscow districts confined themselves to vague exhortations for the "struggle on two fronts." As it was later officially confirmed, the district secretaries had divided in their allegiance between Uglanov and the central leadership. The party organization at Moscow University, reflecting the intellectuals' predilection for any form of opposition, took a firm pro-rightist stand.

To appease the central leadership, Uglanov issued a declaration to the Moscow membership early in October, in which he heavily stressed the danger of the Right deviation as well as the Left. But he did not put an end to the tolerance of rightist opinions within his organization and lamely had to plead the "sickness" of himself and his two cosecretaries as the excuse. Uglanov was evidently encouraged by the publication of Bukharin's thoughtful critique of the Stalinist economic program, his "Notes of an Economist," in *Pravda* on September 30. On October 3 he warned publicly that Soviet agriculture was now seriously lagging, to the detriment of both industry and consumers. On the following day, one of Uglanov's district secretaries, Penkov, echoed these agriculture-first remarks and urged the study of Bukharin's article, but he met with an ominous response—direct contradiction by his own subordinates in the debate which ensued.

On or about October 11, the central leadership initiated a violent press and organizational campaign against the still anonymous "Right deviation," and simultaneously took direct action against the Moscow Opposition. Uglanov suddenly found that he could no longer control transfers in his own organization. While the bureau of the Moscow Committee was compelled to share responsibility for the move, it was on the acknowledged initiative of the Central Committee that the two most recalcitrant district leaders in Moscow, Penkov and Riutin, were removed, on the grounds that they had "recently allowed individual deviations from the correct Leninist line of the party." Confirmation of the central victory came at the meeting of the Moscow Committee on October 18 and 19. Uglanov made the customary report but was given a portent of his coming fall as the committee members withheld the usual applause. Sensing the forces against him, Uglanov remarked ironically that his removal would be justified if the membership really wanted it. He admitted weaknesses in his organization and vaguely conceded "lack of clarity in evaluating the economic situation," but he tried to stand his ground against the Stalinists' attacks: "We will consider it our duty . . . to defend ourselves by struggling against slander." Guardedly he recalled Lenin's warning about Stalin's character.

Uglanov's defensive gestures were fruitless, for the great majority of the Moscow Committee had evidently gone over to the Stalinists. The proceedings of the session were largely taken up with criticism of Uglanov's errors, attacks on the Right deviation, and appeals for discipline and self-criticism. The oppositionists were accused of a "keep it in the family" attitude and of conniving against the Central Committee. A number of Uglanov's supporters, including the ousted district secretaries Penkov and Riutin, made their confessions and boarded the band wagon. "The party is *exclusively* correct," declared district secretary Safronov, "and I find in myself enough courage to admit my errors." A hold-out, the dismissed agitprop chief Liadov-Mandelshtam, pleaded that his friends had no honor because they avoided him as "a traitor to the party line."

On October 19 Stalin appeared in person before the Moscow Committee to deliver a long warning against the Right deviation, though he still allowed it to remain anonymous. Affirming that a Right deviation did in fact exist among the Russian Communists as well as in the Comintern, he described it as "a tendency, an inclination of a part of the Communists, not yet formulated, it is true, and perhaps not yet consciously realized, but nevertheless a tendency, to depart from the general line of our party toward bourgeois ideology." This was not, Stalin argued, a new development, but it had been revealed more clearly by the "vacillations" which the government's recent economic problems had produced. Cleverly he twisted the rightist efforts to defend the old party line and created an antiproletarian scapegoat: "In order to overcome the difficulties we must first defeat the Right danger . . . which is hindering the fight against our difficulties and is trying to shake the party's will to fight to overcome these difficulties."

. . . Uglanov's resistance collapsed completely in the face of the General Secretary's attack. The Moscow Committee confessed the "mistake" in its work and approved without reservation the removals which had been ordered by the Central Committee. The disgrace of Uglanov was confirmed by his subordinates' criticizing him to his face for "insufficient" recognition of his "errors.". . .

While Stalin was destroying the foothold of the Right Opposition in the party organization and in the trade unions, the policy cleavage between his forces and the Right grew wider. From the specific issue of the kulaks and the grain problem the controversy broadened to include the most general problems of economic life and the country's future prospects. Ramifications of the controversy reached to the core of Marxian doctrine and into the most abstruse philosophical matters.

The political origins of the industrialization policy formulated by the Stalinists late in 1928 are abundantly clear when the problem is viewed in the context of the debates of 1925–1927. The issues were essentially the same, with the Stalinists taking the position of Preobrazhensky and the Trotskyists, against the rightists who adhered to the earlier official position. Stalin's new affinity with the former leftist program of intensive planned industrialization at the expense of the peasantry was only emphasized by the vigorous efforts which he made to refute the insinuation that he was merely copying the Trotskyist policy two years too late. (As late as November 1928, the charge "superindustrialist" was still being hurled at the Trotskyists.) The "capitulations" of exiled Trotskyists who decided that Stalin's program was close enough to their own show clearly enough how the new line actually appeared. In part, Stalin's espousal of the leftist program was an acknowledgment of the country's economic impasse as the Left Opposition had analyzed it. His immediate interest in industrialization, however, was mainly political. It was a device to provoke the rightists into making protests that could be called deviation.

While the Right-Left political battle raged in 1926 and 1927 over the speed of industrialization, a parallel cleavage developed among the professional economists. Two distinct conceptions of the nature of planning had emerged by 1927, represented respectively by the "geneticists" and the "teleologists." The geneticists stressed the work of predicting uncontrollable economic tendencies, and adapting plans accordingly, while the teleologists argued that the laws of economics could be transcended by the action of the socialist state. "Our task is not to study economics but to change it," wrote the leading professional exponent of the latter view, S. G. Strumilin, in a paraphrase of Marx. "We are bound by no laws. There are no fortresses which Bolsheviks cannot storm"—a slogan which Stalin was later to plagiarize. "The question of tempo is subject to decision by human beings.". . .

While Gosplan [the State Planning Commission] wrestled with the formulation of a plan that would take all such contingencies [as defects of organization and accounting, and the uncertainties of the harvest and of foreign trade conditions] into account, a rival organization was moving into the planning field. This was the Supreme Economic Council (which actually functioned as the commissariat of industry), headed since 1926 by Kuibyshev, the former chairman of the Central Control Commission and a dedicated, if somewhat colorless, Stalinist. Under Kuibyshev, the Supreme Economic Council proceeded to draw up its own drafts of a five-year plan, with considerably more emphasis on heavy industry. "Castles in air," scoffed the Gosplan economists. . . .

Kuibyshev's speech to the Leningrad party organization on September 19 was the firmest declaration yet heard of a determination to drive ahead and to eliminate any discontent engendered by the drive. "We must be fully aware," Kuibyshev asserted, "that it would be wrong from every point of view to speak of a reduction of the rate of industrialization. . . . We are told we are 'overindustrializing,' and 'biting off more than we can chew.' " This was a patent reference to the warnings from the Bukharin-Rykov group—but the objection was overruled: "Any careful student of our economy will, I am sure, agree with me that the most serious disproportion . . . is the one between the output of the means of production and the requirements of the country." The vindication of Preobrazhensky could not have been more explicit. . . .

The reflection of the party split in the work of economic planning reached the point of crisis in the winter of 1928–1929. The right-wing Gosplan could not overcome its scruples and repeatedly failed to give the party leadership what was wanted, while the Supreme Economic Council went forging ahead with ever more optimistic visions. "Our planning," read a statement of the latter organization, "must include not only forecasting, not only the discovery of economic laws, but a creative, deliberate building of a socialist economy." This was the teleological approach with a vengeance.

At the end of November 1928, too late for the Central Committee to act upon it, the planners in the Supreme Economic Council finally produced an optimal five-year plan which was acceptable to the leadership. The draft had been completed under such pressure for haste that Kuibyshev was unable to carry out his promise to go through the motions of "mass participation" in the preparation of the plan. According to this new version, industrial investment would not only be undertaken at a high rate, but the percentage of the national income devoted to it would increase, year after year, through the five-year period. The party leadership immediately turned, for a convenient forum, to the Eighth Trade Union Congress, and Kuibyshev appeared there to expound at great length the virtues of the new plan, which excluded all previous versions—"Only this variant can be placed under consideration." Brought to heel by party pressure, the trade-unionists gave their endorsement to the plan. Gosplan still remained critical. Bazarov warned, with courage that was remarkable at this late date, "Here there can be the worst results, here you can get such a clearly irrational distribution of resources as will discredit the whole idea of industrialization."

By the early months of 1929, the party leadership was locked in bitter controversy with Bukharin, Rykov, and Tomsky. The Stalinists became unalterably committed to the highest conceivable speed of economic development, if only to assure that the Right would be branded as fainthearted deviators. At the same time they accused the rightist critics of playing politics—compunctions about economic equilibrium were dismissed as "a mere convenient screen for political rather than methodological attacks."

In the meantime, the uncooperative economists were disposed of. Quietly but thoroughly Gosplan was purged; everyone associated with the geneticist position was ousted. The planning efforts already accomplished were rejected for following the "wrong class approach," and the party leadership proclaimed the exclusive orthodoxy of the "purposive-teleological method." A number of the former Gosplan economists, especially those who had originally been associated with the Mensheviks,[5] were involved on charges of "sabotage" in the "Industrial Party" trial of 1930 and the Menshevik trial of 1931. But the shake-up did not stop here. The Stalinist drive for heavy industrial development transcended even what the teleological economists thought feasible, and they in their turn were thrust aside into academic positions. . .

In March 1929, the renovated Gosplan finally produced a full-dress plan with two complete variants. The times were changing fast, however; Kuibyshev now replied, "The optimal variant of the Five-Year Plan is the plan for building socialism." The rightists protested and vainly proposed alternatives—Rykov suggested a "middle variant" and a subsidiary two-year program for agriculture. This brought down on him the charge that he opposed the Five-Year Plan and defended the kulaks.

The First Five-Year Plan was finally approved as official party policy at the Sixteenth Party Conference in April 1929, and confirmed in May by the Council of People's Commissars and the Congress of Soviets. The new optimal variant was declared to have been in effect as of October of the previous year. The role of chance was dismissed by governmental decree. Any concern for such bothersome economic considerations as statistical relationships or laws of equilibrium was swept aside as "class-alien." The new mentality was epitomized in the slogan, "There are no objective obstacles—obstacles must be overcome." Speaking at the Seventeenth Party Congress in 1934, Stalin declared that "objective conditions" could no longer be admitted as factors limiting the will of the Soviet government. Hence-

[5] Mensheviks: The more moderate wing of the Russian Marxists, who had opposed Lenin and the Bolsheviks since 1903.—Ed.

forth, there was no excuse for failure—treason could be the only explanation.

Raymond A. Bauer

IDEOLOGICAL REVISION

The New Man in Soviet Psychology, *by Raymond A. Bauer (b. 1916), professor of industrial psychology at the Harvard Business School, is a survey of psychological thought in Soviet Russia during the first twenty years after the revolution. Professor Bauer found it necessary to clarify the ideological background of Soviet psychology, and in so doing he produced a challenging explanation of Stalin's use of Marxist theory. Marxism was no longer to be understood as a mechanistic theory of the inevitable laws of economic change. Instead, with emphasis on the "dialectic," Marxism was interpreted as "purposive," to justify the ambitions of Stalin's government and the requirements imposed on the Soviet citizens. Any adherence to the older Marxist view was henceforth outlawed as a "bourgeois" deviation.*

Stalin has stressed the activist element in Leninism. He cited, for example, Lenin's opposition to the theory of "spontaneity" on the ground that reliance on the elemental forces in the social process undermined the active role of the party. Stalin has said that if the interpretation of social processes held by some groups at the beginning of the century had been accepted there would have been no need "for an independent working-class party." He suggests a mock conversation with a person who overemphasizes the importance of relying on spontaneous forces. Suppose, he queries, you were to ask such a person what the role of the party should be.

"What are you talking about?" comes the ready answer.

"Can the party do anything to affect the working of so decisive a factor as 'the level of the forces of production'?"

Thus, the party, in the eyes of such a person can have no effective role in shaping history.

Reprinted by permission of the author and publishers, from Raymond A. Bauer, *The New Man in Soviet Psychology,* Russian Research Center Studies no. 7 (Cambridge, Mass.: Harvard University Press, 1952), pp. 17–19, 23–24, 26, 32, 33, 103–104. Copyright 1952 by the President and Fellows of Harvard College.

Lenin, says Stalin, revived the revolutionary aspects of Marxism, which had been played down by the moderate socialists, and in addition adapted Marxism to the demands of modern conditions: "It is a fact that Lenin brought to light once more the revolutionary social content of Marxism, which had been glossed over by the opportunists of the Second International, but that is only a fragment of the truth. The whole truth is that Leninism is a development of Marxism adapting it to the new conditions of capitalism and to the class struggle of the proletariat." Thus Stalin places himself and Lenin firmly on the side of those who favor action rather than rely on the determinate course of events.

For particular historical reasons the question of determinism and freedom has been a central problem in the development of Marxist-Leninist thought and action. All social action—and implicitly all social theory—involves some compromise between determinacy and indeterminacy, some judgment of the extent to which one is free to act and the extent to which one is constrained by circumstance. As practical experience has made the limitations of circumstances more explicit, an ever greater emphasis has had to be placed on the power of the individual to act in such a way as to overcome these limitations. This condition evolved because early predictions based on assumed determinate relationships gave a sanguine picture of the trend of social developments—thus minimizing the emphasis which had to be placed on the role of the individual—whereas later predictions forecast conditions which could not be accepted—therefore necessitating reliance on individual action to negate the trend of determined (that is, predicted) events. An optimism based on predicted immanent developments became replaced with an "optimism" based on man's ability to make his own fate. It is not true that in every instance early predictions were optimistic and later predictions were pessimistic. It is true, however, that a particular set of early optimistic predictions about the withering away of the state and about the nature of socialist institutions were not realized, and it is also true that the relative weight to be assigned to spontaneous, or determinate and noncontrolled, forces in a situation was a recurrent question in problem after problem.

The social postulates of extreme mechanistic Marxism certainly include the following:

(1) Man is a product of his inheritance and his environment; therefore society is responsible for man's character and behavior,
rather than man's being responsible for society.
(2) All social events are determinately related; therefore the trend
of future events can be predicted.
(3) Essentially, the course of events is determined by abstract
forces external to man himself, and there is little that he could
or should do to direct them.
(4) Since all oppressive and repressive institutions are a function
of conflict in class society, a classless society will speedily do
away with repression.
(5) Class society is a result of a particular form of economic relations, and a change in the economic base of society will eliminate class divisions, which in turn will result in the withering
away of the state and bring about ideal social conditions.
(6) Man is inherently rational and inherently good; and once he is
freed from the institutions of a class society, he will revert
spontaneously to rationality and goodness.

In addition to these premises, mechanistic Marxism posits the desir-
ability of a freely developed and fully expressed personality, of freeing man from excessive burdens and of respecting his dignity.

Many of the premises involved in this type of thinking, and in fact
some of the specific postulates outlined above, could be found in the
work of virtually every Bolshevik at one time or another, and they
found expression briefly in most of the Soviet social institutions. However, as the history of the Soviet Union unfolded, it became evident
that these postulates were untenable in various areas of society, and
factions began to develop on the basis of whether they gave predominant emphasis to the determinate trend of events or to the shaping of
these events to a given goal. What had been a conflict in the minds of
men became a conflict between men of different minds.

The conflict between these two sets of postulates was resolved in
two critical events. The first was a crisis in economic planning in
connection with the First Five-Year Plan, and the second, a controversy between the mechanists and the dialecticians in philosophy.
Beginning independently, these two events converged in the late
twenties to precipitate a series of parallel crises in other areas of
Soviet life. . . .

Two broad methodological issues were at stake, the first of which, as Bukharin himself put it in the early thirties, after accepting the defeat of his position, was between two orders of lawfulness: the lawfulness of events impinging on each other and working out their own resolution, and the lawfulness of events consciously organized and directed by man. The second issue involved the nature of evolution in general. The mechanistic conception of evolution or development sees events as proceeding linearly and sees the future as a direct projection of the past. The other point of view sees evolution as a discontinuous course of development involving periods of crisis and revolution producing sudden basic reorganizations of the elements in the system. This results in a new form of organization, subject to different laws—the dialectical law of quantity changing into quality. According to the dialectical point of view an accelerated program of industrialization and collectivization would produce such a "leap" in development and would result in restructuring of social relationships that would negate the predictions of the mechanists.

Further, the supporters of Stalin said that mechanists had no place for chance (accident) in their scheme of thinking.

> *They undertook a mystical view that everything was defined by preceding events. For this, we inevitably slip down to fatalism in practice, to an excuse for abandoning the revolutionary fight, for reaction and all subjective errors. This mechanistic necessity forces us to dig in the past, seeking there the causes of the actual event, to look—not forward, but—backward.*

In other words, the Right opportunist has used scientific analysis to make man the slave rather than the master of events.

The victory of the Stalinist position had a number of important consequences for the future of Soviet society.

1. The primacy of "teleological" over "genetic" considerations was established in economic and social planning. There was, in effect, a basic redefinition—or clarification—of man's relation to his environment. It made official the view that man is the master of his own fate.
2. The controversy in planning crystallized the controversy in philosophy by underscoring the practical implications of the contesting philosophical positions. Under the pressure of the fight over the Five-Year Plan, the "dialectical" position became

clarified, and was established as the "correct" Marxist (Stalin-ist) philosophy. This, in turn, meant that dialectical materialism (as opposed to mechanistic materialism) became the accepted methodology of science.

3. The scope of the plan itself precipitated a series of social crises, social needs, and problems which set their own chain of causation working. Social institutions (some soon, some late) became more tightly integrated, more explicitly directed toward the service of specific functions. Demands on and opportunities for the individual increased. At the same time the government actually had to be stricter in its control of the individual be-cause of the large number of persons—kulaks, Nepmen, and so on—against whom it had taken action. It also had to demand more of the individual in the service of the rapidly expanding economy.

The period of the twenties in Soviet Russia was marked by an extended controversy in science and philosophy over the relative merits of dialectical and mechanistic materialism. There were actually two prongs to the discussion. One issue was whether or not the principles of dialectics, part of the official Marxist philosophy, were applicable to the natural sciences. The other issue was the actual definition of the principles of dialectics. . . .

The victory of the dialecticians was announced in April 1929, the same month in which Bukharin and other members of the Right Opposition were stripped of much of their political power. The Sec-ond All-Union Conference of Marxist-Leninist Scientific Institutions passed a resolution labeling the view of the mechanists "a clear departure from the Marxist-Leninist philosophical position" and stat-ing that "the theoretical discussion with the mechanists is really finished." Shortly after this the Central Committee of the party issued a decree instructing the Communist Academy to implement the introduction of the dialectical point of view in the natural sciences. . . .

. . . What is significant in this philosophical discussion is that in each instance the dialecticians chose the point of view that left the party free to act in reconstructing society and provided a rationale for holding the individual responsible for his behavior.

Fighting out the battles of everyday practical politics and economics in so scholarly an arena as philosophy may seem somewhat out of place to anyone not versed in the history of Bolshevism, but it was standard procedure in the Bolshevik manual of tactics to use every weapon available, from the most prosaic to the most esoteric.

Consider the situation in which the philosophical controversy reached its peak. Stalin was coming into ascendancy as the leader of the party. While by no means handicapped by an inferior intellect, he had neither stature nor experience as a theorist. But he is and was a man of far more than average shrewdness and common sense, who realized that the Soviet Union had reached a crisis. At the same time he was maneuvering for position with contending factions in the party. It seems to have become obvious to Stalin about 1928 that the program of the Left, which had been rejected two years before, was originally correct, or that the situation had changed so that the leftist program either had to be or could be put into effect. In any event, he espoused essentially the program of industrial expansion that the Left had originally proposed, and then found himself opposed by the "learned arguments" of the newly developed Right Opposition. Without considering the merits of the two positions, we know that there were substantial temperamental differences between men like Nikolai Bukharin and Michael Tomsky, on the one hand, and Stalin and his supporters, on the other. The latter group were primarily men of direct action, men who favored active intervention to passive waiting. They were, further, men who were used to bending philosophy to the service of action. The position of the dialecticians offered a way out of the dilemma of determinism, of escaping from a fatalistically determined course of history. Also, the arguments of the dialecticians were a powerful weapon against the theories of Stalin's chief remaining competition, the party's leading thinker, Bukharin. Thus, by force of circumstance, the least theoretically minded of Bolshevik leaders seems to have become the sponsor of one of the most sophisticated and possibly the most sophistic of theories. . . .

Beyond affirming the purposive nature of man, the establishment of the "Leninist line" in philosophy amounted to a very strong statement of the necessity for "a unity of theory and practice" in all science. The latter point is of primary concern here.

The slogan of the "unity of theory and practice—with practice leading theory" is integrally related in Bolshevik thinking with the idea of *partinost,* literally "partyness," which can best be translated as "party vigilance" or "political acuity in the interest of the party." The principle of political vigilance means that every citizen must always be alert to sense the implications of any theory or action from the point of view of the political program of the party, and that the "truth" of any theory or the value of any action is determined on the basis of whether or not it contributes to the party's program.

It is typical of the Bolshevik system that such a highly political, virtually anti-intellectual approach to science is based in a very sophisticated manner on a highly intellectual foundation, Lenin's theory of epistemology.

As developed by Soviet theoreticians after 1930, the essential point in Lenin's theory of knowledge (known in Soviet literature as the Leninist theory of reflection) is that there is an *absolute* truth, but that at any point in time man knows only relative truth, and that he knows this relative truth by virtue of his action on the real world. Absolute truth is approached by successive approximations as each partial truth is discarded and revised in the light of man's attempt to apply it in practice. However, the nature of man's activity, the nature of his understanding of the real world is conditioned by the social order in which he lives, and by his class membership in that order. Every theory is conditioned by *and* serves the interest of some social class. (Note the conjunctive *and*; the fallacy in the argument which follows hinges on the addition of the second verb in the sentence.) Membership in any social class places limitations on one's ability to perceive reality as it is. But the further advanced in the historical sequence any class is, the better equipped its members are to know reality. Each successive order of society permits its members to approach more closely absolute truth, and the most advanced type of society, socialist society, in which the proletarian class (the only class which is not blinded by prejudices and rationalizations) rules, creates the most favorable conditions for discovering truth. Since all truth is relative and serves some class interest, and since the proletarian class has the closest approximation of truth, thus the theory which serves the interest of the proletariat is the closest approximation to absolute truth. Therefore, the primary criterion for validating a scientific theory is the exercise of "party vigilance." A theory is true if it serves the interests of the proletariat, or, more accurately, the vanguard of the proletariat, the Bolshevik Party.

II THE REVOLUTION FROM ABOVE

J. V. Stalin

THE SOCIALIST DRIVE

Joseph Vissarionovich Stalin *(1879–1953) rose from humble beginnings in a worker's family (real name Dzhugashvili) in the Transcaucasian region of Georgia, to become General Secretary of the Russian Communist Party in 1922 and unchallenged dictator of the Soviet Union in 1929. During the middle part of his career—from the mid-1920s to the mid-1930s—he recorded his achievements and intentions extensively in his many speeches, the most important of which were collected and translated in the various editions of* Problems of Leninism. *In speeches of November and December 1929, Stalin set forth a résumé of the new industrial and agricultural policies he had initiated. In Stalin's mind there were only two possibilities—his own policy, "forward—to socialism," or the retreat to capitalism which he charged his Communist opponents with advocating.*

The past year witnessed a great change on all fronts of socialist construction. The change expressed itself, and is still expressing itself, in a determined *offensive* of socialism against the capitalist elements in town and country. The characteristic feature of this offensive is that it has already brought us a number of decisive *successes,* in the principal spheres of the socialist reconstruction of our national economy.

We may therefore conclude that our party has made good use of the retreat effected during the first stages of the New Economic Policy in order to organize the *change* in the subsequent stages and to launch a *successful offensive* against the capitalist elements.

When the New Economic Policy was introduced Lenin said:

> *We are now retreating, going back, as it were; but we are doing this, retreating first, in order to prepare for a longer leap forward. It was only on this condition that we retreated in pursuing our New Economic Policy . . . in order to start a persistent advance after our retreat. (Lenin, Selected Works, Vol. IX, p. 376.)*

The results of the past year show beyond a doubt that the party

From J. V. Stalin, "A Year of Great Change (On the Occasion of the Twelfth Anniversary of the October Revolution)" and "Problems of Agrarian Policy in the USSR (Speech Delivered at the Conference of Marxist Students of the Agrarian Question, December 27, 1929)," in *Problems of Leninism* (Moscow: Foreign Languages Publishing House, 1940), pp. 294–298, 302–305, 308–309, 325–326.

is successfully carrying out this decisive advice of Lenin in the course of its work. . . .

The expansion of the creative initiative and labor enthusiasm of the masses has been stimulated by three main factors:

(a) the fight—by means of *self-criticism*—against bureaucracy, which shackles the labor initiative and labor activity of the masses;

(b) the fight—by means of *socialist emulation*—against the labor-shirkers and disrupters of proletarian labor discipline; and finally

(c) the fight—by the introduction of the *uninterrupted* week—against routine and inertia in industry.

As a result we have a tremendous achievement on the labor front in the form of labor enthusiasm and emulation among the millions of the working class in all parts of our vast country. The significance of this achievement is truly inestimable, for only the labor enthusiasm and zeal of the millions can guarantee the progressive increase of labor productivity without which the final victory of socialism over capitalism is inconceivable. . . .

. . . During the past year we have in the main successfully solved the *problem of accumulation* for capital construction in heavy industry; we have *accelerated* the development of the production of means of production and have created the prerequisites for transforming our country into a *metal* country. This is our second fundamental *achievement* during the past year.

The problem of light industry presents no exceptional difficulties. We solved that problem several years ago. The problem of heavy industry is more difficult and more important. It is *more difficult* because it demands colossal investments of capital, and, as the history of industrially backward countries has shown, heavy industry cannot be developed without extensive long-term loans. It is *more important* because, unless we develop heavy industry, we can build no industry whatever, we cannot carry out any industrialization. And as we have never received, nor are we receiving, either long-term loans or credits for any lengthy period, the acuteness of the problem becomes more than obvious. It is precisely for this reason that the capitalists of all countries refuse us loans and credits; they believe that, left to our own resources, we cannot cope with the problem of accumulation, that we are bound to fail in the task of reconstructing our heavy industry, and will at last be compelled to come to them cap in hand and sell ourselves into bondage.

But the results of the past year tell us a different story. The significance of the results of the past year lies in the fact that the calculations of Messieurs the capitalists have been shattered. The past year has shown that in spite of the open and covert financial blockade of the USSR we did not sell ourselves into bondage to the capitalists; that, with our own resources, we successfully solved the problem of accumulation and laid the foundation for heavy industry. Even the most inveterate enemies of the working class cannot deny this now. Indeed, since capital investments in large-scale industry last year amounted to over 1.6 billion rubles[1] (of which about 1.3 billion rubles were invested in heavy industry), and capital investments in large-scale industry this year will amount to over 3.4 billion rubles (of which over 2.5 billion rubles will be invested in heavy industry); and since the gross output of large-scale industry last year showed an increase of 23 percent, including a 30 percent increase in the output of heavy industry, and the increase in the gross output of large-scale industry this year should be 32 percent, including a 46 percent increase in the output of heavy industry—is it not obvious that the problem of accumulation for the building up of heavy industry no longer presents insuperable difficulties? How can anyone doubt that in developing our heavy industry, we are advancing at an accelerated pace, exceeding our former speed and leaving behind our "traditional" backwardness?

Is it surprising after this that the estimates of the Five-Year Plan were exceeded during the past year, and that the *optimum* variant of the Five-Year Plan, which the bourgeois scribes regarded as "wild fantasy," and which horrified our Right opportunists (Bukharin's group), has actually turned out to be a *minimum* variant?

"The salvation of Russia," says Lenin,

lies not only in a good harvest on the peasant farms—that is not enough; and not only in the good condition of light industry, which provides the peasantry with consumers' goods—this, too, is not enough. We also need

[1] In 1929 the ruble was officially valued at about 50¢ U.S.—Ed.

heavy industry. . . . *Unless we save heavy industry, unless we restore it, we shall not be able to build up any industry; and without heavy industry we shall be doomed as an independent country. . . . Heavy industry needs state subsidies. If we cannot provide them, then we are doomed as a civilized state—let alone as a socialist state. (Lenin,* Selected Works, *Vol. X, p. 328.)*

These are the blunt terms in which Lenin formulated the problem of accumulation and the task of our party in building up heavy industry.

The past year has shown that our party is successfully coping with this task, resolutely overcoming all obstacles in its path.

This does not mean, of course, that industry will not encounter any more serious difficulties. The task of building up heavy industry involves not only the problem of accumulation. It also involves the problem of cadres, the problem (a) of *enlisting* tens of thousands of Soviet-minded technicians and experts for the work of socialist construction, and (b) of *training* new Red technicians and Red experts from among the working class. While the problem of accumulation may in the main be regarded as solved, the problem of cadres still awaits solution. And the problem of cadres is now—when we are engaged in the technical reconstruction of industry—the decisive problem of socialist construction. . . .

The assertions of the Right opportunists (Bukharin's group) to the effect (a) that the peasants would not join the collective farms; (b) that the speedy development of collective farming would only arouse mass discontent and drive a wedge between the peasantry and the working class, (c) that the "high-road" of socialist development in the rural districts is *not* the collective farms, *but* the cooperative societies; and (d) that the development of collective farming and the, offensive against the capitalist elements in the rural districts may in the end deprive the country of grain altogether—all these assertions have also collapsed and crumbled to dust. They have all collapsed and crumbled to dust as old bourgeois-liberal rubbish.

Firstly, the peasants have joined the collective farms; they have joined in whole villages, whole volosts, whole districts.

Secondly, the mass collective-farm movement is not weakening the bond, but, on the contrary, is strengthening it by putting it on a new, production basis. Now even the blind can see that if there is any serious dissatisfaction among the great bulk of the peasantry it is not because of the collective-farm policy of the Soviet government, but because the Soviet government is unable to keep pace with the growth of the collective-farm movement in supplying the peasants with machines and tractors.

Thirdly, the controversy about the "high-road" of socialist development in the rural districts is a scholastic controversy, worthy of young petty-bourgeois liberals of the type of Eichenwald and Slepkov. It is obvious that, as long as there was no mass collective-farm movement, the "high-road" was the lower forms of the cooperative movement—supply and marketing cooperatives; but when the higher form of the cooperative movement—the collective farm—appeared, the latter became the "high-road" of development. The high-road (without quotation marks) of socialist development in the rural districts is Lenin's cooperative plan, which embraces all forms of agricultural cooperation, from the lowest (supply and marketing) to the highest (productive collective farms). To *draw a contrast* between collective farming and the cooperative societies is to make a mockery of Leninism and to acknowledge one's own ignorance.

Fourthly, now even the blind can see that without the offensive against the capitalist elements in the rural districts, and without the development of the collective-farm and state-farm movement, we would not have had the decisive successes, achieved this year in the matter of grain collections, nor the tens of millions of poods[2] of permanent grain reserves which have already accumulated in the hands of the state. Moreover, it can now be confidently asserted that, thanks to the growth of the collective-farm and state-farm movement, we are definitely emerging, or have already emerged, from the grain crisis. And if the development of the collective farms and state farms is accelerated, there is not the slightest ground for doubt that in about three years' time our country will be one of the largest grain countries in the world, if not *the* largest grain country in the world.

What is the *new* feature of the present collective-farm movement? The new and decisive feature of the present collective-farm movement is that the peasants are joining the collective farms not in separate groups, as was formerly the case, but in whole villages,

[2] One pood equals approximately 36 pounds.—Ed.

whole volosts, whole districts, and even whole areas. And what does that mean? It means that *the middle peasant has joined the collective-farm movement.* This is the basis of that radical change in the development of agriculture which represents the most important achievement of the Soviet government during the past year.

Trotskyism's Menshevik[3] "conception" that the working class is incapable of leading the great bulk of the peasantry in the cause of socialist construction is collapsing and being smashed to atoms. Now even the blind can see that the middle peasant has turned towards the collective farm. Now it is obvious to all that the Five-Year Plan of industry and agriculture is a five-year plan of building a socialist society, that those who do not believe in the possibility of building socialism in our country have no right to greet our Five-Year Plan.

The last hope of the capitalists of all countries, who are dreaming of restoring capitalism in the USSR—"the sacred principle of private property"—is collapsing and vanishing. The peasants, whom they regarded as material for manuring the soil for capitalism, are abandoning *en masse* the lauded banner of "private property" and are taking the path of collectivism, the path of socialism. The last hope for the restoration of capitalism is crumbling. . . .

We are advancing full steam ahead along the path of industrialization—to socialism, leaving behind the age-long "Russian" backwardness. We are becoming a country of metal, a country of automobiles, a country of tractors. And when we have put the USSR on an automobile, and the muzhik on a tractor, let the esteemed capitalists, who boast so loudly of their "civilization," try to overtake us! We shall see which countries may then be "classified" as backward and which as advanced.

. . . Can we advance our socialized industry at an accelerated rate while having to rely on an agricultural base, such as is provided by small peasant farming, which is incapable of expanded reproduction, and which, in addition, is the predominant force in our national economy? No, we cannot. Can the Soviet government and the work of socialist construction be, for any length of time, based on two *different* foundations: on the foundation of the most large-scale and con-

---

[3] Moderate Marxist (imputing this deviation to Trotsky).—Ed.

centrated socialist industry and on the foundation of the most scattered and backward, small-commodity peasant farming? No, they cannot. Sooner or later this would be bound to end in the complete collapse of the whole national economy. What, then, is the solution? The solution lies in enlarging the agricultural units, in making agriculture capable of accumulation, of expanded reproduction, and in thus changing the agricultural base of our national economy. But how are the agricultural units to be enlarged? There are two ways of doing this. There is the *capitalist* way, which is to enlarge the agricultural units by introducing capitalism in agriculture—a way which leads to the impoverishment of the peasantry and to the development of capitalist enterprises in agriculture. We reject this way as incompatible with the Soviet economic system. There is a second way: the *socialist* way, which is to set up collective farms and state farms, the way which leads to the amalgamation of the small peasant farms into large collective farms, technically and scientifically equipped, and to the squeezing out of the capitalist elements from agriculture. We are in favor of this second way.

And so, the question stands as follows: either one way or the other, either *back*—to capitalism or *forward*—to socialism. There is no third way, nor can there be. The "equilibrium" theory makes an attempt to indicate a third way. And precisely because it is based on a third (nonexistent) way, it is Utopian and anti-Marxian. . . .

Now, as you see, we have the material base which enables us to *substitute* for kulak output the output of the collective farms and state farms. That is why our offensive against the kulaks is now meeting with undeniable success. That is how the offensive against the kulaks must be carried on, if we mean a real offensive and not futile declamations against the kulaks.

That is why we have recently passed from the policy of *restricting* the exploiting proclivities of the kulaks to the policy of *eliminating the kulaks as a class.*

Well, what about the policy of expropriating the kulaks? Can we permit the expropriation of kulaks in the regions of solid collectivization? This question is asked in various quarters. A ridiculous question! We could not permit the expropriation of the kulaks as long as we were pursuing the policy of restricting the exploiting proclivities of the kulaks, as long as we were unable to launch a determined offensive against the kulaks, as long as we were unable to substitute for kulak output the output of the collective farms and state farms. At that time the policy of not permitting the expropriation of the kulaks was necessary and correct. But now? Now the situation is different. Now we are able to carry on a determined offensive against the kulaks, to break their resistance, to eliminate them as a class and substitute for their output the output of the collective farms and state farms. Now, the kulaks are being expropriated by the masses of poor and middle peasants themselves, by the masses who are putting solid collectivization into practice. Now, the expropriation of the kulaks in the regions of solid collectivization is no longer just an administrative measure. Now, the expropriation of the kulaks is an integral part of the formation and development of the collective farms. That is why it is ridiculous and fatuous to expatiate today on the expropriation of the kulaks. You do not lament the loss of the hair of one who has been beheaded.

There is another question which seems no less ridiculous; whether the kulak should be permitted to join the collective farms. Of course not, for he is a sworn enemy of the collective-farm movement. Clear, one would think.

Alec Nove
ECONOMICS AND PERSONALITY

The complex issues of economics underlying Stalin's five-year plans and the collectivization of the peasants have been succinctly evaluated by the British economist Alec Nove (b. 1915), a leading authority on the Soviet economic system. Nove surveys the problem in the political and psychological respects as well as the strictly economic, in an effort to judge what personal choices or political requirements caused Stalinism to become an economically unavoidable outcome.

Stalin has suffered a dramatic postmortem demotion, and a monu-

From Alec Nove, "Was Stalin Really Necessary?" *Encounter* (April 1962), pp. 86–92. Reprinted by permission of the editors.

ment to his victims is to be erected in Moscow. The present Soviet leadership is thus disassociating itself publicly from many of the highly disagreeable features of Stalin's rule, while claiming for the party and the Soviet system the credit for making Russia a great economic and military power. Is this a logically consistent standpoint? How far was Stalin, or Stalinism, an integral, unavoidable, "necessary" part of the achievement of the period? How much of the evil associated with the Stalin system is attributable to the peculiar character of the late dictator, and how much was the consequence of the policies adopted by the large majority of the Bolshevik party, or of the effort of a small and dedicated minority to impose very rapid industrialization on a peasant country? . . .

. . . The idea of "necessity" does not of course mean that the leader had to be a Georgian with a long moustache, but rather a tough dictator ruling a totalitarian state of the Stalinist type. What were the practical alternatives before the Bolsheviks in the late twenties, which contributed to the creation of the Stalinist régime, or, if one prefers a different formulation, gave the opportunity to ambitious men to achieve so high a degree of absolutism?

The key problem before the Bolsheviks concerned the linked questions of industrialization and political power. They felt they had to industrialize for several reasons, some of which they shared with non-Bolshevik predecessors. Thus the tsarist minister, Count Witte, as well as Stalin, believed that to achieve national strength and maintain independence, Russia needed a modern industry, especially heavy industry. The national-defense argument, relabelled "defense of the revolution," was greatly strengthened by the belief that the Russian Revolution was in constant danger from a hostile capitalist environment, militarily and technically far stronger than the USSR. Then there was the belief that the building of socialism or communism involved industrialization, and, more immediately, that a "proletarian dictatorship" was insecure so long as it ruled in an overwhelmingly petty-bourgeois, peasant, environment. There had to be a large increase in the number and importance of the proletariat, while the rise of a rich "kulak" class in the villages was regarded as a dangerous (or potentially dangerous) resurgence of capitalism. It was clear, by 1927, that it was useless to wait for "world revolution" to solve these problems. These propositions were common to the protagonists of the various platforms of the middle twenties. Thus even the "moderate" Bukharin wrote: "If there were a fall in the relative weight of the working class in its political and its social and class power, . . . this would subvert the basis of the proletarian dictatorship, the basis of our government." He too spoke in principle of the "struggle against the kulak, against the capitalist road," and warned of the "kulak danger." He too, even in the context of an attack on Zinoviev and the Left Opposition, argued the need for "changing the production relations of our country."

Until about 1927, a rapid rise in industrial production resulted from (or, "was a result of") the reactivation of prerevolutionary productive capacity, which fell into disuse and disrepair in the civil war period. However, it now became urgent to find material and financial means to expand the industrial base. This at once brought the peasant problem to the fore. The revolution had distributed land to 25 million families, most of whom were able or willing to provide only small marketable surpluses. Supplies of food to the towns and for export fell, peasant consumption rose. Yet the off-farm surplus must grow rapidly to sustain industrialization, especially where large-scale loans from abroad could scarcely be expected. As the Left Opposition vigorously pointed out, the peasant, the bulk of the population, had somehow to be made to contribute produce and money, to provide the bulk of "primitive socialist accumulation."

The arguments around these problems were inextricably entangled in the political factional struggles of the twenties. The moderate wing, led by Bukharin, believed that it was possible to advance slowly towards industrialization "at the pace of a tortoise," a pace severely limited by what the peasant was willing to do voluntarily. This was sometimes described as "riding towards socialism on a peasant nag." The logic of this policy demanded priority for developing consumers' goods industries, to make more cloth to encourage the peasants to sell more food. At first, Stalin sided with the moderates.

The case against the Bukharin line was of several different kinds. Firstly, free trade with the peasants could only provide adequate surpluses if the better-off peasants (that is, those known as *kulaks*) were allowed to expand, since they were the most efficient producers and provided a large part of the marketable produce. Yet all the

Bolshevik leaders (including, despite momentary aberrations, Bukharin himself) found this ideologically and politically unacceptable. A strong group of independent, rich peasants was Stolypin's dream as a basis for tsardom. It was the Bolshevik's nightmare, as totally inconsistent in the long run with their rule or with a socialist transformation of "petty-bourgeois" Russia. But this made the Bukharin approach of doubtful internal consistency. This was understood at the time by intelligent nonparty men. Thus the famous economist Kondratiev, later to perish in the purges, declared in 1927: "If you want a higher rate of accumulation . . . then the stronger elements of the village must be allowed to exploit (the weaker)," in other words that the kulaks must expand their holdings and employ landless laborers. The "peasant nag" could not pull the cart; or it, and the peasant, would pull in the wrong direction.

A second reason concerned the pace of the tortoise. The Bolsheviks were in a hurry. They saw themselves threatened by "imperialist interventionists." Even though some war scares were manufactured for factional reasons, the party as a whole believed that war against them would come before very long. This argued not merely for speed, but also for priority to *heavy* and not light industry, since it provided a basis for an arms industry. Still another reason was a less tangible but still very real one: the necessity of maintaining political *élan,* of not appearing to accept for an indefinite period a policy of gradualism based on the peasant, which would have demoralized the party and so gravely weakened the regime. It was widely felt, in and out of Russia, that by 1927 the regime had reached a *cul-de-sac.* I have in front of me a contemporary Menshevik pamphlet published abroad, by P. A. Garvi, which describes its dilemma quite clearly, and indeed the political and economic problem was extremely pressing: to justify its existence, to justify the party dictatorship in the name of the proletariat, a rapid move forward was urgent; but such a move forward would hardly be consistent with the "alliance with the peasants" which was the foundation of the policy of the moderates in the twenties. Stalin at this point swung over towards the Left, and his policy of all-out industrialization and collectivization was a means of breaking out of the *cul-de-sac,* of mobilizing the party to smash peasant resistance, to make possible the acquisition of farm surpluses without having to pay the price which any free peasants or free peasant associations would have demanded. He may well have felt he had little choice. It is worth quoting from the reminiscences of another Menshevik [N. Valentinov], who in the late twenties was working in the Soviet planning organs: "The financial base of the First Five-Year Plan, *until Stalin found it in levying tribute on the peasants, in primitive accumulation by the methods of Tamerlane,* was extremely precarious. . . . (It seemed likely that) everything would go to the devil. . . . No wonder that no one, literally no one, of the well-informed economists, believed or could believe in the fulfillment (of the plan)."

It does not matter in the present context whether Stalin made this shift through personal conviction of its necessity, or because this seemed to him to be a clever power-maneuver. The cleverness in any case largely consisted in knowing that he would thus strengthen his position by becoming the spokesman of the view which was widely popular among party activists. The leftists, destroyed organizationally by Stalin in earlier years, had a considerable following. Stalin's left-turn brought many of them to his support—though this did not save them from being shot in due course on Stalin's orders. It is probably the case that he had at this time genuine majority support within the party for his policy, though many had reservations about certain excesses, of which more will be said. But if this be so, the policy as such cannot be attributed to Stalin personally, and therefore the consequences which flowed from its adoption must be a matter of more than personal responsibility.

Let us examine some of these consequences. Collectivization could not be voluntary. Rapid industrialization, especially with priority for heavy industry, meant a reduction in living standards, despite contrary promises in the First Five-Year Plan. This meant a sharp increase in the degree of coercion, in the powers of the police, in the unpopularity of the regime. The aims of the bulk of the people were bound to be in conflict with the aims of the party. It should be added that this conflict is probably bound to arise in some form wherever *the state* is responsible for financing rapid industrialization; the sacrifices are then imposed by political authority, and the masses of "small" people do not and cannot provide voluntarily the necessary savings, since in the nature of things their present abstinence cannot be linked with a future return which they as individuals can identify.

However, this possibly unavoidable unpopularity was greatly increased in the USSR by the sheer pace of the advance and by the attack on peasant property, and, as we shall see, both these factors reacted adversely on production of consumers' goods and so led to still further hardships and even greater unpopularity. The strains and priorities involved in a rapid move forward required a high degree of economic centralization, to prevent resources from being diverted to satisfy needs which were urgent but of a nonpriority character. In this situation, the party was the one body capable of carrying out enormous changes and resisting social and economic pressures in a hostile environment; this was bound to affect its structure. For a number of years it had already been in process of transformation from a political into a power machine. The problems involved in the "revolution from above" intensified the process of turning it into an obedient instrument for changing, suppressing, controlling.

This, in turn, required hierarchical subordination, in suppression of discussion; therefore there had to be an unquestioned commander-in-chief. Below him, toughness in executing unpopular orders became the highest qualification for party office. The emergence of Stalin, and of Stalin-type bullying officials of the sergeant-major species, was accompanied by the decline in the importance of the cosmopolitan journalist-intellectual type of party leader who had played so prominent a role earlier.

The rise of Stalin to supreme authority was surely connected with the belief among many party members that he was the kind of man who could cope with this kind of situation. Of course, it could well be that Stalin tended to adopt policies which caused him and his type to be regarded as indispensable, and he promoted men to office in the party because they were loyal to him. Personal ambition, a desire for power, were important factors in shaping events. But this is so obvious, so clearly visible on the surface, that the underlying problems, policy choices and logical consequences of policies need to be stressed.

Let us recapitulate: the Communists needed dictatorial power if they were to continue to rule; if they were to take effective steps towards industrialization these steps were bound to give rise to problems which would require further tightening of political and economic control. While we cannot say, without much further research, whether a Bukharinite or other moderate policy was impossible, once the decision to move fast was taken this had very radical consequences; the need for a tough, coercive government correspondingly increased. Given the nature of the party apparatus, the mental and political development of the Russian masses, the logic of police rule, these policies were bound to lead to a conflict with the peasantry and to excesses of various kinds. Thus, given the premises, certain elements of what may be called Stalinism followed, were objective "necessities." In this sense, and to this extent, Stalin was, so to speak, operating within the logical consequences of Leninism.

It is an essential part of Lenin's views that the party was to seize power and use it to change Russian society; this is what distinguished him from the Mensheviks who believed that conditions for socialism should ripen within society. Lenin also suppressed Opposition parties and required stern discipline from his own followers. (It is impossible to ban free speech outside the party without purging the party of those who express "wrong" views within it.) Indeed Lenin promoted Stalin because he knew he was tough, would "prepare peppery dishes," though he had last-minute regrets about it. While it would be going too far to describe Stalin as a true Leninist, if only because Lenin was neither personally brutal nor an oriental despot, Stalin undoubtedly carried through some of the logical consequences of Lenin's policies and ideas. This remains true even though Lenin thought that the peasant problem could be solved by voluntary inspiration, and would probably have recoiled at the conditions of forced collectivization.

Is it necessary to stress that this does not make these actions right, or good? Yes, it is, because so many critics assume that to explain is to justify. So it must be said several times that no moral conclusions follow, that even the most vicious acts by politicians and others generally have causes which must be analyzed. We are here only concerned to disentangle the special contribution of Stalin, the extent to which Stalinism was, so to speak, situation-determined. This is relevant, indeed, to one's picture of Stalin's personal responsibility, but in no way absolves him of such responsibility. If in order to do A it proves necessary to do B, we can, after all, refuse to do B, abandon or modify the aim of attaining A, or resign, or, in extreme circumstances—like Stalin's old comrade Ordzhonikidze—commit suicide.

But Stalin's personal responsibility goes far beyond his being the voice and leader of a party majority in a given historical situation. For one cannot possibly argue that all the immense evils of the Stalin era flowed inescapably from the policy decisions of 1928–1929. In assessing Stalin's personal role in bringing these evils about, it is useful to approach the facts from two angles. There was, first, the category of evils which sprang from policy choices which Stalin made and which he need not have made; in other words we are here concerned with consequences (perhaps necessary) of unnecessary decisions. The other category consists of evil actions which can reasonably be attributed to Stalin and which are his direct responsibility.

Of course, these categories shade into one another, as do murder and manslaughter. In the first case, the evils were in a sense situation-determined, but Stalin had a large hand in determining the situation. In the second, his guilt is as clear as a politician's guilt can be.

The most obvious examples of the first category are: the brutality of collectivization and the madly excessive pace of industrial development. In each case, we are dealing with *"excessive excesses,"* since we have already noted that collectivization without coercion was impossible, and rapid industrialization was bound to cause stresses and strains.

Take collectivization first. Some overzealous officials were presumably bound to overdo things, especially since the typical party man was a townsman with no understanding or sympathy for peasants and their problems. But these officials received orders to impose rapid collectivization, to deport *kulaks,* to seize all livestock, and Stalin was surely the source of these orders. The deportation of the *kulaks* (which in reality meant anyone who voiced opposition to collectivization) removed at one blow the most efficient farmers. There had been no serious preparation of the measures, no clear orders about how a collective farm should be run. Chinese experience, at least before the communes, suggests that milder ways of proceeding are possible. In any event, the attempt to collectivize all private livestock ended in disaster and a retreat. It is worth reproducing the figures from the official handbook of agricultural statistics:

Livestock Population (Million of Head)

	1928	1934
Horses	32.1	15.4
Cattle	60.1	33.5
Pigs	22.0	11.5
Sheep	97.3	32.9

Yet already by 1934 private livestock holdings were again permitted, and in 1938 over three-quarters of all cows, over two-thirds of all pigs, nearly two-thirds of all sheep, were in private hands. This is evidence of a disastrous error.

Its consequences were profound. Peasant hostility and bitterness were greatly intensified. For many years there were in fact no net investments in agriculture, since the new tractors merely went to replace some of the slaughtered horses. Acute food shortage made itself felt—though the state's control over produce ensured that most of those who died in the resulting famine were peasants and not townsmen. But once all this happened, the case for coercion was greatly strengthened, the need for police measures became more urgent than ever, the power of the censorship was increased, freedom of speech had still further to be curtailed, as part of the necessities of remaining in power and continuing the industrial revolution in an environment grown more hostile as a result of such policies. So Stalin's policy decisions led to events which contributed greatly to the further growth of totalitarianism and the police state.

The same is true of the attempt to do the impossible on the industrial front in the years of the First Five-Year Plan. Much of the effort was simply wasted, as when food was taken from hungry peasants and exported to pay for machines which rusted in the open or were wrecked by untrained workmen. At the same time, the closing of many private workshops deprived the people of consumers' goods which the state, intent on building steelworks and machineshops, was quite unable to provide. Again, living standards suffered, the hatred of many citizens for the regime increased, the NKVD had to be expanded and the logic of police rule followed. But Stalin had a big role in the initial decisions to jump too far too fast. (It is interesting to note that Mao, who should have learnt the lessons of history, repeated many of these mistakes in China's "great leap forward" of 1958–1959, which suggests that *there are certain errors which Communists repeatedly commit,* possibly due to the suppression, in "antirightist" campaigns, of the voices of moderation and common sense.)

One of the consequences of these acute hardships was isolation from foreign countries. Economists often speak of the "demonstration effect," that is, of the effect of the knowledge of higher living standards abroad on the citizens of poor and underdeveloped countries. This knowledge may act as a spur to effort—but it also generates resistance to sacrifice. Stalin and his regime systematically "shielded" Soviet citizens from knowledge of the outside world, by censorship, by cutting off personal contacts, by misinformation. The need to do so, in their eyes, was greatly increased by the extent of the drop in living standards in the early thirties.

But we must now come to Stalin's more direct contribution to the brutality and terrorism of the Stalin era.

There was, firstly, his needless cruelty which showed itself already in the methods used to impose collectivization. The great purges were surely not "objectively necessary." To explain them one has to take into account Stalin's thirst for supreme power, his intense pathological suspiciousness, that is, matters pertaining to Stalin's personal position and character. These led him to massacre the majority of the "Stalinist" Central Committee elected in 1934, who had supported or at the very least tolerated Stalin's policies up to that date. The facts suggest that they believed that relaxation was possible and desirable; many of them seem to have died for the crime of saying so. . . .

. . . One could argue that the myth about "voluntary collectivization" was an objectively necessary lie, in the sense of transcending Stalin's personality; indeed, this lie figures in the party program adopted by the Twenty-second Congress last November. But Stalin's lies went very much beyond this, and beyond the distortions and myths which can be ascribed to other politicians in other countries.

Throughout Russia, officials at all levels modelled themselves on Stalin, and each succeeded in imposing more unnecessary misery on more subordinates, stultifying initiative, penalizing intelligence, discouraging originality. The price of all this is still being paid.

The urgent need to prepare for war has often been advanced as an excuse for Stalin's industrial "tempos" and for the terror. This can hardly be accepted. In the worst years of social coercion and over-ambitious plans, that is, 1929–1933, Hitler was only just climbing to power, and Comintern policy showed that he was not then regarded as the main enemy. It is possible that Stalin was liquidating all potential opponents in the purges of 1936–1938 as a precaution in case war broke out, though this seems doubtful for a variety of reasons. But it is quite false to use the result of the war as ex-post-factum justification of Stalinism. Perhaps, with less harsh policies, the greater degree of loyalty in 1941 would have offset a smaller industrial base? In any event the purges not only led to the slaughter of the best military officers but also halted the growth of heavy industry.

The attentive reader will have noticed that this analysis has some features in common with Khrushchev's. Before 1934, Stalin had been carrying out policies which commanded the assent of a majority of the party and which, like collectivization, had been accepted as necessary and irreversible by the bulk of party members, whatever their reservations about particular mistakes and acts of brutality. However, after that date he took more and more personal, arbitrary measures, massacred much of the party, behaved like an oriental despot. It is true that he was also arbitrary before 1934, and that he took some wise decisions after that date; but there is a case for placing a qualitative change around then.

But this is by no means the end of the matter. It is not only a question of making some obvious remarks concerning Khrushchev's own role during the terror. Of much more general significance is the fact that the events prior to 1934, including the building-up of Stalin into an all-powerful and infallible dictator (by men many of whom he afterwards massacred), cannot be disassociated with what followed; at the very least they provided Stalin with his opportunity. This is where the historian must avoid the twin and opposite pitfalls of regarding what happened as inevitable, and regarding it as a chapter of "personalized" accidents. At each stage there are choices to be made, though the range of possible choices is generally much narrower than people suppose. In 1928 any practicable Bolshevik program would have been harsh and unpopular. It might not have been so harsh and unpopular but for choices which need not necessarily have been made. If before 1934, that is, in the very period of maximum social coercion, Stalin truly represented the will of the party, and Khrushchev argues that he did, some totalitarian consequences logically follow. One of these as already suggested, is the semimilitarized party led by a *Fuehrer,* a dictator, because without an unquestioned leader the consequences of the policies adopted could not be faced.

But, even if it is true that the triumph of a dictator may be explained by objective circumstances which certainly existed in the Soviet situation, the acts of a dictator once he has "arrived" involve a considerable (though of course not infinite) degree of personal choice. Those who gave him the opportunity to act in an arbitrary and cruel way, who adopted policies which involved arbitrariness and coercion on a big scale, cannot ascribe subsequent events to the wickedness of one man or his immediate associates and claim that their hands are clean, even indeed if they were shot themselves on Stalin's orders. The whole-hog Stalin, in other words, was not "necessary," but the possibility of a Stalin was a necessary consequence of the effort of a minority group to keep power and to carry out a vast social-economic revolution in a very short time. And *some* elements of Stalinism were, in those circumstances, scarcely avoidable.

The serious problem for us is to see how far certain elements of Stalinism, in the sense of purposefully-applied social coercion, imposed by a party in the name of an ideology, are likely or liable to accompany rapid economic development even in non-Communist countries.

For it is surely true that many of the problems tackled by Stalin so brutally are present elsewhere, though events in the USSR were, of course, deeply affected by peculiar features of Russia and of Bolshevism. The West should indeed emphasize the high cost in human and material terms of a Stalin, and show that the rise of such a man to supreme power in the Soviet Union was, to use the familiar

Soviet-Marxist jargon phrase, "not accidental." Indeed, some Western historians who normally write "personalist" and empiricist history will begin to see the virtues of an approach they normally deride
as "historicist"; they will analyze Soviet history to establish patterns,
regularities, "necessities" which lead to Stalin. By contrast, an em-
barrassed Khrushchev will be—is being—forced to give an un-Marx-
ist emphasis to personal and accidental factors.

But, of course, we must not confine our search for "necessities"
in history only to instances which happen to serve a propagandist
purpose. This would be a typically Soviet approach to historiography,
only in reverse. It is particularly important to think very seriously
about the interrelationship of coercion and industrialization, about
the nature of the obstacles and vicious circles which drive men to
think in totalitarian terms. Unless we realize how complex are the
problems which development brings, how irrelevant are many of
our ideas to the practical possibilities open to statesmen in these
countries, we may unconsciously drive them towards the road which
led to Stalin. They cannot be satisfied with "the pace of a tortoise."

Manya Gordon
THE FATE OF THE WORKERS

*To a non-Communist socialist, the First Five Year Plan meant the complete
betrayal of the workers' interests for the sake of building new state-owned
industry. This is the view argued by Manya Gordon (1882–1945), a native of
Russia and at one time a member of the Socialist Revolutionary Party, who
came to America and became the wife of the Russian-American editor and
author Simeon Strunsky. In her book,* Workers Before and After Lenin, *Miss
Gordon undertook to show just how the so-called proletarian revolution had
affected the condition of the Russian working class.*

The Communists began by being sincerely loyal to labor, but Lenin soon discovered that the interests of labor were not always the same as the employer's—the state. Tomsky endorsed this stand in the 1920 resolutions. In other words, the Marxist Lenin, acknowledged leader of the socialist state, and Tomsky, the Marxist trade union leader, agreed that the interests of the workers were not the same as those of the employer in a so-called socialist state. If that is so, then the state as sole employer can always find a way of prohibiting strikes and other defensive activities of the workers. Any real labor grievance can be declared antigovernment. This is precisely the difficulty that Tomsky faced and endeavored to surmount. He did, in fact, accomplish a great deal in the period up to 1928. But ultimately the Communist state as employer had no difficulty in undermining his entire position.

The year 1928, the beginning of the First Five-Year Plan, witnessed a complete change in the position of labor. Stalin, Molotov, Kaganovich and others were bent on making of the trade unions an ordinary instrument for the execution of the government plans, completely subservient to the Soviet state. Tomsky and the other trade union leaders opposed this "merging" of the labor organizations with the government because it would turn their representatives into impotent state officials. Stalin and his associates replied to this protest by quoting from the resolutions of the Ninth Congress of which Tomsky was one of the signatories and which declared: "Under the dictatorship of the proletariat the trade unions cease to be organizations which sell labor power to an employing class. There can be no question of trade union opposition to the institutions of the Soviet state. Such opposition is a deviation from Marxism to bourgeois trade unionism." Thus, when convenient the Soviet government declares the trade unions a separate institution concerned only with the interests of the workers, but when necessary the unions become the government.

Tomsky's accusation that Stalin had really adopted Trotsky's doctrine of "merging," so strongly opposed by Lenin, had no effect. The result is history. Tomsky, Bukharin and Rykov were compelled to resign from the Politbureau and the Central Committee of the Communist Party, and Stalin packed these powerful agencies with his own followers who did not hesitate to subordinate the interests of labor to the Five-Year Plan. In April 1929, when the subject of the position of the trade unions in the Soviet state was again to the fore Stalin had no difficulty in finding a majority which declared: "In the matter of the trade unions, Bukharin, Rykov, and Tomsky have launched a dangerous trade union opposition to the party, are actually seeking to weaken the party's supervision over the trade union movement, and are concealing their 'trade unionistic' tendencies by describing the party struggle against the shortcomings in the unions as a Trotskyist shake-up of the unions."

The American reader may consider this a very mild statement in an extremely serious discussion, but in reality it turned out to be a death sentence on these outstanding Communist leaders and on the trade unions. Stalin and his associates declared: "The trade unions are called upon to play a decisive role in the task of building socialist industry by stimulating labor productivity, labor discipline and socialist competition, and extirpating all remnants of guild isolation and 'trade unionism.' " Tomsky refused to acquiesce in this method of virtually destroying the trade unions by converting them into agencies of exploitation and was removed from the central committee of the unions. He was succeeded by Shvernik, completely unknown but Stalin's favorite. In order to strengthen Shvernik's authority Stalin made him, in November 1929, a member of the Central Committee of the Communist Party and there followed the speeding up of the struggle against Tomsky's "bourgeois 'trade unionism' " and the nullification of every trade union prerogative without which the labor organizations became meaningless.

Henceforth the trade unions were compelled to drive the workers, to organize "shock brigades" and "socialist competition" and bring to trial workers who lagged behind in their quantitative "norms" or in quality. As a result the trade unions in Soviet Russia are today a misnomer, and have nothing basically in common with similar organizations in other countries. They are merely a whip over the workers, as plainly shown in the resolutions adopted in the second year of the Five Year Plan, at the Sixteenth Congress of the Communist Party in 1930. The most important part of the declaration reads as follows:

> *The present phase of socialist construction raises the problem of the complete reorganization of the activities of the proletarian mass organizations, and among others the trade unions. It is necessary to concentrate*

on production. The opportunistic ruling group of the old executive of the All-Russian Trade Union Central Committee not only showed itself unable to understand the problems of the proletarian dictatorship but opposed the party's reorganization of the work of the trade unions. Displaying "trade unionistic" tendencies, this opportunistic leadership actually carried on a campaign to weaken the party's supervision over the trade union movement. Under the leadership of the party, the trade unions have now removed their bankrupt leaders and have begun a determined fight against the elements of "trade unionism" and opportunism in the trade union movement. Today the basic factor in energizing and improving the entire work of the trade unions must be socialist competition and its offspring, the shock brigades. Socialist competition and the shock brigades must become the primary concern of all the constructive activities of the unions. The problem of the trade unions is the organization of socialist competition and the shock brigades. The trade unions must organize fraternal trials between the best shock brigadiers in order to make the necessary impression on persons who violate labor discipline. The chief concern of all union organizations must be the promotion of outstanding workers to the position of factory directors, officials of departments and their assistants. This reconstruction period demands the participation of the trade unions in the socialist reconstruction of agriculture. The trade unions must make it their particular business to draw women into production. In approving the dispatch of 25,000 workers for the construction of the kolkhozes [collectivized farms] the congress declares that the trade unions must make careful preparation and produce new thousands of workers as organizers and directors of kolkhoz construction.

The congress pledges the party organizations and the trade union bodies to increase the propaganda of Leninism in the entire system of the cultural-political work of the unions, to impregnate it with Communist dogma, to remove completely all nonpolitical and narrow cultural elements. The trade unions must fight petty bourgeois leanings and forms of thinking in the labor sphere. The Sixteenth Congress approves the attitude of the new leadership of the trade unions in regard to the absolute support and strengthening of the Profintern [Communist Trade Union International] and trade union amalgamation with the Communist International. The Soviet trade unions must use the Profintern to strengthen their relations with the working class of the Communist and colonial nations for the purpose of waging an unceasing struggle against the reformists in the trade union movement and to promote union with Amsterdam and the strengthening of the revolutionary world trade union movement. The problems which are submitted to the unions can only be solved by a complete reorganization of the work of the trade unions. The basis of the reorganization of the unions is the shock brigade movement.

Here, then, it is bluntly stated that socialist competition and its "offspring" the shock brigades must be the primary concern of all constructive work in the unions. Instead of defending the interests of the workers the labor organizations are obliged to disseminate Stalin's brand of Leninism. Actually, it will be recalled, Lenin insisted that the trade unions must be nonpolitical. Stalin now demands that in their Leninist propaganda the unions shall wipe out all nonpolitical elements. This decree was not without a purpose. It was directed against the trade union movement and the solidarity of the workers as well as the Opposition—and it succeeded.

This period of 1929–1930 marks the virtual annihilation of the trade unions. Terrorized by threats of execution, by the trials of the nonpartisan engineers in 1930, by the purges of the Mensheviks in 1931, by the expulsion from the trade unions of all of Tomsky's associates and the appointment of Shvernik as head, the trade unions became completely passive. They no longer had the courage to pose any question concerned with the protection of labor. The trade unions were silent when in 1931 it was decreed that a worker could not change his job without the permission of the head of the plant. They were silent when the railroad workers were threatened with years of imprisonment because they had failed to fulfill the prescribed quota in transportation. They were silent when the Soviet [council] of People's Commissars, on February 13, 1931 condemned technically untrained peasant boys to three years' imprisonment because they had unintentionally wrecked some tractors. They were silent on December 4, 1932 when the Soviet of People's Commissars and the Central Committee of the Communist Party issued the amazing decree putting food supplies and other necessities under the control of the factory directors "in order to strengthen the power of directors of enterprises." In other words, as Pravda saw it, the administrator was given the right to prescribe "the amount of food that should be used."

Beginning with 1930 "the primary purpose of the trade unions," as one secretary of the central committee put it, "was to direct the fight for the completion and overfulfillment by every worker of his prescribed norm of work." The "merging" of the trade unions with the government was so speedy and complete that wages, sanitation and other labor interests were left in abeyance and the unions concentrated their entire attention on extracting from their members the maximum amount of work. In their anxiety to prove their loyalty to the government the new trade union leaders were more severe than the factory directors. For example, the central committee of the machinists' union called to the attention of the government, that is the employer, the fact that in several machine works the wage budget was "exceeded," and took steps to turn the matter over to the government prosecutor for bringing criminal charges against the factory directors.

Collective bargaining was relegated to the waste basket. The factory managers became the sole authority on wages and the "amount" of provisions each worker might consume. Without the right to strike or protest in any other way against oppressive measures by the employer the Soviet workers were reduced to the position occupied by labor at the very beginning of Russia's industrialization seventy-five years ago. In fact, Stalin's attitude towards labor was precisely the same as that of the early Russian capitalists towards the erstwhile serfs. The new phraseology and the avowed purpose was different, but that did not make the subjugation of labor any pleasanter.

One might cite as an example the national economic plan of 1931 with two very interesting items. It prescribed for industrial workers an increase in production of 28 percent, and for that they were to receive a 6 percent increase in wages. A brief study of these figures will reveal the psychological similarity of government and capitalist as employer. The gross industrial production of 1930 amounted to 25.8 billion rubles. During that year heavy industry employed 4,263,000 workers. Therefore the gross production per person was 6,000 rubles. For the following year the government demanded an increase of 28 percent, that is, an increase of 1,700 rubles. In 1930 the annual average wage of industrial workers was 1,035 rubles and the government was willing to grant a 6 percent increase, that is 62 rubles. In other words the Communist government asked for a 1,700 ruble increase in production in return for which it was willing to pay the workers 62 rubles. Actually, instead of an increase there was a reduction in wages. It is an interesting example not only of Communist reasoning about wages but of the method of determining wages. Everything was done by the administration. Labor had not the slightest share in it. . . .

Disorganization of agriculture, the only profitable enterprise in the Soviet Union, was not conducive to higher wages. In fact, the decline in real wages began in 1928. This in turn compelled the official statisticians more energetically to manipulate the wage indexes, but notwithstanding their efforts it became apparent that the industrial worker had to be satisfied with less food. The beginning of farm collectivization in 1929 helped still further to increase the shortage of food in the cities.

The catastrophic state of the country did not, however, prevent the government from writing into the resolutions of the Sixteenth Congress of the Communist Party in July 1930: "During the last five years wages have increased more than 70 percent, reaching 139 percent of prewar real wages." Four months later at a meeting of the Central Executive Committee and the Central Committee of the Communist Party the utterances were more tempered but not devoid of exaggeration. The resolution declared: "Wages have increased during the first two years of the Five Year Plan (1929–1930) by 12 percent." It did not take the trouble to explain the difference between nominal and real earnings. Actually the rise in nominal wages failed to keep pace with the ever-increasing cost of provisions. . . .

In 1928–1929 the government statisticians declared: "Because of the shortage of a number of products there took place in the course of the year a curtailment of the consumption of bread, meat and sugar." The following year it was officially acknowledged: "The composition of the workers' diet has undergone a great change in comparison with the previous year. The decrease in the consumption of breadstuffs was 4.8 percent, meat 10.1 percent, sugar 14.2 percent." Butter, eggs and milk were no longer mentioned. The tightening of the belt continued. In 1930 the shortage became so grave that the government considered it expedient to stop the publication of the food indexes. . . .

As between 1928 and 1930 it is true that the nominal wage of an industrial worker rose from 69 rubles to 83 rubles or 18 percent; but it has been seen that the cost of food in the same period rose nearly 89 percent. . . .

. . . The Communist government did not cease to export grain in exchange for its precious machines. Of course, the tsars also exported grain at a time of scarcity, in 1891–1893, but their inhumanity was condemned by everybody, including the future Communists. Furthermore, the tsar was not a Marxist. He did not confuse his loyalties. Exporting foodstuffs during a national shortage did not conflict with his class interests. His immediate entourage of land-owners, bureaucrats and capitalists did not suffer. Stalin's agrarian policy weighed down on the very people who had a right to expect protection from the Soviet government. The exportation of food while the industrial workers were starving was proof that the Soviet govern-ment was more interested in its industrialization formulas than in the proletariat. It revealed a capitalist-employer attitude towards production.

The plan was the thing, and not the life of the workers. To be sure, it was all done for the good of future generations and in the name of the socialist state. The exploitation of the Congo by Leo-pold II, J. D. Rockefeller's early Standard Oil activities and other capitalist aggressions have been defended with the same kind of cant. During the tsarist regime Leo Tolstoy and other great-hearted Russians, with a majority of Russia's "bourgeois capitalists," came to the aid of the starving masses. The Communists, on the other hand, insisted that the Russian people were not starving while the all-powerful OGPU stifled every protest. Instead of appealing for foreign aid as in 1921–1923 when the American people came to the rescue, every effort was made to conceal the catastrophic situation. Foreign correspondents were forbidden to enter the famine stricken areas and the censor deleted all "undesirable" information from their dispatches. "The greater the toll, the more effective the lesson."

But for one very serious qualification the plan to subjugate the peasantry was thus proceeding according to schedule. This excep-tion consisted in the fact that punishment descended not alone upon the officially proclaimed guilty peasant, but upon the innocent indus-trial worker. To use Lenin's graphic description of the condition of the workers in 1921, more than ten years later in 1931–1933, "the en-feeblement of the workers is near the point of complete incapacity for work." Lack of food endangered the execution of the Five-Year Plan. Had Lenin been alive he would have very likely taken drastic measures against this suicidal agricultural policy. Joseph Stalin was of sterner metal than the founder of Russian Communism. To be sure, Lenin in his courageous retreat in 1921—the New Economic Policy

—was in some degree motivated by the fact that the Communists were not sufficiently entrenched to risk a showdown. By 1930 thirteen years of Communist rule fortified Stalin's belief in the invincibility of the Soviet state and his personal authority. Power developed in him the capitalist-employer psychology, but an autocrat who sees himself as an industrialist without actually understanding the industrial requirements of the country is a menace.

M. Lewin
COLLECTIVIZATION: THE REASONS

A growing body of Western scholarship has begun to challenge the view that Russia's economic difficulties made forcible collectivization of the peasants a necessary accompaniment of the industrialization drive. The Polish-born, Israeli- and French-educated historian Moshe Lewin (b. 1921), who presently teaches at the University of Birmingham in England, has re-examined the background of collectivization in great detail, particularly in his book Russian Peasants and Soviet Power. *In an earlier article based on this work he demonstrates the existence of real alternatives facing the Soviet leadership.*

The Role of the Grain Crisis

. . . It would be wrong to look upon the great leap at the end of 1929 as having been conceived all of a piece at the very last moment. For, in a sense, the decision to undertake overall collectivization had its roots in the grain crisis at the beginning of 1928. Stalin's ideas on policy germinated during the testing time of this crisis, though only in essentials, for *at that stage he was concerned only with a short-term policy of moderate aims,* but by reason of the growing crisis he was constantly obliged to extend the objectives with which he had set out at the beginning of the year.

Indeed, the grain crisis was of crucial importance in the shaping

From M. Lewin, "The Immediate Background of Soviet Collectivization," *Soviet Studies* 17 (October 1965): 170–172, 179–197. Reprinted by permission of the publisher, Basil Blackwell.

of future events, among other reasons because Stalin derived from it a whole series of new conclusions and the elements of a new plan of campaign. During his visit to Siberia, where he had gone to urge and compel the party officials to take the grain ruthlessly, he had felt that, in addition to the weapons of compulsion, he ought to have something to offer these officials in the way of a long-term policy and a more optimistic perspective. None of his statements in Siberia was published at the time, but we now know in what terms he spoke.

It was at this juncture that he became aware of the urgent necessity for establishing strongpoints in the countryside, similar to those the regime had built up in the towns. So it appeared that the hitherto accepted thesis to the effect that cooperation could serve as this strategic position was in practice dropped. This was replaced by the discovery, which was new coming from Stalin, of kolkhozy [collective farms] and sovkhozy [state farms]—those feeble organisms hitherto the Cinderellas of the regime. It is at this point also that he expressed the thought that the Soviet regime was "walking on two unequal legs"—the socialist sector in the towns and the private sector in the villages—and that this could not go on indefinitely. It can be deduced from this (and Stalin in fact admitted it explicitly the same year) that he no longer believed in NEP as a viable policy. The more his methods intensified the crisis, the more his scepticism increased.

Towards May [1928], his faith in the kolkhozy and sovkhozy as the sovereign remedy was further strengthened. He discovered that these organisms had a considerable marketing potential; it was suggested that this was four times greater than that of the private peasants. At this time Stalin was also greatly preoccupied with another important problem; how was the regime to ensure that kolkhozy and sovkhozy would hand their grain over to the state? Here he went straight to the heart of the matter. He believed, and rightly so, that what would be impossible with the existing 25 million farms would become more practicable if they were merged into a smaller number of large farms.

Stalin's strategy, as it emerged at this stage, took the following form: there was an imperative need for a new policy, comprising a renewed effort on the industrial front and the establishment of a powerful kolkhoz-sovkhoz sector. The private sector in the countryside would remain, and would in fact continue to function as an essential element in grain production, but this was no longer enough. In Stalin's view, the scale of the socialist operation in the country-side would be determined by the quantitative target which he had set himself. As he saw it, matters must be so arranged that the state would be absolutely sure of having at its disposal some 250 million poods of grain (in other words, about a third of the quantity required by the end of the Five-Year Plan). Sovkhozy, kolkhozy and contracts signed with peasants' associations would produce this quantity, and the state would thus be able to supply the key sectors of the economy and the army, and to operate on the national (and international) markets, thereby forcing the peasants to sell their surpluses to the state because of competition due to the reserves it had in hand. Stalin would have liked to achieve this objective within three to four years. His colleagues were of the opinion that it would take four to five years.

The regime was, therefore, still a long way from any kind of total collectivization but, as we know, it was already on the road, although it was hardly aware of it at the time.

Stalin's thoughts about the situation had crystallized by the July plenum and still followed the same main lines, irrespective of his maneuvers in the internal struggle against the right wing, which, brought into the open by the procurement crisis, was now at its height. Stalin knew, and told the Central Committee in a speech which was secret at the time, that the peasants would have to pay a tribute (*dan*) for the requirements of industrialization. This was Preo-brazhensky's theory, but with none of the latter's scruples or reservations. Stalin realized that the workers, too, would have to be made to pay, and that this would give rise to increasing social contradictions. How, then, were things to be kept going for another four years or so, until such times as the state and collective sector would bring an improvement in the situation? Stalin had made up his mind: in the meanwhile, the regime would use emergency measures to collect the grain. He had already done this in the course of the year. He suggested it again in July, and had made official policy of it by April 1929. Bukharin scarcely exaggerated when he said to Kamenev: "He will have to drown the risings in blood,"—but this Stalin was prepared to do. . . .

The Five-Year Plan and Stalin's Attitude

. . . The Five-Year Plan had no convincing answer to the question of easing current supply difficulties while waiting for the plan to bear fruit. At all events, it was decided that, until the end of the Five-Year Plan, there would be no export of grain.

No one had yet dreamed of mass collectivization as a rapid and effective means of solving both current and long-term problems at one and the same time. The plan was ratified by the Congress of Soviets in May 1929. The great majority of the *Party leadership* did not, either at this stage or in the autumn, foresee what decisions were to be taken some six months later.[1] At that time, everyone was uttering warnings about over-hasty action in relation to changes of organization in the countryside. The party were convinced, as Kalinin and Rykov put it at the time,[2] that the scale of collectivization must be related and adapted to the state's actual ability to provide machines and specialists. They all sincerely believed that the entire operation would be carried out exclusively on the basis of voluntary membership.

But it was precisely at this moment, when the plan, with its relatively moderate and feasible aims for the agricultural sector, had just been launched, that Stalin arrived at quite different conclusions. At the plenum in April 1929, his lack of faith in the private agricultural sector and in NEP finally came to the surface. Just about this time another procurement campaign had been carried through in the face of enormous difficulties, and had yielded *less grain than in the previous year,* despite the use of a whole body of coercive measures, which had been applied more or less throughout the country but especially in the Urals and in Siberia.

[1] Bauman, Moscow party secretary and head of the rural department of the Central Committee, said in June (*Pravda,* 16 June 1929) that Moscow oblast [province] was preparing to collectivize 25 percent of its peasants in five years and that in general, a period of twenty years was necessary to collectivize all.

[2] Kalinin, Fifth Congress of Soviets, stenographic report, bulletin no. 15, p. 39, declared: "Whoever thinks that these [good agricultural enterprises] can be established in a hole-and-corner way, primitively, without highly qualified mechanics and specialists, whoever thinks this is neither a Marxist nor a Communist but a man of petty-bourgeois mentality, a man stricken by peasant narrowness"(!); Rykov, ibid. bulletin no. 7, p. 8 spoke against setting up kolkhozy on the basis of the *sokha* (wooden plow); Stalin said the same thing in April 1929 (*Bolshevik,* 1929, nos. 23–24, p. 34).

It was clear that Stalin was already planning to launch a really large-scale operation. He informed the Central Committee that the kulaks and other hostile forces were preparing to undermine the Soviet regime—a type of assertion which, as we now know, was a sign that he was either preparing to attack or to drive home his attack. Indeed, he told the Central Committee (it should be borne in mind that his speech was secret at the time) that "the days of the capitalists and the kulaks are numbered." . . .

The violent and impetuous character of the decisions which were taken is more readily explicable by certain internal factors. Stalin expressly stated in April that he was relying on emergency measures to solve the grain crisis. He was well aware that such a policy could not last long without leading to a disastrous clash with the peasantry. This was the reason behind the attack on the Nepmen and industrial specialists in the towns, and on the better-off peasants in the countryside, for care must be taken to weaken any elements which might eventually rally an outraged peasantry. The same motive underlay subsequent decisions (towards the end of 1929). Again, the antikulak measures, apart from their role in the campaigns for wresting grain from the peasants, were a maneuver aimed at the social encirclement of the middle peasants, designed to divide them and to block all their escape routes, leaving them only one way out.

Here one recognizes the hand of Stalin, the master tactician. In fact, his social and political tactics were much better than his strategy, for the latter calls for a greater capacity for theoretical analysis, which he did not possess. At all events, could it be said in April-May 1929, when he had already made his intentions quite clear, that the practical program embodying ideas on the scale of the reforms which were to take place and the methods by which they were to be achieved had received consideration, preparation or ratification from any organization whatsoever?

In the writer's view, Stalin at this point still did not know where his actions would lead six months later. It would seem that his aims, and those of his immediate lieutenants, were still in line with the provisions of the Five-Year Plan, although in certain respects going beyond these. Several months were still to elapse, until about the end of September, before the economic results of the year would be known, when Stalin and his Politburo would *once more revise* the existing plans, involving decisions on an unprecedentedly large scale.

The Results of the Year 1928/29 and the Part Played by Them

The economic results of the year 1928/29 were much worse than had been expected. This was admitted by Mikoyan. The better-off peasants had cut down their sowings and the authorities struggled to make good the loss by increasing the areas sown by the rest of the peasants. The results thus obtained were not encouraging. Worse still, the numbers of livestock began to decline for the peasants were short of fodder and food. The towns too were short of food. Ration cards were introduced in February 1929, while in the factories the management were putting increasing pressure on the workers to step up production. The workers retaliated by mass defections from one factory to another, and by an enormous wave of *brak* (faulty production) for which they could not of course be held entirely responsible. The rise in the price of bread grains and other agricultural products caused a rise in prices throughout the economy. Speculation was rife; bread tended to disappear from the towns into regions which had none, especially those which did not produce bread grains, or into provincial towns which the government was not supplying. Living standards dropped and all the time administrative pressure and state tyranny were growing. Grain procurements, as we know, had been very inadequate, whereas the private middlemen had succeeded in buying more that year from the peasants than in previous years.

Thus, the upheavals taking place in agriculture were clearly having repercussions on the national economy. In the view of the majority of the Politburo, the bad state of agriculture was entirely to blame for the crisis.

However, in addition to the part played by faulty economic policy, the great effort which was going into industrialization contributed enormously to the strain and was very largely responsible for the crisis because, as Bukharin had said, it was excessive. And yet the leadership were convinced that their only hope lay precisely in an ever higher rate of industrial growth. Moreover, they were borne out in this by the fact that, to all appearances, the annual industrial plan for 1928/29, which had been officially declared to be the first year of the Five-Year Plan, was going well. However, this was in appearance only, a point of capital importance in understanding the change in policy which took place at the end of the year. . . .

On the agricultural front the plan failed utterly. Agricultural production, including industrial crops, was on the downgrade. The food-processing industry also declined and the chemical industry and agricultural machinery plans were not fulfilled. It should be recalled that the trade networks had been gravely disorganized as a result of the offensive against the private traders.

It can readily be understood that in a situation of this kind the leaders would feel that they had their backs to the wall and that the regime would be impelled to bring to bear the full coercive power of its dictatorship.

In the view of the party leaders, it was exclusively the rural sector which was to blame for the disequilibrium. This sector had recently opened a second front against the regime, being now engaged on a livestock offensive, in addition to the grain offensive which had already assumed serious proportions by the beginning of 1928.

The pace of industrialization was not thought to be excessive; on the contrary, the Politburo thought it both desirable and possible to step up rates of growth, a decision which was to be taken at the Central Committee meeting in November 1929. In this way, the authorities hoped to rescue the country from its troubles and steer it into calmer waters with the minimum of delay. In the minds of the leadership, the state of agriculture was the biggest obstacle to their aims.

In September 1929, when the leadership were already aware of the year's economic results, it seems that the small Stalinist leadership, having evaluated the situation, made up their minds: if in the course of the coming months, which were the only ones in which a state campaign could be launched in the countryside (before sowing was begun) some radical change did not take place on the rural front, the drive for industrialization would unquestionably have lost its impetus by 1931, if not sooner.

It was this reasoning, at this precise moment, which dictated Stalin's change of policy at the end of 1929, particularly in view of the fact that the results of the forced collectivization which had been started in the summer seemed to give grounds for much optimism.

On to the Attack

It was not until June 1929 that any significant and far-reaching attempt at implementing the new policy in the countryside became apparent, and even then the exact nature and extent of the course which was to be followed had still not assumed any definite form. The development of the new program, or rather the new course of action (for there was as yet no definite program, in the accepted sense of the term) seems to have been characterized by a continual process of sliding, as it were, towards the objectives in question, while the latter were continually being enlarged. This curious process lasted from the beginning of 1928 to the end of 1929, with a period of extreme acceleration which set in in the summer of 1929. The incessant changes which the plans for agriculture underwent will serve to illustrate this sliding process.[3]

The Politburo were constantly changing their directives because they had no definite system of objectives. Events, some of a negative character, and others which appeared positive and encouraging, spurred the leadership to action. Thus, from summer onwards, a whole series of measures showed that the center had begun to act in earnest, and in great haste. . . .

In summer 1929 the Soviet press was already mentioning a new phase, that of mass collectivization. The countryside was mobilized by thousands of agitators and activists of all sorts. The rural Communists, under threat of disciplinary measures for the first time, were instructed to join the kolkhozy in order to set an example.

The *Kolkhoztsentr* was granted wider powers and began to set up

[3] The Five-Year Plan spoke of 5 million households collectivized towards the end of the quinquennium, covering an area of 21–22 million hectares. In June 1929 *kolkhoztsentr* [the Kolkhoz Center] announced an aim of 8 million hectares with 7–8 million souls for the single year 1930, and half the rural population (and three times the area envisaged in the initial plan) by 1933. In August Mikoyan spoke (for 1930) of 10 million hectares. In September Gosplan fixed, still for 1929/30, a target of 13 million hectares with 10 percent of the total population in kolkhozy. In October and November the "control figures" for 1929/30 were altered to 15.2 million hectares with 12 percent of the population. In December Sovnarkom wanted to collectivize 30 million hectares—and this was not the end.

its network at oblast, okrug and raion[4] level, while another organization, *Traktortsentr,* was set up to administer the MTS [machine-tractor stations] and to create a fairly large number of these stations as quickly as possible.

For the first time, the trade unions found themselves faced with an imperative demand to assist in the collectivization of the villages, an unfamiliar task for which they were in no way equipped. In fact, at this period almost all the state and party organizations were called upon to collectivize and to direct the process of collectivization. In its feverish haste, the Politburo delegated responsibility to so many organizations that there was soon a veritable administrative tangle, the results of which were harmful in the extreme.

In addition, the party and the specialized services spent that year preparing, with a degree of energy and efficiency rarely to be encountered in other fields, for the procurement campaign, which in fact was to be more successful than ever before because of the unprecedented extent of the resources mobilized for the purpose. Once the procurement task had been accomplished, the enormous forces which had been concentrated in the countryside were redeployed and instructed to apply themselves to the task of collectivization. After the procurements, the bulk of these forces were available mainly as from January 1930. The actual process of organizing the kolkhozy now began to develop in a number of interesting ways. There was marked progress. *Kolkhoztsentr* decided to double (between June and October) the area occupied by the giant kolkhozy, and during this period the kolkhoz movement as a whole was doubled, increasing from 3.9 to 7.6 percent of holdings collectivized. At this stage the movement consisted mainly of poor peasants who had been influenced by propaganda and attracted by the quite unrealistic promises showered on them and by the state aid which was being channelled to the kolkhoz sector. This success ought to have been consolidated before any further advance was attempted, but the effect of it was rather to encourage the leadership to step up the campaign and to exert even greater pressure.

In its initial stages this movement, although not strictly speaking a spontaneous one, was nonetheless not the result of coercion, al-

---

[4] Region, sub-province, and district.—Ed.

though some elements of administrative pressure had been in evidence as far back as the beginning of 1928. According to recent statements from Soviet sources, coercion began to play an increasing part from the early autumn of 1929, and one might add that, with the onset of winter, it had become the regime's main weapon. . . .

The more specific decisions about the great turn in collectivization appear to have been taken by the Politburo in the month of October, though the evidence for this assumption is still incomplete. At all events, a short time previously no such decisions had existed.

Towards the end of October, *Pravda* finally stated the problem in unequivocal terms: all the forces which had been massed for the procurements campaign, it said, must be thrown into collectivization. In view of what is known about the methods employed during the procurements campaign, the order is not without significance. In fact, from this time onward the press was to be full of denunciations of the kulaks and appeals for mass collectivization. The incitement to violent methods was barely concealed, though no definite indication was given about the nature or extent of these methods, or how they were to be applied. This was no accident. The leadership had now opted not for reforms but for revolution.

On 7 November Stalin published his famous article on the "Great Turn," in which almost every element of his appraisal of the situation was incorrect. In particular, he stated that "the middle peasant has opted for the kolkhozy," which according to present-day Soviet sources, was not at all the case. According to these same sources, Stalin was anxious to induce the forthcoming meeting of the Central Committee (the November meeting) to adopt the decisions he wanted by presenting the members of the Central Committee with a view of reality colored to suit his own aims.

The November meeting accordingly complied, though with certain reservations attested by present-day sources. The plenum adopted an unrealistic plan for industrial growth, called for a more rapid rate of collectivization, with a move towards "kolkhoz-sovkhoz composites"—mythical organizations which never in fact existed. At this meeting, it was decided to set up a new all-Union commissariat for agriculture, to build two new tractor factories and two more for combine-harvesters.

Molotov, who presented the principal report on the problem of collectivization, suggested "dekulakization" without explicitly saying so (and indeed, there were instances of confused antikulak measures in a number of places very shortly after); he spoke disparagingly of the five-year plans for agriculture, since in his view it was "the coming months, weeks and days which counted." He said that before long not only okrugs but whole republics would be completely collectivized, and the time which he thought such an undertaking should take was exactly five months.

The leadership were plainly reluctant to impose any terms of limitations on the activities of the officials. Some members of the Central Committee insisted that a commission be set up within the Politburo to direct collectivization and to see that the whole operation, particularly the process of dekulakization, was carried through in an orderly manner. We can but guess at the reasons why the Politburo took three weeks to set up this commission, which was made up of the most experienced representatives of the oblast authorities and specialists from the central departments.

Two weeks later the commission produced a draft resolution and a detailed plan of action, but Stalin altered their proposals to give them greater urgency and wider scope, his main preoccupation apparently being to give the least possible excuse for delay, and the freest possible rein to uninhibited action.

The subcommittee responsible for the draft proposal on dekulakization was even dismissed and replaced by another in January 1930. Without waiting for its conclusions, Stalin on 27 December publicly gave the green light to the "liquidation of the kulaks as a class," without putting forward at the time any suggestions or directions about the manner in which this terrible operation was to be carried out.

Some weeks previously, on his fiftieth birthday, Stalin had been hailed, for the first time, as the greatest Marxist-Leninist and the greatest strategist of all time, and so forth. From now on, he was the infallible leader, the object of a cult.

Was There Any Choice?

The historian is often perplexed when faced with the question: was there any other way out? And yet this is not a question which one can easily evade unless one is convinced that in fact no alternative existed.

As for the problem at present under discussion, the following argument suggests a number of replies:

Compulsory collectivization was launched under pressure from a crisis which threatened not only the country's drive for industrialization but also the stability of the regime itself. There may be reservations about the truth of this allegation, but the fact remains that this is how the situation appeared to the effective leaders of the party at the time.

It is true that the weaknesses inherent in the structure of agriculture had a disruptive effect on the national economy, that they threatened to reduce the country to famine and served as a breeding-ground for a number of adverse social elements, and so forth. But it is undoubtedly true that agriculture was not exclusively to blame for the crisis.

1. The measure of industrialization which was already going on at the time represented an enormous burden, the size of which was largely the result of the excessive rate of industrialization. But a particular rate or speed of growth is not exclusively dictated by the pressure of objective needs (in the case of Russia rapid industrialization as such may be accepted as an objective necessity); *they are also the result of a choice, an appraisal, a certain level of political and economic planning and administrative capacity.* Here there exists an enormous margin of error in decision-making and the conduct of affairs. In this particular context, it is our view that the leaders did in fact make mistakes over a whole number of questions, and that the quality of their administration was poor, and at times disastrous. In particular, the rate of industrial growth was excessive, and the decisions taken by the leaders were often quite arbitrary, since the leaders themselves had little inclination to listen to the suggestions put forward by experts or those of moderate opinions. Bukharin was right (and Trotsky agreed with him) when he said that it was absurd to embark on a building program knowing in advance that the requisite materials would not be available.

In fact, the excessive rate of growth and the lack of administrative skill in the handling of affairs were such that:

a. In practice the progress of industrialization during the First

Five-Year Plan was not the result of the Five-Year Plan or of any other coherent plan. Such was the extent of the confusion in the administration of the Five-Year Plan that it led, among other things, to the famous method of priority (shock) projects (*udarniye stroiki*) in which everything was sacrificed for the achievement of a handful of objectives which were judged to be of key importance. The method was a salutary one, no doubt, in the given situation, but it originated in confusion and gave rise to excessive waste. This was not planning in any sense of the term.

   b. The excessive growth rates which ruined the Five-Year Plan as a planned and properly organized operation also contributed to the resultant wastage of resources. It is impossible to say just what the *excess* cost of the Five-Year Plan was, but it is a fact that, in a country which was short of resources, what human and material resources they had were all too often recklessly squandered and consequently yielded no advantage. . . .

   2. An analysis of the second major contributory factor in the crisis, that is the state of agriculture, discloses a number of ills which might have been avoided or mitigated if steps had been taken in time:

   a. During the years of NEP, especially from 1925 onward, the leaders placed overmuch reliance on the ability of NEP to function automatically and either did not perceive, or neglected, a number of factors which were to cause them untold difficulties at a later stage; in this connection, the future right wing undeniably bears a great deal of the responsibility. At this stage, there was already some substance in the allegation made by the Left Opposition that a more serious attempt at industrialization could have been begun at a much earlier date. We previously cited as a significant example the case of the tractor factory at Stalingrad. Whatever might have been the practical considerations which led to a failure to implement this project in 1924, they reflect a poverty of statesmanship.

   b. We have referred to agricultural price policy during the NEP period, which Molotov described . . . as a series of colossal stupidities. If these colossal stupidities had been avoided, could it possibly be said that subsequent events, particularly the grain crisis in the winter of 1928, need have been as severe as they in fact were?

   c. The total neglect of the collective movement in the countryside was a blatant and unpardonable error. The same was true of the sovkhozy, which were in a notoriously backward state. We have already mentioned the views of Rykov, when he asked in 1928: Why was a major campaign on the sovkhozy not launched earlier? He had in mind a number of other measures which might have encouraged agricultural progress, but which were never introduced.

The idea of a powerful state and collective sector, which would be limited in scope but well-organized, might have played a part of the very greatest importance. Nor can it be said that the Bolsheviks were incapable of conceiving such an idea prior to 1928. And yet the fact remains that it was not until 1929 that this discovery was made, and energetic action was taken to build up this sector. How it was done, in what conditions and with what results, is well known. Having failed to pursue a reasonable policy, the regime found itself thrown back on the disastrous alternative of mass collectivization.

d. Prior to 1928, and for some time after this date, there were a number of elements in the social structure of village life which could have been of the greatest importance as a starting-point for promising developments in the collective and cooperative field. The institution of the *mir* itself could have been used to form one of the many variants of the producers' association (*tovarishchestvo*), as had been suggested by Gosplan in 1929. But this avenue was first neglected and then finally left unexplored.

There were abundant examples in the countryside of spontaneous cooperative movements, particularly the simple producers' associations (*prostiye proizvodstvenniye tovarishchestva*). We cannot discuss these at length in the present context, but they were in fact spontaneous, owing nothing to the initiative or support of the authorities. In most cases they did not even form part of the official cooperative movement (the same was true of a great many of the kolkhozy) and they were, therefore, described as wild or beyond the pale. But this need not have been so.[5]

e. The way in which the authorities handled the cooperative movement, both before and after the grain crisis, left much to be

---

[5] Molotov affirmed at the Fifteenth Congress (*stenotchet,* p. 1074) that these simple associations contained one million householders (the figure is probably exaggerated) but that only 6 percent of this number was embraced by cooperation, the rest being wild.

desired. Behind the figures which recorded quantitative results, one could discern a movement stifled in the grip of a bureaucracy which left the mass of the peasantry no scope for genuine initiative and hence for constructive education. Lenin's dream of cooperation was in no way utopian. Furthermore, "kulak domination" of the cooperative movement was neither as real or as unavoidable as it was made out to be in the subsequent official interpretation. The party never deployed any appreciable forces in this sector, either in terms of quantity or quality, nor did it devote much thought to the problem. This is why the future process of collectivization, curious and paradoxical though it may seem, was in fact carried out on the ruins of the cooperative movement.

f. Up until the end of 1929, the kolkhoz movement consisted for the most part of *tozi,* a not very highly collectivized form of organization which was plainly favored by the peasants, and also by the majority of the party activists concerned with this problem. The directive calling for the abolition of these organizations and the imposition of the *artel*; the fact of *having made one single form of organization obligatory* in a country which had a whole range of such structures; the fact that no opportunity was afforded for experimentation with other possible types of organization—all these facts add up to a policy which it is impossible to endorse with the seal of inevitability. We have no hesitation in suggesting that these were fatal errors.

3. Whatever the circumstances may have been which led the Stalinist group to interpret the grain crisis as a sign that NEP was doomed, and which set them on the road to mass collectivization, all of their decisions and appraisals are open to criticism and to question.

a. It may be admitted that the grain crisis in the winter of 1928 called for a series of administrative measures, although this point of view was in fact disputed at the time by certain party experts, as well as by the Right Opposition. What is open to question is the exclusive reliance on coercive measures which consequently became increasingly violent and further aggravated the existing difficulties. If some pressure had to be exerted, it could have been accompanied by the social and economic measures proposed by the (future) right wing. Some imports of grain, a rise in the procurement prices, imports of manufactured goods—all of these might have helped to ease the nature and the extent of the pressure, and might perhaps have lessened the impact of the crisis and gone some way to improving relations with the peasantry. But these measures were rejected, or worse still, they were first of all rejected and then adopted (in part) later, in fact *too late.*

b. The decision to collectivize the greatest possible number of peasants, and to dispossess and deport the better-off peasants, which was taken towards the end of 1929, and which certain observers accept as having been inevitable, is equally open to question, at least in respect of its scope and timing. It is true that at that moment, because of the failures of the past, some of which we have already mentioned, there are strong indications that the leadership felt themselves compelled to take exceptional and very dangerous measures. But it is significant that a number of Soviet scholars nowadays express doubts not only about the speed and the excessively administrative nature of the collectivization, but also about the timing of the dekulakization measures undertaken at this stage. They maintain that the mass of the peasants, and particularly the middle peasants, were as yet unprepared for collectivization on such a massive scale, and therefore not ready for liquidation of the kulaks. By making such a statement, they call into question the whole of the spectacular change of policy at the end of 1929.

Our present analysis is not so much concerned with the sudden change as with the long period which led up to it, and we have tried to focus attention on certain factors in this period which have tended to be disregarded by the policy makers, or certain errors which appear particularly blatant. The purpose is not one of speculation about other courses which history might have taken, and so this is not an essay in "if history." It is simply an attempt at isolating a fairly large number of concrete factors which together might have gone to make up a different body of measures, or in other words a different policy, though within the same institutional framework. This might in itself suffice to answer the question: was there any alternative? Let us conclude, however, with a few general observations.

The situation in which Soviet Russia found itself was such that a vigorous campaign of industrialization became a matter of prime necessity, and this could not be achieved without "tribute" from the peasants, the workers, and in fact the entire population. As Preobra-zhensky had accurately predicted, this was bound to involve a period of social strain, particularly during the initial phases of the industrial effort. In addition, it may be said that to meet with success in its efforts, the regime had to be a tough one, a resolute dictatorship.

This precondition does not, however, exclude the element of choice in respect of the behavior of such a regime and the policy which it pursued. Granted that tribute was inevitable, its size was still a matter for choice and not a fixed quantity rigidly laid down by some immutable law of history; granted that, in the given situation, some form of dictatorship was necessary, it should not be overlooked that dictatorship, like democracy, can assume many different forms. In this situation, dictatorship would seem to have been a logical necessity, but not necessarily in the autocratic, terroristic, cult-producing guise which it in fact assumed; granted the need for industrialization, the problems of "how much" and "how" were still open to choice. While it is agreed that the process of industrialization was bound to involve sweeping changes in the countryside, it is, in our view, wrong to suppose that these changes could not have been effected otherwise than by collectivization as Russia experienced it. Why the insistence on the kolkhoz as the exclusive form of collective, when village structures suggested several alternatives? Is there any reason why the time-limits which the Politburo chose to set should be accorded the status of immutable historical laws? And what of the wholesale condemnation of any private sector?

Changes in the structures of rural life, necessary as they undoubtedly were, need not have followed a uniform pattern but could have been effected by the setting up of several different sectors, the nucleus of which already existed during the NEP period, and which could have been either sovkhozy, kolkhozy (of which there were several types) or other forms of cooperative or joint association with varying degrees of socialization and varying degrees of integration of private farms and private property, including (why not?) a private peasants' sector.

If we agree that the road which Soviet Russia had to travel left the regime so little room for maneuver that it had to choose between its own destruction and the path which it in fact took, then it would be logical to see in Stalin's policy the direct expression of historical necessity, and to accept all the methods which were used as having been justified, with reservations only in respect of certain errors or excesses; in this case, one might logically argue that what was achieved could only have been achieved by a dictatorship of the most despotic kind, and by one individual—Stalin. This is the logical conclusion of the opinions expressed by Dr. Schlesinger in *Soviet Studies*.[6] His theory that the elimination first of the left wing and then of the right wing were indispensable if the regime was to survive and to succeed in its task of industrialization, fits logically into this pattern.

In our view, there are certain weaknesses in this argument. As the present study has shown, there were a series of factors which could have been combined to form an alternative. Again, it is an indisputable fact that Stalin had no foreknowledge of the great leap forward which he was to take, and of all its consequences, and that he had no such ambitions, least of all in 1926 and 1927 when he was concerned with the liquidation of the Left. Doubtless, he was already an "industrializer," as Dr. Schlesinger suggests, but no more so than his associates at that time, for example Rykov (was the intensification of the industrialization drive in 1926 embarked upon against the wishes of someone like Rykov or Bukharin?). Generalizations about an industrialized Russia, which everybody accepted at the time, are of less account than practical measures. In practical terms, Stalin was a supporter both of industrialization and of NEP (he was simply more cautious in his statements than an unskillful politician like Bukharin) and therefore he moved with prudence and moderation in this domain. For these reasons the theory that the Left, which was enthusiastically pro-industrialization and antikulak, had to be liquidated as an essential prerequisite for future industrialization, and by a Stalin who at that time had still so little thought of what his future policy was to be, is a rather odd theory. It may be accepted, if one accepts another equally odd theory, which presents Stalin as a sort of *deus ex machina,* the only man in the party who was capable of transforming Russia into an industrial country. If this were so, then one would in fact have to accept the elimination of the Left as hav-

[6] See his "Note on the Context of Early Soviet Planning," *Soviet Studies* (July 1964).

ing been necessary, not because of its "sectarian appeal" to the workers (there is no reason to believe that the Left was incapable of demanding sacrifices from the proletariat) but because anything that might have stood in the way of "the only man who was able to act" and so forth had to be sacrificed for the good of the cause.

As for the elimination of the Right, in order to show that this too was indispensable one would have to prove, first of all, that all of their proposals were basically wrong whereas everything that Stalin proposed, and did, was basically right. This was far from being the case. The sequence of events after 1928, and the results of Stalinist policy, suggest that what the Stalinist administration particularly needed (we leave aside here the eventual need for its own abolition) was precisely the moderating influence which the Right could have exerted. What was called for, therefore, in the case of the Right was not elimination but at most restriction of its responsibilities within the framework of its rights as a minority. The methods which were used by the leaders of the right wing in their struggle against Stalin show that these same leaders were perfectly capable of remaining within the bounds of discipline, and of refraining from carrying on their controversy before the general public, or even the party as a whole, provided they had some assurance that their views would not be rejected out of hand, and that they would be given some opportunity of exerting a restraining influence.

And so events took their course. Historians, and other analysts, record these events and try to interpret them. But an essential precondition for analysis is the ability on the one hand to identify urgent social needs dictated by circumstances, and on the other to judge the practical solutions to these problems which were the result of subjective choice on the part of the leaders. By making this distinction, we are able to appraise the actions of historical personages, and to pass judgment on the quality of the leaders.

Merle Fainsod

COLLECTIVIZATION: THE METHOD

In 1941 the advancing German army captured most of the Communist Party archive in the city of Smolensk. In 1945 this material fell into the hands of the American army and was microfilmed before being returned to the Russians. Merle Fainsod (1907–1972), late Professor of Government and Director of the Russian Research Center at Harvard University, wove this secret documentary material of the 1920s and 1930s into a unique book on the inner workings of the Soviet government in an individual province. The Smolensk documents show, through official Communist eyes, the uncensored story of the collectivization of the peasants in 1929 and 1930.

The Liquidation of the Kulaks as a Class

The grain collection campaign of 1929, as it turned out, was merely a prelude to a far more drastic operation, the decision to liquidate the kulak as a class and to lay the groundwork for total collectivization. The signal for the all-out drive was given at the end of 1929, and soon after the turn of the year the operation was launched in various parts of the Western Oblast [Province]. The Smolensk Archive provides a particularly rich record of the execution of the operation in Velikiye Luki okrug [sub-province]; it will be described here in some detail.

On January 28, 1930, the party committee of Velikiye Luki okrug approved a proposal to deport kulaks from the okrug and to confiscate their property. Two OGPU officials (Kolosov and Dabolin) were designated to prepare a plan of action. On January 30 the party committee approved the following arrangements: (1) to enlarge the okrug OGPU apparatus by four more members and to mobilize an additional eleven people from the OGPU reserve; (2) to make 10,000 rubles available to the OGPU to finance the added personnel; (3) to release okrug militia forces from other duties and to use them in the dekulakization campaign; (4) to supply arms from the "mobilization reserves" to all participants; and (5) to postpone putting into effect an earlier okrug decision to take down all church bells and close churches in order not to arouse general peasant resistance.

March 1, 1930, was set as a target date for the completion of the operation. On February 6 special okrug and raion [district] troikas were designated to direct activities. In each case the troika consisted of the first secretary of the party committee, the chairman of the soviet executive committee (ispolkom) and the head of the OGPU. The okrug party committee also arranged to dispatch twenty-six people to the raions to assist the local authorities.

On February 12, a top-secret letter was sent to all raitroikas [district troikas] outlining detailed instructions for the conduct of the operation. Working through the raikoms [district party committees] and the village soviets, the raitroikas were to undertake a prompt inventory of all kulak property, meanwhile warning the kulaks that if they were caught in the unauthorized sale of any of their property, all of it would immediately be confiscated. The inventory was to be completed within a two-week period.

The letter ordered the raitroikas to divide all kulak households into three groups, according to the degree of danger which they presented to the soviet authorities and the severity of the punishment which was to be imposed on them. The first and most dangerous group, described as "the counterrevolutionary kulak aktiv [active group]," was to be arrested by the OGPU. The raitroikas were authorized to make additions to this "list" on the basis of recommendations emerging from meetings of poor peasants and agricultural laborers. Incriminating material was to be forwarded to the OGPU. The second category consisted of "certain (separate) elements of the kulak aktiv," especially from among the richest peasants and "quasi-landowners," who were to be deported to "far-off" parts of the Soviet Union. The remaining kulaks were to be removed from areas scheduled for "total collectivization," but were not to be deported from the okrug. For such kulaks the raion executive committees were to provide special land parcels carved out of eroded areas, "swamp-lands in woods," and other soil "in need of improvement."

Families of Group I and II kulaks were to be deported from the okrug on the approval of the okrug troika. Property of Group I households was to be confiscated immediately and handed over to

FIGURE 3. A state farm in Kazakhstan, 1969 (*Novosti from Sovfoto*).

neighboring collective farms either in existence or in process of organization. In the absence of such farms, the property was to be
delivered to the nearest functioning kolkhoz. Property of Group II
households was to be confiscated gradually, with confiscation timed
to coincide with deportation schedules. In order to guide the raions
in conducting the operation, the okrug troika supplied each raion
with an orientation number of Group I kulaks who were to be arrested and Group II kulaks who were to be deported. . . .

Protocols of the okrug troika mirror the confusion and disorganization of the period. Despite apparently precise directives and instructions, many raion and village authorities went their own way,
interpreting the kulak category broadly to embrace middle and even
poor peasants who were opposed to collectivization, evicting kulak
families with Red Army connections, and rarely bothering to supply
the okrug troika with supporting data to justify their decisions. In
the first flush of the dekulakization campaign, excesses were
commonplace. An OGPU report of February 28, 1930, provides a
matter-of-fact recital of some of the antics of the dekulakizers.
According to the report, in many villages "certain members of the
workers' brigades and officials of lower echelons of the party-soviet
apparatus" deprived members of kulak and middle peasant households of their clothing and warm underwear (directly from the body),
"confiscated" head-wear from children's heads, and removed

shoes from people's feet. The perpetrators divided the confiscated goods among themselves; the food they found was eaten on the spot; the alcohol they uncovered was consumed immediately, resulting in drunken orgies. In one case a worker tore a warm blouse off a woman's back, put it on himself with the words, "You wore it long enough, now I will wear it." The slogan of many of the dekulakization brigades was: "drink, eat—it's all ours." One commune, in search of more and richer confiscations, commenced to dekulakize kulaks of the bordering village soviet. As the kulaks in question were administratively under the jurisdiction of another kolkhoz, a struggle ensued between the communards and the kolkhozniks [collective farmers]. The communards under the direction of their party secretary absconded with much of the money and property of the kulaks before the kolkhoz could act. In the process, even eyeglasses were torn from the peasants' faces; kasha [porridge] was confiscated straight from the oven and either eaten or used to smear the ikons When the OGPU investigated the whereabouts of the confiscated property, the commune destroyed the original inventory lists and wrote new ones.

Another OGPU report, dated February 23, 1930, noted that middle and even poor peasants were being arrested by "anybody"—by raion emissaries, village soviet members, kolkhoz chairmen, and any one in any way connected with collectivization. People were being transported to militia prisons without the slightest grounds or evidence. Although the raion authorities were aware of this, they were reluctant to interfere so as "not to undermine the authority of the village soviet" responsible for the arrest. Some poor peasants and activists were blackmailing the richer peasants, taking bribes for removing them from the confiscation or deportation lists. In many cases, confiscated cattle was not being fed and was starving to death.

Still another report pointed out that the looting in the villages had induced an atmosphere of panic among the well-to-do peasants. According to this report, a wave of suicides was sweeping the richer households; kulaks were killing their wives and children and then taking their own lives. In order to prevent complete property confiscation, many kulaks and their wives were entering into fictitious divorces, in the hope that at least some property and the lives of

FIGURE 4. Harvesting on a Soviet farm in 1936 (*Wide World Photos*).

wives and children would be spared. Sensing their impending doom, kulaks in growing numbers were fleeing to the east (Moscow, the Urals, Siberia). They dekulakized themselves by selling out all they owned, or leaving their property with relatives and friends, or simply abandoning their fields and homes.

Occasionally kulaks also found friends and protectors at court. Chairmen of village soviets were reported as befriending kulaks by exempting valuable kulak property from confiscation; some party members defended kulaks because of their previous humanitarian behavior toward poor peasants. Many poor and middle peasants considered dekulakization unjust and harmful, refused to vote approval of deportation and expropriation measures, hid kulak property, and warned their kulak friends of pending searches and requisitions. In many cases poor and middle peasants were reported as collecting signatures to petitions testifying to the loyalty and good character of kulaks, millers, and other well-to-do elements. The high-handed tactics of indiscriminate and arbitrary confiscation and deportation turned many poor and middle peasants into bitter opponents of the regime.

At this point the party leadership decided to call a halt to the excesses it had set in motion. On February 20, 1930, Rumyantsev[1] addressed a letter to all okrug party secretaries, calling attention to the fact that, despite "exhaustive and precise instructions" from the obkom [provincial party committee], deviations in dekulakization policy were continuing. Among these he particularly condemned: (1) the dekulakization of middle peasants and the "mass-inclusion" of such peasants in kulak lists based only on "vicious rumor" and "possible provocation"; (2) the lawless actions of dekulakization brigades which "interfere with normal administrative processes"; (3) the use of Red Army units in carrying out dekulakization; (4) the spreading of the slogans of dekulakization (with the same inadmissible methods) to the city Nepmen; (5) the actions of drunken soldiers and Komsomols [young Communists] who "without mass preparation" were "arbitrarily closing village churches, breaking ikons, and threatening the peasants."

The Rumyantsev letter was followed by a top-secret obkom circular of March 2 reprimanding the okrug party committees for "brutal" abuses committed by raion and village officials against the "dekulakized." Brought up short by these warnings and Stalin's "Dizziness from Success" article (published in *Pravda* on March 2), the okrug troikas initiated a review of all raion decisions on dekulakization. In a typical action in Velikiye Luki okrug involving a list of 121 dekulakized households in Siebezhsky raion, the raitroika's decisions were rejected in forty-four cases, and eight cases were referred to the OGPU for further investigation. The OGPU quickly adjusted to the new line and followed the lead of the okrug troikas in overruling raion decisions. The raitroikas were instructed to return confiscated property to those peasants who had been "unjustly" dekulakized.

[1] Ivan P. Rumyantsev, first secretary of the Communist Party for the Smolensk Province, until he was purged in 1937.—Ed.

Like other posthumous efforts to render justice, the instructions proved easier to issue than to execute.

Kulak Deportations

Meanwhile, kulak deportations gathered momentum. The most detailed description of the deportations in the Smolensk Archive are to be found in OGPU reports of March 1931[2] dealing with the situation in the Roslavl area. In the rural district of Roslavl preparations for deportation began on February 15, 1931.[2] Lists of all kulaks and well-to-do peasants were collected from the village soviets. But these lists, the OGPU emissary complained, "failed to provide the information necessary to do the impending job." Consequently, personal questionnaires were circulated to 215 potential victims under the guise of checking the correctness of their tax liabilities. On March 18, the raitroika reviewed the questionnaires and condemned seventy-four households to liquidation. On the evening of March 19, the raitroika assembled its emissaries at a central point, gave them instructions, and assigned two households to each emissary. The operation was to be completed that same night. But not all went smoothly. In a number of cases the emissaries stalled, conducted drawn-out meetings with poor peasants, and in general "failed to arrange the job in a tightly conspiratorial fashion." As a result kulaks were forewarned, and the emissaries failed to find those marked for deportation. Some emissaries allowed tearful goodbyes to be drawn out during which many able-bodied men slipped away. A number of kulaks succeeded in smuggling their property to poorer relatives. All in all, thirty-two families were deported from the raion; the rest fled, and the OGPU head stated that measures were being taken to find them. He complained that many emissaries had made "grave mistakes"; the wife of one emissary, a Komsomol, publicly expressed grief and sympathy for the deported. "We are no longer people," she was quoted as having said; "we are animals." But most Komsomols were lauded for having done an outstanding job, "better than that of responsible officials." According to the report, poor peasants were "generally pleased" with the progress of events. But

[2] Evidently a misprint which should read "1930."—Ed.

middle peasants were "confused and unnerved." "Our turn will come soon," they kept repeating. . . .

Problems of Kolkhoz Organization

Prior to the application of this pressure, the kolkhoz movement was slow to take root in the Western Oblast. Indeed, the First Five-Year Plan for the oblast contemplated that only 8.6 percent of the peasant households would be enrolled in kolkhozes by 1932–1933. On October 1, 1928, the actual percentage of collectivization was an almost infinitesimal 0.8 percent. By October 1, 1929, it had increased to only 2.5 percent. From that point on, in accordance with directions from the center to liquidate the kulak and intensify the organization of kolkhozes, the tempo of collectivization mounted swiftly. On March 1, 1930, the Western Oblast reported that 38.8 percent of all hired-labor, poor-peasant, and middle-peasant households were collectivized.

What happened in the intervening five months is perhaps best portrayed in the language of the peasants themselves. The Smolensk Archive contains a collection of peasants' letters (most of them unpublished) written during this period to the editors of the oblast peasant newspaper, *Nasha Derevnya* (Our Village). They vividly convey what was happening in the countryside and how the letter writers felt about it. "Dear Comrades," wrote Ivan Trofimovich Chuyunkov from the village of Yushkovo:

> *For a long time I have wanted to write you about what you have written on collectivization in your newspaper* Nasha Derevnya.
> *In the first place I will give you my address so that you will not suspect that I am a kulak or one of his parasites. I am a poor peasant. I have one hut, one barn, one horse, three dessiatins[3] of land, and a wife and three children. Dear Comrades, as a subscriber to your newspaper . . . I found in No. 13/85 for February 15 a letter from a peasant who writes about the life of kolkhoz construction. I, a poor peasant, reading this letter, fully agreed with it. This peasant described life in the kolkhoz completely correctly. Isn't it true that all the poor peasants and middle peasants do not want to go into the kolkhoz at all, but that you drive them in by force? For example, I'll take my village soviet of Yushkovo. A brigade of soldiers came to us. This brigade went into all the occupied homes, and do you think that they organized a kolkhoz? No, they did not organize it. The*

[3] One dessiatin = approx. 2.6 acres.—Ed.

hired laborers and the poor peasants came out against it and said they did not want corvée, they did not want serfdom . . . I'll write more of my village soviet. When the Red Army brigade left, they sent us a kolkhoz organizer from Bryansk okrug. And whom do you think this Comrade signed up? Not poor peasants, not hired laborers, but kulaks, who, sensing their own ruin, enter the kolkhoz. And your organizer . . . takes to evil deeds. At night, together with the Komsomolites, he takes everything away from the peasants, both surpluses and taxes, which you fleece from the peasants. Of course agricultural taxes are necessary, self-taxation is necessary, fire taxes are necessary, tractorization is necessary. But where can the toiling peasant get this money if not from the seeds of his products? And these party people stay up all night and rob the peasants. If he brings a pud, if he brings five, it's all the same. I would propose that you let the peasant live in greater freedom than he does now, and then we won't beg you to get rid of such a gang, for we ourselves will eliminate them.

Wrote one Pyotr Gorky:

In the first place, I, a citizen of the village of Muzhyno . . . tell you, our government and also the editors, that we toiling peasants, poor peasants, and also the middle peasants see that life is bad, but nevertheless we have endured it. But when we got to the year 1930, we saw that we were ruined. We have bad land and little of it in the village of Muzhyno, and we had grain and potato requisitions, and they took them from us by force, both from the poor peasants and from the middle peasants. Simply speaking, it was robbery . . . We ourselves do not know what to do. Every day they send us lecturers asking us to sign up for such-and-such a kolkhoz for eternal slavery, but we don't want to leave our good homes. It may be a poor little hut, but it's mine, a poor horse, but it's mine. Among us, he who works more has something to eat. We peasants are used to working, but you, our government, change the pay every day arbitrarily . . . We ourselves don't know what to do. There aren't any nails, there is nothing and life is bad. We will not be able to eat in the kolkhoz . . . Therefore we beg you to turn the rudder of the kolkhoz movement and let the peasant own property. Then we assure you that everyone will be able to put more surpluses on the market, and trade will be free. We poor peasants ask you to change everything, to give us freedom, and then we will be glad to help the state.

Wrote still another peasant:

Comrades, you write that all the middle peasants and poor peasants join the kolkhoz voluntarily, but it is not true. For example, in our village of Podbuzhye, all do not enter the kolkhoz willingly. When the register *made the rounds, only 25 percent signed it, while 75 percent did not. They collected seeds by frightening [the peasants] with protocols and arrests. If any one spoke against it, he was threatened with arrest and forced labor. You are deceived in this, Comrades. Collective life can be created when the entire mass of the peasants goes voluntarily, and not by force . . . I beg you not to divulge my name, because the party people will be angry. [Signed] POLZIKOV.*

Another peasant wrote:

They [the kolkhoz organizers] use force and threats against those who do not enter the kolkhoz—they take away their land and deport them out of the bounds of the village. I ask you . . . whether they can behave like that and take away the land and deport an invalid poor peasant like me?

The following letter is in a similar vein:

Comrade editor . . . If, as you write, they [the peasants] join the kolkhozes voluntarily, why do you send brigades who send you to prison for the slightest resistance against the kolkhoz? Did the people think that they would live this way after they received freedom? Now it happens that freedom is not a word, but prison is a word. Say something against collectivization, and you're put in prison . . . If you took a vote, you would only find half of a percent who joined the kolkhoz voluntarily. Each one thinks it is a terrible thing; each one wants to be a master and not a slave . . .

The same hatred of the kolkhoz was expressed by Ivan Bogdanov from the village of Lodosh:

My household consists of one horse, three sheep, four dessiatins of land for seven consumers . . . I ask you to answer the question whether it is compulsory to enter the kolkhoz. I think not, but they gave us compulsory collectivization in Usvyatsk raion. I am sure that if you came and took a vote that not more than 15 percent would be in favor of the kolkhoz. All the people destroy their livestock, saying, "It doesn't matter, you have to go into the kolkhoz against your will" . . . Do not force the people to join the kolkhoz—there isn't any sense to it . . . It's better to hang yourself than to join the kolkhoz; it's better not to be born than to join the kolkhoz . . .

These extracts, which are culled largely from the letters of poor peasants, underline the role that force played in accelerating the tempo of collectivization. Nor was the opposition to collectivization confined to verbal protests. In some instances, at least, violence was met with violence, and the reports of the procurator [prosecutor] and the OGPU for this period are replete with examples. On September 30, 1929, Lebedev, the oblast procurator, reported the following incident to the obkom:

> On September 2, of this year, in the village of Lyalichi, Klintsy okrug, a mob of 200 people made an open attack on the kolkhozniks who were going out to work the fields. This attack consisted of the dispersal of the kolkhozniks from the field, the destruction of their equipment, clothes, and so forth. They chased after the leaders of the kolkhoz, but the latter succeeded in saving themselves by fleeing. The majority of the attackers were women, who were armed with staves, pitchforks, spades, axes, and so forth. On the night of September 3 a threshing floor with all the harvest, belonging to a member of the kolkhoz, was destroyed by fire.

Thirty-nine persons were brought to trial for their participation in this affair. According to a special Information Bulletin of the Procurator of the Western Oblast for July-October 1929, "The most widespread means of struggle against kolkhoz construction (after its organization) is arson." Numerous instances are cited where barns, haystacks, and houses belonging to kolkhozes were burned. Also listed as "very typical" are "cases of mass outbursts against the kolkhozes, primarily by women, under the leadership of kulaks and wealthy people." One such incident in the village of Golshino where a kolkhoz was being organized is described as follows:

> The local priest came out as an ardent oppositionist, carrying on open agitation among the women to resist the organization of the kolkhoz. On . . . the day designated for the division of land under the future kolkhoz, a crowd of women went to the fields, armed with axes, staves, and pitchforks, to beat the kolkhozniks. Meeting the surveyor and the secretary of the village soviet on the way, they began to insult them, tried to break the surveyor's instruments, and beat the secretary. Then they went on to the field and pulled out all the posts which bounded the kolkhoz. In the investigation of this case it was found that not enough mass work had been done by the local party organs while the kolkhoz was being organized. The local priest occupied himself with "agitation work" . . . coming out openly against the closing of the church, and he went around to the peasants in their yards and summoned the women to demonstrate against the kolkhoz. Nobody from the volost party and soviet organs knew

about the agitation, for the organization of the kolkhoz had been entrusted to the surveyor . . .

The story of the first great collectivization drive (1929–1930) as it unfolds in the Smolensk Archive is a record of "storm" tactics and stubborn peasant opposition, of grandiose projects and "paper" victories. The regime in many cases could not trust its local soviet functionaries to carry the brunt of the drive, and as a result workers were mobilized from the factories to organize the kolkhozes. The "25,000ers," as they were called, did not find their task easy. Here is a letter which a group of them wrote to their responsible superior, one Comrade Stolbov:

We workers have been sent to the Western Oblast, Voskresensk raion, Vyazma okrug, to work in the kolkhozes. But our living conditions do not permit us to work as we should. They have placed us in kolkhozes which have only been established a month or less. They sent us into leading work in kolkhozes where there were supposed to be funds, and they told us we would be paid out of the funds of the kolkhoz, but it didn't happen that way at all. They put most of us 16 people in such conditions in Voskresensk raion that we beg for help. They put us in kolkhozes with economies where there are no funds, where property has not yet been socialized, and we workers must be the organizers of the kolkhozes. Those of us who have arrived in the small kolkhozes are not given either money or food; they receive us worse than beggars. There are no living quarters . . .

In view of all these conditions, the work is not progressing; we live and do not know what the future will bring, how and what we will eat. What they told us when they sent us to work in the country is not at all so; they said that we would work in kolkhozes and would receive up to 30–40 rubles per month, but we didn't even receive 5 rubles a month, and there is not even food, and we don't eat.

The local organizations take a miserable attitude toward this and do not know themselves how we will eat and do not do anything about it.

Under such conditions of life as we have described above, it is impossible to work, and there is only one way out. To work longer is impossible, and to live in such circumstances is impossible; we must flee home, and then see what will happen. We ask the okrug committee of the party to answer this and to tell us what to do.

III THE COUNTER-REVOLUTION FROM ABOVE

David J. Dallin

THE RETURN OF INEQUALITY

David Dallin (1889–1962) was a young Menshevik leader at the time of the revolution who was forced to emigrate and went on to pursue a writing career in the United States. In a pioneering analysis of actual social evolution in the Soviet Union he found that in the course of the Stalin Revolution Sov'et society had returned rapidly to a hierarchy of power and privilege.

. . . Inequality inevitably proved victorious in practice, while equality was remembered only as a synonym for misery. But it was very difficult to incorporate the idea of inequality into the framework of Communist ideology.

After 1921 the retreat from the initial system of universal equality was for a certain time manifest; but the concessions were confined to the field of economics (commerce, wages, foreign concessions); there still remained a good deal of simplicity and emphasized novelty in human relations between superiors and subordinates, between officers and men, between chiefs and employees. Even in regard to individual income, the retreat was considered to be of a strictly temporary nature—a matter of expediency rather than a new civilization *sui generis,* or a new Soviet system of a class society.

Lenin, Trotsky, and Stalin ventured to adopt the NEP with all its deviations from equality in 1921, admitting it to be a retreat from the Communist achievements of the earlier Soviet period. But a year later, in March 1922, Lenin proclaimed "the end of the retreat." A little later Bukharin addressed the peasants with the slogan, "Enrich yourselves"; but he came to regret these words, which continued to plague him to the very day of his execution.

A new period began with the second Soviet revolution—the sweeping industrialization and collectivization. The instructions given from above were, "Down with equalitarianism!" Those who attempted to resist were ruthlessly eliminated. In his conflict with the left-wing factions, Stalin frequently denounced in sharp terms the

Reprinted by permission of the publisher, from David J. Dallin, *The Real Soviet Russia,* trans. Joseph Shaplen, rev. and enl. ed. (New Haven: Yale University Press, 1947), pp. 113–116, 142–144, 154–159, 165. Copyright © 1944, 1947 by Yale University Press.

"nonsense that money was unnecessary" and "trade was a dead letter." He assailed the demand for social equality by dubbing it ironically the *uravnilovka*—contemptuous Russian slang for equalitarianism.

"These people think that socialism requires equality, equality in the needs and personal life of the members of society," Stalin declared in January 1934. "These are petty bourgeois views of our left-wing scatterbrains. We know how greatly our industry has been injured by the infantile exercises of our left-wing scatterbrains. The left wingers do not understand that money and moneyed economy will remain with us for a long time."

Michael Tomsky, leader of the Soviet trade unions, objected to any further differentiation in wage scales, to any additional distinctions of wages between higher and lower paid workers. He was removed and his place taken by the more subservient Shvernik (now president of the USSR[1]); Tomsky ultimately committed suicide.

"More inequality!" was now also the cry in the army; officer ranks were restored, fraternizing between higher and lower ranks was forbidden, and the authority of officers over privates was extended. The idea was adopted of "Distinguished Men in the Soviet Land," that is, persons who had distinguished themselves in one way or another, and had thus won the right to a higher standard of living. This new aristocracy *in spe* won its rights by labor and sacrifice; it was more reminiscent of those ancient conquerors from whom, through storm and stress, stemmed the future lords, junkers, and noblemen, than of the modern men of property. But the new Soviet aristocracy no longer engaged in the coquetry of unselfishness and equality with the "common man." It demanded earthly compensation, at once and as much as possible. Let each be paid for his deeds, and in accordance with the deeds.

A new class society was in the process of development.

"Socialism Is Inequality"

It became Stalin's task to bring this chaos of ideas into some sort of unity, to reconcile the new system of inequality with Communism, and to combine the new concepts with the traditions of Lenin's epoch.

---

[1] To 1953.—Ed.

This task appeared all the more difficult because in the late twenties it was no longer possible to blame the ugly reality, the great poverty of the overwhelming majority, upon the avarice of capitalism, or to charge that this reality was the legacy of capitalism. The inequality now in force was a *new* inequality.

Stalin's concept was based on a distinction between socialism and communism.

When the Communist League was founded a hundred years ago, and Marx and Engels proclaimed their "Communist Manifesto," the term "communism" was used in reference to the future classless society. Later, for various reasons, the term "socialism" came to mean the same thing. Particularly in Russia, since the beginning of this century, the term "socialism" alone was used to express the ideal of a harmonious, happy, just social order—an order without poverty, war, and violence.

To be sure, there have been many efforts, in political literature, to distinguish between communism and socialism. Marx and Engels themselves (and later, Lenin) spoke, in passing, of the "lower" and "higher" stages of communism as a matter of the near future, the realization of which required only the attainment of a certain technological level. "Communism," he said, "is the Soviet power plus electrification," that is, a matter of a few years as far as its realization was concerned.

It became Stalin's task, proceeding from the ideas expounded by Lenin, to develop the theory of socialism as a specific social order, distinct from both capitalism and communism. According to Stalin's theory, the order now existing in Russia represents complete socialism. In such an order there is no private economy, there are no persons who live without working, but social equality does not exist. People are paid not "according to need" but "according to deed." In November 1935, Stalin declared in an address that "the distinction between intellectual and manual labor continues to exist," and that "the productivity of labor is not yet so high as to insure an abundance of consumer goods."

Communism will represent a higher stage of development, he said: "Communism means that in a Communist society everyone works according to his abilities and receives consumer goods not in accordance with what he produces but in accordance with his needs as a culturally developed human being." He assailed those who thought of "material equality on the basis of poverty.". . .

Fluctuations in Policy

A new crop of intellectuals made its appearance. Young people of the Soviet generation were being graduated from secondary and higher educational institutions. They were carefully sifted before being admitted to study courses, and most of them were members of the Communist Youth League who had no recollection or knowledge of either the old regime or democracy. Ignorant of the traditions of the old intelligentsia, but familiar with the required Soviet political terminology, these people at first evoked no suspicion or fears on the part of the regime. On the contrary, the road to the solution of the accursed problem of the intelligentsia now appeared to have been opened through the succession of generations, and through selection and training. Among the new elements there were many children of workers, and this served as an added guaranty of loyalty. Many of the new young intelligentsia joined the party, increasing the percentage of Communist engineers, lawyers, doctors, and so on.

Six months after the trial of the Industrial Party, the regime's anti-intelligentsia attitude was succeeded by another policy: the government seemed to turn its face toward the intelligentsia. In June 1931, Stalin declared that whereas, only two years before, the intelligentsia "had been infected with the wrecking disease," leaving the government no recourse but ruthlessness, "new sentiments among the old technological intelligentsia" had now taken shape. "Even the confirmed wreckers of yesterday are beginning to cooperate with the working class," said Stalin. "The attitude of the old technological intelligentsia has already begun to change."

For this reason Stalin now promised a new policy. "Our policy now," he said, "must be to attract the intelligentsia and show concern for it." "We must alter our attitude toward the technological intelligentsia of the old school." This was an attempt at *rapprochement* with the old as well as the new intelligentsia, for it was the period of feverish industrial construction and collectivization.

Half a year later, however, Stalin again thundered public threats against wreckers and saboteurs, including those "professors who in their wrecking go to the length of infecting cattle in collectives and on Soviet farms with plague germs and the Siberian anthrax, spreading meningitis among horses, and so on." He accused them of "organizing mass looting and theft of state property and of the property of cooperatives and collectives." "Theft and plunder in plants, warehouses, and commercial enterprises—these are the main activities of these people," he charged. Addressing his associates, Stalin accused them angrily of "gazing indifferently upon such manifestations." This time the accusations and repressions fell upon both the old and new intelligentsia.

Soon after came another change. From 1934 to 1936 arrests among the intelligentsia diminished, and working conditions improved. The general policy was directed toward the promotion of national unity and class collaboration; the lack of legal status of various Soviet social groups, as reflected in the former constitutions, gave way to nominal equality before the law. For the intelligentsia, this appeared to indicate a readiness on the part of the regime to overlook past sins: the sins of bourgeois origin, of earlier sympathy with oppositionist parties and groups, past offenses that had led to arrests, and other dark spots in biographies. Indeed, in his address dealing with the new constitution (November 1936), after speaking of the status of the workers and peasants, Stalin declared: "The intelligentsia has suffered many changes . . . It is now united in its roots with the working class and peasantry . . . The intelligentsia is now a full-fledged member of Soviet society, and participates together with the workers and peasants in the building of the new classless society.". . .

Rapid Increase

To understand the fantastic growth of the new higher class, we must bear in mind that the total number of government employees, about 1 million at the time of the revolution, had reached 2,767,000 by 1924. Ten years after the Soviet revolution, when industry had barely been restored to prewar levels, although Russia meanwhile had lost 20 percent of her population by being deprived of the territories previously mentioned, the number of government employees had reached 4 million. Neither the workers nor the peasants had increased in number during that ten-year period; only the total number of government employees had increased fourfold. It was strange to see the army of intellectual workers overtaking all others numerically. Two years later their number rose to 4.6 million.

But then came the years of "the great upheaval," 1929–1930, the period of industrialization and collectivization. The number of industrial workers began to grow rapidly, but the hosts of government employees remained far in advance. By 1933 they had reached the gigantic total of 8,011,000, and by 1935, 8,780,000.[2]

The 1937 census disclosed the fact that the intelligentsia had reached a total of 9,591,000, or between 13 and 14 percent of the population. Its numbers continued to rise, reaching more than 10 million by June 1941.[3]

To understand the significance of these figures, we must remember that all the higher classes of prerevolutionary Russia, including the government apparatus and private industry, totaled about 7 percent of the population. If we add to this the prerevolutionary intelligentsia and the office workers, the total came to 8 or 9 percent. These were the organizers of the national economy and the administrators of the old empire.

The present situation indicates that the state and economic apparatus, organizing and directing the physical labor of the masses, has more than doubled. To support the apex of the social pyramid was a great burden before the revolution, when it was necessary to maintain from 10 million to 12 million members of the propertied and middle classes. But far greater is the burden of maintaining 24 million to 28 million government employees (these figures include their families) simultaneously with intensified investment in industry.

What is the explanation of this phenomenon? Is it the fact that the government is now spending more money and using more people in

---

[2] These figures are actually underestimates, for they do not include the figures covering the following state agencies: NKVD; the apparatus of the Communist Party and the Komsomol; the Commissariat of Defense. These three groups added several hundred thousand to the army of government employees. The exact figures are a state secret.

[3] There are an additional 2 million employees, or 3 percent of the population, who cannot be included either in the intelligentsia or in the ranks of manual labor; these are minor employees. The total number of government employess on the eve of the war was therefore between 12 million and 13 million, or about 17.5 percent of the population.

education, science, medicine, and sanitation? True, the number of teachers has reached 970,000; the number of doctors, 130,000. But all these changes in policy, education, and public health do not begin to solve the riddle of the many millions of government employees.

What is more, despite their constant increase, their numbers were never sufficient; new cadres were being sought uninterruptedly. Even during the period of great industrial unemployment in the twenties, government employees were never discharged. "We have no people!" is the cry heard from the provinces whenever instructions covering new tasks and new plans arrive "from the center." The shortage of manpower for the Soviet machine was a constant subject of discussion in the Soviets and at party meetings. Young people graduated from secondary and higher schools were snapped up without delay; tens of thousands were thus poured annually straight from the schools into the administrative and economic machine. But it was like drinking salt water; the greater the amount swallowed, the greater grew the thirst, and again and again rose the cry to Moscow: "We have no people." Moscow replied angrily: "You must find them! Seek and ye shall find!" And once more the search was resumed.

Efforts were also made to reduce the dimensions of the monstrously swollen machine, for it constituted an intolerable burden on the state budget. Although the matter was not discussed publicly, the higher circles understood perfectly that the millions of government employees weighed very heavily upon the national economy, for 12 or 14 percent of the population consumed as much as 30 or 35 percent of the national income. "Reduction of the apparatus" was constantly discussed by the central and provincial authorities. Periodically draconic measures were resorted to with a view to achieving this purpose, when by a stroke of the pen chiefs were ordered to cut their staffs 10 to 20 percent. There were scores of such orders. But, contrary to many other decrees of the Soviet government, these failed to produce results. At first the orders were obeyed, but the work began to suffer and then, gradually, almost imperceptibly, new cadres of employees were engaged, and frequently the new total exceeded the old in many a Soviet institution. The central authorities, their attention being engaged in other drives, could only shrug their shoulders.

For example, there was a big leap forward during the First Five-Year Plan, when the total number of government employees increased from 4 million to 8 million. The plan had modestly envisaged that the "number of government employees will increase by 6 to 10 percent during the five-year period"; in reality, the increase was unprecedented. The Second Five-Year Plan provided for a reduction of 600,000 in the number of government employees. Instead of the prescribed decrease, there was a marked increase. . . .

The Leviathan

The unprecedented expansion of employees in the government service is rooted in the insolubility of the basic problem—the impossibility of controlling from a single center the administration of the whole economic, political, cultural and scientific, material and intellectual, urban and rural life of a great country. The more the functions of the state expand, the more difficult becomes their performance. When they become all-embracing, the Soviet state makes gigantic efforts to cope with them. The growing pressure finds expression in the recruiting of new cadres of employees and directors. The greater the burden upon the state, the more numerous the bottlenecks and the more frequently does it seek extraneous remedies.

The frequently unsatisfactory performance of the state machine has given rise to chronic shake-ups and readjustments, transfers and regroupings. There have been a great many of these in the history of the Soviet government apparatus, but they have never produced adequate results. For this reason another measure resorted to has been the establishment of new divisions, sectors, institutes, and commissariats, whose task it has been to correct mistakes. These new institutions soon developed their own shortcomings and they, in turn, were subdivided, expanded, or multiplied, adding new masses to the army of government employees. . . .

Government employees feel they must remain employees but at the same time must try to live better. To establish oneself, to learn the entrances and exits, to master the formulas, to obtain contacts—in short, to find one's place and to hold it is the course to be pursued, for upon this depends life itself, one's own and one's family's. Under such circumstances all those questions which formerly occupied first place in the life of Russian government employees and which have always concerned officialdom in all countries assume primary significance: salary, expenses, per diem compensation, allowances for quarters, extra allowances, and so on; added to these, in Soviet Russia are extra payments in cash—bonuses and rewards—as well as in foodstuffs, quarters, hospitalization facilities, and trips to summer resorts, to the Volga, the Crimea, and the Caucasus. Thousands of medals and ribbons grace human breasts, each carrying with it certain rights and privileges. But most important of all is advancement up the administrative ladder, the kind of success that gives a person inner satisfaction, a sense of dignity, a feeling of pride, for advancement signifies recognition of one's services by the omnipotent state.

A hierarchal society like that of Soviet Russia needs all this not less but more than any other. Rigid subordination, strict differentiation of rank, glorification of discipline—all the devices on which the old Prussian and Austrian idea of government service was based—find even greater application under the Soviet order: the chief of department and his subordinate; the army commander and the rank-and-filer; the general and the colonel; the director and the staff man; the secretary and the clerk; the people's commissar and the vice-commissar; the General Secretary and the member of the *Politbureau*; in the party apparatus, first secretary, second secretary, and third secretary; in the theater, "people's artist" and "distinguished artist."

George S. Counts
THE REPUDIATION OF EXPERIMENT

George S. Counts (b. 1889), Professor Emeritus of Teachers College, Columbia University, is a long-standing authority on education in the Soviet Union. In the historical section of his most recent work he describes the drastic changes made in Soviet educational policy in the early 1930s. This was

Reprinted with permission of McGraw-Hill Book Co., Inc. from *The Challenge of Soviet Education* by George S. Counts, pp. 60–65, 68–74. Copyright © 1957 by the McGraw-Hill Book Company, Inc.

part of the general movement by Stalin and his supporters to put an end to the radical cultural and social experiments of the 1920s and institute more traditional and highly disciplinarian standards instead.

Soviet educators have called the period from 1921 to 1931 the "experimental" period in the history of Soviet education. It might also be called the "romantic" period. And the student of Soviet politics might with good reason call it the period of the capture of the school, the pupil, and the teacher by the party. At any rate, during these years the mastery of knowledge was clearly subordinated to the political education of the younger generation. The party did not give the close attention to details of school management that characterized the later period. To be sure, it endorsed certain broad conceptions of education, such as the "unified labor school" and "polytechnical education," to which it gave the Marxian label. But this left broad areas in which educators and teachers could conduct discussions, engage in experimentation, and espouse divergent approaches to educational tasks and objectives. Moreover, the Soviet educator took pride in his knowledge of the educational ideas and practices of capitalist countries. There was abundant evidence in the 1920s of the persisting influence of the liberal and humanist movement of the two preceding generations.

Several of the leading educators of the period had actually worked in this movement. N. K. Krupskaia, wife and widow of Lenin, and head of the important department of political education of the Commissariat of Education, had taught in the Sunday schools before the revolution. Invariably she impressed all who came to know her as a person of deep human sympathies. Albert Pinkevich, whose books on the theory and practice of education were widely used in teacher-training institutions, had been principal of a secondary school for boys in St. Petersburg which was renowned for its progressive methods—progressive in the Western meaning of the word. And then there was S. T. Shatsky, a remarkable personality who had been influenced by Jane Addams and John Dewey and who after the revolution was appointed head of the First Experimental Station in People's Education in Moscow. All these persons, and many others, had experienced harsh treatment at the hands of the Russian autocracy. Little wonder that they interpreted the revolution as a sort of

FIGURE 5. Soviet architecture before and after the Stalin Revolution.

The Lubianka, headquarters and prison of the NKVD, built in the 1920s.

The University of Moscow, built in the 1940s (*Tass from Sovfoto*).

key to the gates of an educational paradise. In his memoirs Shatsky contrasted the old school which he had attended as a boy with the new school of the Soviet regime. The former was marked by harsh discipline, mastery of subject matter, and preparation for adult life; the latter, by regard for the child as a human being and the organization of instruction around his current interests. And Paul Blonsky, father of Soviet pedology and author of *The Unified Labor School* published in 1919, was a devout advocate of freedom for the child. An admirer of Rousseau, he suggested that Robinson Crusoe on the desert island provided a sound method for the education of the younger generation. He condemned as "prejudices of the old school" the recitation, the teaching plan, the separate subjects, the gradation of classes, the system of marks, the lack of faith in the child, and the passion for book learning.

In the light of developments in the 1930s, to be reported later, it is important to note that in this period a Soviet educator might express his own ideas and take exception to pronouncements by the state authorities. The case of Pinkevich may serve as an illustration. In his preface to the American edition of his *Outlines of Pedagogy,* which went through several editions in the Russian language, he addresses the following words to the English reader:

> *I wish to make it perfectly clear . . . that the system expounded in the present book is not the generally accepted system, nor is it the official system. Although the basic principles upon which Soviet educators are striving to build a system of Marxian pedagogy are everywhere the same, there may be wide differences in details and in the handling of individual questions. Moreover, the development of a uniform theory of education is neither possible nor desirable. In the present case it is sufficient to note that my position on fundamental issues is typical of the great majority of Soviet educators.*

In discussing the Programs of the Primary School prepared by the State Scientific Council of the Commissariat of Education, Pinkevich says that, while they "contain extremely valuable material," they are subject to the "fundamental criticism" of violating the "principle of objective teaching." After giving an example, he argues that there is "danger of the blind acceptance on faith of the dogmatic statements of the instructor" and that in "our opinion the entire program is threatened with dogmatization." He disappeared in the purges of 1937.

In this period there was widespread interest in the development of education in other lands. A writer in the field of pedagogy would invariably present the theories of leading educators in Europe and America, and do so in a friendly spirit and with a considerable measure of objectivity. Thus Pinkevich could say that he found the works of American educators "a rich source of materials" and "the most valuable source" from beyond the borders of the Soviet Union. Also, after reviewing the ideas of leading Western educators, he speaks of "the great American philosopher, John Dewey," and ranks him "among the bourgeois forerunners of the true labor school." And Blonsky, perhaps the most erudite Soviet scholar in the whole field of education, followed very closely the work of E. L. Thorndike, Charles H. Judd, and others. Incidentally, his subject of pedology was declared a pseudo-science by the Central Committee of the party in 1936. The subject was forthwith abolished and Blonsky disappeared. A. V. Lunacharsky, a friend of Lenin and the first commissar of education in the Russian Republic, was something of a cosmopolitan, a man of broad cultural interests, a connoisseur and patron of the arts who intervened with Lenin at the time of the revolution to save from destruction the art treasures of old Russia. In 1928,[1] four years after the death of Lenin, he was removed from office. A visitor to the Soviet Union in the 1920s was generally impressed by the eagerness of Soviet teachers and educators to learn about educational practices in other lands. As a rule, however, they would state explicitly that the techniques, and not the purposes, of education in capitalist countries would be of value to them.

The school which these people and their collaborators built under the directives issued by the party was called the "unified labor school." It was "unified" because it was organized at three levels as a single school, with provision for the unimpeded progress of the child from the first grade to the ninth or tenth. It was called "labor" because in Marxian theory human labor is the source of all value and the laboring class is the builder of the new society. Thus labor is endowed with that mystical quality in a Communist order which

[1] Actually 1929.—Ed.

marks the role of the proletariat in the history of the present epoch. By labor even a member of the despised bourgeoisie may redeem himself and become whole. And so the education of the young must be linked with labor as theory must be linked with practice, words with deeds. Here, the Soviet leaders contended, was the greatest and most fruitful invention in the whole history of education, but an invention which could be put to use only under the rule of the proletariat.

This school was an activity school, a school in which children learned by doing. In contrasting their school with the school of the past, the Soviet educators were fond of saying that their school was a "school that does" rather than a "school that talks." But the word "activity" in the Soviet context was given a meaning which distinguished it radically from that prevailing in the so-called progressive schools of the West. It carried a moral and social content. As one enthusiast said, "The question of 'the socially useful activities of the school' must be regarded at the present moment as the most important question of Soviet pedagogy, because it constitutes the sharpest and brightest trait which distinguishes the Soviet school, not only from the tsarist school, but also from every other contemporary school." The Soviet school must be as "bright and unique" as the "Soviet Union which gave it birth." And this basic characteristic is not found in the "complex method, self-government, or the social work of the teacher. Relatively speaking, all of these are trivialities." The Soviet school, "being created in the epoch of the stupendous sweep of a program for building the country, *must itself participate in the building of life.*" In a word, education must be a central factor in the direct transformation of both man and society. . . .

The point should be emphasized that socially useful labor was not merely a method of teaching. Nor was it a substitute for the traditional curriculum. As a matter of fact, it was both method and curriculum. In the opinion of Soviet educators it added content and gave vitality to the entire program of instruction. The school continued to teach the native tongue, natural science, social studies, and mathematics, but it did all these things in relation to contemporary life and the tasks of Soviet society as determined by the Bolshevik dictatorship. Socially useful labor gave a new dimension to the curriculum and profoundly altered its structure. The mastery of academic subjects as such was relegated to a subordinate position. Some Soviet educators contended that subjects should be abolished and that the child should acquire necessary skills and knowledges as a by-product of the pursuit of socially desirable ends. This led to the development of interest in the "method of projects" and convinced many American visitors that the Bolsheviks had adopted the philosophy and program of "progressive education." The Soviet educators also were attracted to the "Dalton plan" [that is, using the brighter students as tutors] and the "laboratory method," not only for the natural sciences, but also for other subjects. One of the most enthusiastic advocates of socially useful labor was V. N. Shul'gin, director of the Institute of School Methods in Moscow. Taking seriously the Marxian prophecy that the state would "wither away" after the establishment of socialism and confident that socialism was not far away, he developed and expounded the doctrine of the "withering away of the school." He saw the child of the future acquiring his education by participating in the life of society, each of whose institutions would perform its appropriate educational function. The child would grow up, "not in a school, not in a kindergarten, not in a retort of a chemical laboratory," but in the "factory, the mill, the agricultural economy, the class struggle." And he would be taught, "not by a teacher in a box, in a knit cap," but "by the entire order of things." Also, "industry will be placed at the service of education. It will be organized for educational purposes, as will be the street." According to a report received by the writer in Moscow in 1936, Shul'gin himself was at that time "withering away" on an engineering project in the region of the North Caucasus. And he was not serving as an engineer. . . .

With the launching of the great program for the industrialization of the country in the autumn of 1928 and the complete triumph of Stalin over his rivals by the early thirties, the so-called "experimental period" came to a close. The educational practices of that period had been at least measurably successful in the propagation of Bolshevik doctrines among children and youth. Many of the old teachers had been either reconciled with the revolution or eliminated from the profession by natural or political causes. As early as June 12, 1925,

the Soviet of People's Commissars of the RSFSR[2] "notices a considerable improvement in the ideas and attitudes of the body of
teachers toward the new regime," and "a parallel improvement of the
same order generally among scientists." Also a new generation of
teachers, reared in large part under Soviet institutions and presumably loyal to the regime, was emerging. At the same time, the
program of construction carried through in the early years with
the assistance of foreign engineers, technicians, and even skilled
workers, called for the swift mastery of science and technology. As
a consequence, novel and exacting demands were made on the
schools. They were asked to participate actively in the conversion of a
technically and culturally backward country into a modern industrial
state. In 1936, when the author inquired of teachers and children in
both European Russia and Siberia regarding the first duty of the
pupil, the response was everywhere the same—"the mastery of
knowledge." The immediate fulfillment of the Five-Year Plan was left
to the older generation. The pupil's first responsibility was to study
language, mathematics, and science. Added to all this was the
profound shift in the whole orientation and configuration of Soviet
life and institutions associated with the rise of Stalin and Stalinism.
In the process of adjustment to the new conditions many of the
practices and doctrines of the earlier period were modified, aban-
doned, or reversed. But only in a limited sense were the issues
pedagogical in nature. At bottom, like everything else in the Soviet
Union, including the content of the calendar and the humor of the
circus, they were essentially political issues—political issues of
critical concern to the dictatorship.

The demands of the program of construction and the slogan of
overtaking and surpassing the most advanced capitalist countries
merit an additional word. As the Soviet leaders struggled to achieve
the goals of the First Five-Year Plan, they became painfully aware
of the general backwardness of Russia. This they had all said many
times; indeed, Soviet literature had been filled with this lament all
through the period of the battle to consolidate Bolshevik rule. But
only as they undertook the heavy tasks of industrial construction did

---

[2] RSFSR: The Russian Socialist Federated Soviet Republic, the original Communist state of 1917 and the main constituent republic of the Union of Soviet
Socialist Republics after the latter was formed in 1922.—Ed.

The Repudiation of Experiment 125

they realize fully the truth of the oft-repeated indictment of the past. They found to their sorrow that the rank and file of Soviet citizens did indeed lag far behind the peoples of the West in the most elementary mastery of the skills, knowledges, and understandings required in the building of an industrial economy—skills, knowledges, and understandings which the child in America acquires more or less incidentally in the process of growing up amid complicated tools, machines, motors, and electricity. The unified labor school, with its emphasis on socially useful work, freedom from discipline, unorganized curricula, political indoctrination, and diverse romantic notions about education stemming from Marx and Lenin, simply was not sufficient to the task. As a consequence, practically the entire regimen of the middle school was swiftly transformed by decrees issued either directly or indirectly by the Central Committee of the party. These decrees were directed, not only to broad educational policies, but also to the details of instruction and school management. As a consequence, a new Soviet school emerged which was profoundly different from the school of the 1920s—a school which resembled in many respects the school of old Russia and would have been labeled counterrevolutionary in the earlier period, but one which in fact expresses the basic philosophy of Bolshevism far more faithfully than its predecessor.

The first of these important decrees, issued on September 5, 1931, called for the simple mastery of knowledge. According to the Central Committee, "the basic defect of our school at the present moment" is the "fact that school instruction fails to give a sufficient body of general knowledge" and thus fails to "prepare for the technicums and higher schools fully literate people with a good command of the basic sciences (physics, chemistry, mathematics, native language, geography and others)." While continuing to stress the principle of "polytechnical education," the decree condemns the traditional practice in these sharp words: "Every attempt to separate the polytechnization of the school from a systematic and firm mastery of the sciences, and of physics, chemistry, and mathematics in particular . . . constitutes the most flagrant perversion of the ideas of the polytechnical school." The teaching of these subjects "must be conducted by means of strictly established schedules." In order to emphasize the importance and urgency of the need for a fundamental reorganization of the entire program of instruction, the Central Committee asked the commissariats of education in the Union Republics "to organize immediately a scientific-Marxian revision of the program, making certain that it contains a strictly defined body of systematic knowledge (native language, mathematics, physics, chemistry, geography, history)." The date for the introduction of the "new revised programs" was set for January 1, 1932. In the meantime, all necessary practical measures were to be taken to instruct the teachers and prepare directives for launching the new programs without delay. To expedite the reforms, "all members of the party engaged in the work of people's education" were instructed "to master the new procedures in the shortest possible time." Thus was restored the curriculum of separate subjects—subjects with clearly defined content to be mastered by the pupil. And this curriculum was to be uniform for practically all children from the first grade to the tenth.

The decree of September 5, 1931, ordered corresponding changes in the field of methods of instruction. While recognizing the value of some of the new methods of teaching "in the development of initiative and the preparation of active participants in socialist construction," it demanded the launching of a "decisive warfare against irresponsible projectorizing and the introduction on a mass scale of methods untested in practice." This error assumed its most glaring form in the "adoption of the so-called 'project method.' Stemming directly from the anti-Leninist theory of the 'withering away of the school,' the attempts to place the 'project method' at the basis of the entire school actually led to the destruction of the school." It is interesting to note, incidentally, that Krupskaia had been particularly enthusiastic about this method. The Central Committee warned the entire teaching profession against both "extreme Left tendencies" and "attempts to go back to the bourgeois school." However, the response to this initial decree was quite unsatisfactory. Consequently, on August 25, 1932, the Central Committee issued another decree, which ordered the "liquidation of the perversions of laboratory-brigade methods" and then proceeded to a positive definition of the appropriate method for the Soviet school: "The chief form of the organization of instruction in the primary and secondary school must be the recitation with a given group of pupils following a strict schedule of studies. Under the leadership of the teacher this form must include group, brigade, and individual work of each pupil," and "the teacher must present the subject he is teaching systematically and consistently."

Implicit in the emphasis on the mastery of knowledge and the revival of the recitation is a fundamental change in the relations between teacher and pupil. The decree of September 5, 1931, called upon the commissariats of education to strengthen "individual authority in the management of the school" and to "increase the responsibility of the teaching body in their work by promoting and encouraging loyal and well-trained teachers." At the same time, "the work of children's self-government in the school" was to be "directed chiefly toward the improvement of the quality of learning and the strengthening of school discipline." The decree may be understood also as marking the emergence of a body of teachers presumably loyal to the regime. . . .

The demand of the Central Committee that the mastery of a definite body of knowledge should be the basic purpose of the middle school led speedily to the reversal of a fairly well-established Soviet tradition regarding the role of the textbook in the educative process. Many of the foremost leaders of Soviet education, including Krupskaia, Shatsky, and Blonsky, were fond of saying that "life must be the textbook." This position was officially proclaimed by the Russian Commissariat of Education in the following words contained in a circular letter dated August 1918: "Textbooks in general should be thrown out of the school." As late as May 1930, an all-Russian conference of educators "definitely repudiates the principle of the stabilization of textbooks." In the same year the plenum of the Central Committee of the Professional Union of Educational Workers declared that the standardization of textbooks is "incorrect and politically injurious." But on February 12, 1933, the Central Committee of the party pronounced this attitude toward the textbook "incorrect" and "intolerable." It then proceeded to instruct the Commissariat of Education to prepare "stable textbooks" in the "native language, mathematics, geography, physics, chemistry, biology, etc." And the date of publication was set for "July 15, 1933, in order that they may be ready for the opening of the academic year—September 1, 1933"! In the sense of the committee, a "stable textbook" is one "designed for use over a period of many years" and "approved after a preliminary scrupulous examination by the Collegium of the Commissariat of Education." In such a textbook, as Stalin once said, "every word and every definition must be weighed." And such a textbook must be prepared for "each subject" taught in the school.

The next step to ensure the mastery of knowledge was the development of a rigorous system of marks, examinations, promotion, and awards. . . .

This transformation of the purposes, the curriculum, and methods of the school was accompanied by an expression of widespread concern regarding the behavior of pupils. From the early thirties the Soviet press contained numerous references to "hooliganism" on the part of children and youth in schools and public places. The general lack of discipline on the part of the young was deplored and a widespread campaign to correct these evils was launched. Even Stalin gave the matter his attention, and the famous cavalry leader, General Budenny, almost a legendary figure, went into the school in 1935 to impress on children the necessity of loving and respecting their teachers and elders. The pupil was told over and over again that his first duty was to study and learn. No longer was he to assume responsibility for running the school, correcting his parents, managing the affairs of the community, or even assisting directly in the great program of construction. He was subjected increasingly to strict supervision in school, at home, and on the street. Moreover, he was held accountable for his successes and failures as an individual.

Edward J. Brown
THE MOBILIZATION OF CULTURE

Edward J. Brown (b. 1909), professor of Russian at Stanford University, has investigated a crucial period in the history of Soviet cultural policy—the era of the "Revolutionary Association of Proletarian Writers" (RAPP) under the leadership of Leopold Averbakh. The period of RAPP coincided with the

From Edward J. Brown, *The Proletarian Episode in Russian Literature, 1928–1932* (New York: Columbia University Press, 1953), pp. 60–63, 85–88, 90, 92–93, 220–222. Reprinted by permission of the publisher.

Stalin Revolution, and the primary purpose of the organization was to bring Russian writers under Communist Party control and make literature serve the political purposes of the party. Similar steps were taken at this time in most other cultural fields. In every case, however, the work of these early control agencies failed to satisfy the desire of Stalin and the party leadership for more and simpler propaganda. By the mid-thirties RAPP and its kindred organizations had been dissolved and replaced by new bodies ready to fulfill Stalin's requirements of "socialist realism" without question or complaint.

The works of Averbakh and the official statements of the leadership of RAPP make frequent reference to the necessity for a "cultural revolution." The political revolution and the reorganization of industry and agriculture will be meaningless, they indicate, unless these developments are accompanied by a rise in the cultural level of the working masses. The term "culture" is used in a very broad sense to include not only an increase in the popular utilization of literature and art in all its forms, but most of all a rise in general literacy, in education, and in standards of health and sanitation.

Averbakh's main thesis would appear to be that "the productivity of labor depends not only on the industrialization of the country, but also upon raising the educational and cultural level of the masses." This statement in itself would seem to be fairly obvious and to raise no serious political issues: such a program was, at least in its broad outlines, included in the party program. But the question is one of emphasis. Averbakh's idea is that industrialization at the tempos contemplated by the program of the party will be impossible without a continuous and concomitant rise in the cultural level of the masses.

Averbakh was in 1928 extremely dissatisfied with the results so far achieved in this realm. He adduces figures to show that only very little had been done to liquidate illiteracy, to broaden educational services, to improve health, and to extend medical care. From the figures he gives the conclusion is inescapable that the USSR was not only far behind the nations of Central and Eastern Europe, but had not even been able to make significant strides beyond the achievements of tsarist Russia.

He stresses the extreme cultural backwardness of the country by comparison with Western nations. Apparently in answer to anticipated arguments, he emphasizes that funds expended for such things as education and health care will also contribute to the rise in production figures, for they will improve the quality of the workers.

He quotes speeches made at the Fifteenth Congress of the Party (1927) by Rykov and Bukharin to the effect that further growth in industrialization must be accompanied by a corresponding rise in the cultural level of the masses. He quotes a speech given at the Moscow Party Conference, at which Bukharin had called for an increase in the funds allocated to cultural work. Averbakh concludes:

> *It is clear, then, that we are lagging behind culturally and that we must give special attention to the . . . financing of the cultural revolution.*

The cultural revolution, as Averbakh understood it, involved deep changes in human beings. Such changes of course presupposed the liquidation of illiteracy and the traditional "darkness" of pre-1917 Russia. But they must go much further:

> *The cultural revolution is a lengthy epoch during which human material will be transformed, the toiling masses themselves will be reeducated, and a new type of man produced. In this work a great and serious task falls to the lot of art, with its specific means of influencing the whole human psyche.*

Echoing the conclusions of Averbakh in the brochure quoted above, the resolutions of the RAPP executive emphasize that this cultural work cannot wait for the consolidation of a firm material base for the new society, but must go hand in hand with it. A leading article in one of the early issues of *On Literary Guard,* printed in large type and apparently designed as a major statement of editorial policy, emphasizes that the party and the government cannot wait for the outcome of "socialist construction" and the raising of the material level of the workers before interesting themselves in cultural matters. Cultural progress must go hand in hand with construction, or else the latter will be hampered.

The theoreticians and practitioners of proletarian literature believed that their product should be an important agency of this "cultural revolution." The resolution adopted by the First Congress of Proletarian Writers in 1928 sets forth such ideas in the Marxist jargon of the day:

> *Being one of the means for the cognition of social life and of the whole world which surrounds man, art organizes the feelings and thoughts by means of images influencing the psyche of the reader, listener, etc., through "emotional infection." In the conditions of a class society art is a mighty weapon of the class struggle. In actively influencing all ideological fields, the proletariat makes no exception of art. Therefore one of the main tasks of the cultural revolution is to aid the development of proletarian art and its advanced detachment, proletarian literature.*

"To aid the development of . . . proletarian literature," such is the important task of the "cultural revolution." What exactly was understood by the term "proletarian literature"? There is never any question in the statements of RAPP theoreticians on this subject that the term must include not only the literary product of people who are proletarian in origin but also that of nonproletarians who sympathize with—"take the viewpoint of"—the proletariat. And indeed it could not be otherwise, for the leadership of RAPP and a large proportion of its membership were made up of writers and critics who were not of working-class origin. Averbakh, Libedinsky, Fadeev, Panfyorov, Kirshon, Gladkov, and most of the people active in RAPP, were in their family origins *petit-bourgeois* intellectuals. This was true not only of RAPP but also of the early On Guard group. Unlike the Proletcult,[1] whose tendency was to accept as proletarian only works directly expressing the life of the "labor collective," On Guard and RAPP had a much broader understanding of the term:

> *Proletarian literature we understand as that literature which comprehends the world from the viewpoint of the proletariat and influences the reader in accord with the tasks of the working class. . . . Only from the point of view of the world outlook of the proletariat—Marxism—can social reality be perceived by the artist with maximum objectivity.*

Averbakh at one point clearly underlines the idea that the term "proletarian" has no necessary reference to the class origin of the writer:

> *Proletarian art is not a form of art which must necessarily be created by a proletarian. Proletarian art is such art as aids the proletariat in the building of socialism, and organizes our feelings and thoughts in the direction of the building of a Communist society.*

[1] "Proletcult": "Proletarian Culture," an organization of ultra-left intellectuals in the 1920s.—Ed.

There emerged from this attempt to apply Marxism to literary theory and criticism a body of ideas some of which were not without objective merit. The emphasis on realism and against direct propaganda and obvious tendentiousness was the result of elementary lessons learned at the feet of Voronsky, and confirmed by the reading of Plekhanov.[2] The notion that reality is complex, unstable, and even a little mysterious, and that the "psyche" develops on more than one level and under influences not completely understood was an idea that the proletarians seem to have been groping for in their lengthy disquisitions on the "living man" and "immediate impressions." These ideas were of course woven into the fabric of "dialectical materialism," and the writer was required to portray reality from the viewpoint of the Marxist ideology. That this requirement did inhibit many writers, especially those in whom Marxism was not organic, could easily have been foreseen, and was in fact admitted by Averbakh and Libedinsky. If demanded mechanically of all writers its effect might be to discourage serious literary production. But as a viewpoint elected by a group of writers intent on exploring and perhaps explaining the world, it was capable of producing good results; and the proletarians did produce some works of genuine merit: we may mention Sholokhov's *The Silent Don,* Libedinsky's *Birth of a Hero,* Mitrofanov's *June-July,* and the early chapters of Panfyorov's *Brussky.*

Yet there was a fatal flaw inherent in the nature of RAPP. The literary ideas of the leading group became articles of faith to which all writers within the organization were required to subscribe. The literary attitudes and habits of opposition groups were not granted autonomy. The fictitious and oppressive authority bestowed upon RAPP by the party during these years tended to vitiate literary life, even within its own organization. Just how this happened we shall presently see. . . .

With the adoption of the First Five-Year Plan in 1928 the party had undertaken a program which called for the maximum efforts in the direction of overcoming the industrial backwardness of the Soviet Union. Its program called for tremendous sacrifice and constant

[2] Alexander Voronsky, the leading Soviet literary critic of the 1920s; Georgi Plekhanov, the founder of Russian Marxism and a leader of the Mensheviks until his death in 1918.—Ed.

exertion. All forces were quite frankly "mobilized" for the task, and no exception was made for the forces of literature and art. Literary men, too, were expected to help in the colossal job of "overtaking and surpassing" the advanced countries; they were expected, in plain words, to devote their talents as writers to the humble task of publicizing and propagandizing the plan. The idea that belles-lettres are an "instrument" in the hands of the dominant class—always the contention of the extreme Left in Soviet theory—was now adopted by the party in its simplest and crudest form.

With this change in the party's attitude toward literature, the RAPP theory and practice began to lose favor; for the leaders of RAPP were slow, reluctant, and ineffectual in carrying out the direct "social demand" of the party. Under the pressure of its own program, the party moved gradually but surely into a position of direct antagonism to the announced literary principles of RAPP, as set forth [above].

In the summer of 1928 the Central Committee of the party called an all-Union conference on questions of agitation, propaganda, and cultural work. Among the resolutions adopted in the course of this discussion we find the following:

> *Literature, the theater, and the cinema should all be brought forward and into contact with the widest circles of the population, and should be utilized in the fight for a new cultural outlook, a new way of life, against bourgeois and* petit-bourgeois *ideology, against vodka, philistinism . . . against the resurrection of bourgeois ideology under new labels, and against a slavish imitation of bourgeois culture.*

. . . [RAPP] was an organization made to order for the purposes of the Central Committee; it was composed mainly of Communists willing to undertake social tasks; it was organized and disciplined; it was already actively engaged in developing new writers from the working class; it announced as its chief virtue devotion in carrying out the policy of the Central Committee.

RAPP was the organization to which the party would naturally turn as the chief support of its policy in the field of literary organization, literary production, and literary criticism. And while there is no statement of the Central Committee which definitely names RAPP as the spokesman of the Central Committee, yet it soon became clear that the party depended upon RAPP to consolidate all Communist literary forces, to fight against "deviations" in the literary field, and to aid in carrying out literary directives. . . .

. . . A resolution of the Central Committee "On Publishing Work" was published on August 15, 1931. It lists the "successes" of Soviet publishing, pointing to the increase in number of titles issued, especially in the field of theory (the works of Lenin) and industrial technique. It goes on to point out what, in general, is expected of "the book":

> *The content and character of the book should in every way respond to the demands of socialist reconstruction; it should be militant and deal with political themes of the present day; it should arm the broad masses of the builders of socialism with Marxist-Leninist theory and with technical knowledge. The book should be the mightiest means of educating, mobilizing, and organizing the masses for the tasks of economic and cultural building.*

Such is the Central Committee's description of what literature generally is expected to accomplish. On the subject of belles-lettres the resolution is no less definite as to the utilitarian aims to be pursued:

> *Imaginative literature, which plays such a huge educational role, should reflect far more deeply and fully the heroism of socialist construction and of the class struggle, the transformation of social relations and the growth of new people—the heroes of socialist construction. The publication of imaginative literature should be to a certain extent specialized by the GIKHL [State Publishing House for Belles-Lettres] into different sectors (for example, there should be, alongside synthetic imaginative works, historical literature, agricultural belles-lettres, industrial belles-lettres, classical literature, etc).*

It should be clear that in the view of the Central Committee there was no question of eliminating entirely the production of literary works on historical subjects, or of such as are described as "synthetic," a term which apparently refers to fictional works having no immediate relation to the realities of socialist construction. It is clearly a question of emphasis. The party policy is to increase the weight and relative importance of literature serving the ends of "socialist construction." And the Central Committee gave writers a material incentive for the production of such literature:

In view of the fact that the system of payment of authors has considerable importance in improving the quality of the printed work, it is necessary to differentiate payments, and to set up such a scale of honorariums as will stimulate the promotion of the most talented authors; that is especially necessary in the case of those forms of literary production which have special importance for the present period.

Thus it was the policy of the Central Committee in literature as in other sectors of "the economy" to use the incentive of higher pay in order to increase the production of "better quality" works, and by this they meant works answering the "needs of the day." It has not been possible to get reliable information on the scale of payments for literary works during this period; but it is reasonable to assume that more would be paid for a novel on the Dneprostroi construction than for a novel dealing with the "sufferings of mind" of an intellectual at odds with the epoch. It seems fairly certain on the basis of this official directive that there was, in fact, a wide differential in payments to authors, based in part on the importance of the subjects chosen in promoting the aims of "socialist reconstruction." This assumption is borne out, further, by the fact that Soviet writers generally gave themselves with a will to the depiction and stimulation of the labors of the Five-Year Plan. Thus the incentive of material success was added to the administrative directives, editorial propaganda, resolutions, and enterprises of the Central Committee, all aimed at producing a literature for and about the Five-Year Plan. In addition, there was undoubtedly present in many writers a genuine sympathy for the aims of the industrialization program and a real interest in the transformation of the country which was going on around them. . . .

The theory of proletarian literature dominant in RAPP was its most distinctive and characteristic contribution to the movement. This theory was worked out in the heat of controversy with Proletcult and On Guard ideas on the left, and the views of Voronsky and the Pereval[3] critics on the right. In its final form it included elements of both. The theory described the nature of proletarian literature as cognition of life from the viewpoint of dialectical materialism, and its function as aiding the proletariat in its advance along the road to

---

[3] "Pereval": "The Pass," a group of politically moderate writers, forced out of existence around 1930.—Ed.

communism. It maintained that literature is an important instrument in the hands of the working class, and can be an effective means of changing reality, but only insofar as it deals directly with that reality itself. When it is unfaithful to reality—when it fails as "cognition of life"—then it is not literature and it is not an effective instrument. Proletarian literature must be realistic. It must continue the tradition of nineteenth-century Russian realism and accept as its cultural heritage the great masters of that school, particularly Tolstoy.

During the period of the First Five-Year Plan, this theory of literature and the practice based upon it came into conflict with the tremendous effort to rebuild the country which had been undertaken by the party. In this effort the party endeavored to enlist all forces, and its campaign affected every department of life. The psychology cultivated among the builders was essentially a military one, and the plan itself resembled a military campaign in its scale, its tempo, its slogans, and in the feeling of imminent war nourished by the party. The urgent demand was to expend all energies so as to aid in fulfilling the goals of the plan. No exception was made for literature and the arts. Writers, too, had a function to perform, and literature was regarded as a means for mobilizing the masses. Thus under the pressure of its own program, the party had adopted in its simplest form the traditional viewpoint of the "left" in Soviet literary theory. It proposed to use literature as an instrument of its policy.

This development led to a curiously anomalous situation in which the organization supported by the party and commissioned to mobilize proletarian forces on the literary front was out of harmony with the party program for literature, both disapproving and resisting the effort to make literature an instrument of publicistic aims. Because of its leadership's lack of enthusiasm for carrying out party directives, the organization was constantly torn by inner dissension, and heavily criticized from without by the party press and party spokesmen.

When RAPP was liquidated in April 1932, many reasons were officially advanced for that step. The resolution of the Central Committee claims that a great growth in literature had taken place during the years of its activity, but concludes that RAPP should be liquidated. Kaganovich explained that liquidation was necessary because a few selfish Communists in RAPP had been "holding back the writers' creative powers." Party spokesmen in the years immediately following its dissolution gave a number of additional reasons for this step: the clannishness and isolation of the leading group, their administrative excesses, their theoretical deviations and "idealistic" alienation from the "party spirit" of literature. All of these things may have been factors in the final decision.

The investigation undertaken here has produced evidence that there were two basic reasons for the dissolution of RAPP: its resistance to the party's use of literature as an instrument of direct propaganda for the Five-Year Plan, and its hostility to a talented group of writers—the majority of them outside the Communist and proletarian milieu—of whose value to the party as literary allies there was little doubt. It is suggested further that the dissolution of the proletarian literary organization was one indication of a decisive change in policy regarding the relative position and importance of the proletariat and other social groups. Thus ended the struggle for "proletarian hegemony," and all the discussions and disputes carried out in its name.

The period of the First Five-Year Plan was indeed a devastating one in the history of Russian literature. It marked the ruthless extension by the Communist party of its political power into the field of belles-lettres. Russian literature has never recovered from that experience. RAPP was designed as an agency for the extension of party power and as such it has occupied an unenviable place in literary history. Yet it must be remembered, to its credit, that at some time during this period Averbakh and the literary men associated with him discovered in themselves at least a modicum of care for the literature which others wished to use as an "instrument." Within the narrow limits of their class ideology—and they allowed themselves no other —they tried to save it.

Nikolai I. Bukharin
as told to Boris Nicolaevsky

THE CRACKDOWN ON THE PARTY

In 1936 the Russian Menshevik journal Sotsialistichesky Vestnik *(The Socialist Messenger), then located in Paris, published a long letter from "a veteran member of the Bolshevik Party." It was actually written by the Menshevik historian Boris Nicolaevsky to record the substance of a series of talks that he had in Paris in the spring of 1936 with Nikolai Bukharin (1888–1938), leader of the ill-fated Right Opposition. The letter was translated into English and published in book form in 1938. In it Bukharin recounts the behind-the-scene maneuvering among the Soviet leadership in the early 1930s and the events leading up to the first of the "Moscow Trials" in 1936.*

Among the last testaments left by Lenin there is none to which our "party leadership" had clung more tenaciously than his imperative advice not to repeat the mistake of the Jacobins—to eschew the road of mutual extermination. It was considered an axiom that in the fight against the Party Opposition any methods save the death penalty should be resorted to. True, there had been occasional lapses from this rule: Blumkin and a few other Trotskyites had been shot for penetrating, on instructions of their organization, into the secret recesses of the GPU, and warning their comrades against treachery and impending arrest. These shootings were generally regarded as exceptional measures, imposed not for participation in the struggle within the party, but for betrayal of official duties. Misdemeanors of this kind were always severely punished in the USSR. In 1924–1925 a Menshevik was shot who had forced his way into the secretariat of the Central Control Committee and had taken certain documents in order to send them to the *Socialist Messenger.* Even during the "Menshevik Trial" (1931) recourse to the death penalty had never been seriously considered.

The first occasion when the death penalty for participation in oppositionist activity in internal party politics was discussed was in connection with the Riutin affair. This was at the end of 1932, when

From *Letter of an Old Bolshevik* (New York: The Rand School, and London: George Allen and Unwin, 1938), pp. 14–20, 22–25, 27–29, 69–71, 76. Reprinted by permission of George Allen and Unwin, Ltd. and of the Tamiment Institute of New York (successor to the Rand School).

the situation in the country was similar to 1921—the time of the Kronstadt rebellion. In 1932, it is true, there were no actual revolts, but many believed that it would have been better if the government had had to deal with actual revolts. Half of the country was stricken with famine. The workers were on short rations. The productivity of labor had greatly fallen, and there was no way of raising it, for it was not a question of unwillingness on the part of the workers, but of physical impossibility of working productively on an empty stomach. The predominant view in party circles was that Stalin had led the country into an impasse by his policy, that he had roused the peasants against the party, and that the situation could be saved only by his removal from party domination. Many influential members of the Central Committee were of this opinion. It was said that an anti-Stalin majority was being formed in the "Politburo" as well. Wherever party officials met, the subject of discussion was: what program was to be substituted for Stalin's "general line." It is obvious that, in the process, various proposed programs and declarations were being circulated from hand to hand. Among these, Riutin's program was specially noteworthy. It was definitely propeasant in character. It demanded the abolition of the collectives and the granting of economic self-determination to the peasants. But this was not all that differentiated this program from others. At that time the program of the right-wing Bolsheviks, such as that of Slepkov, was emphatically propeasant, but so was that of the former left-wing Trotskyists, who had been, in fact, politically responsible for Stalin's "general line," since it was they who had been its original ideologists. Riutin's program was remarkable chiefly for its *severe criticism of Stalin.* It was two hundred pages long, fifty of which were devoted to Stalin's personal characteristics, to a consideration of the part he had played in the party, and to the reasons for the basic contention that unless Stalin was removed from party domination there could be no recovery in the party or in the country. These views were expressed with remarkable vigor and made a deep impression. Stalin was depicted as the evil genius of the Russian Revolution, who, actuated by vindictiveness and lust for power, had brought the revolution to the edge of the abyss.

This section of the program, for which the author was to pay a heavy penalty, was particularly responsible for its success. The program aroused a great deal of discussion, and it was not surprising, therefore, that a copy was soon brought to Stalin's desk. This, naturally, led to arrests and house searches. As a result, not only were all those who had circulated Riutin's program arrested, but also those who had distributed other declarations. Riutin, who at that time was in exile or in an "isolator," where he had worked out his plan, was brought to Moscow. Upon examination, he admitted the authorship. As an old party leader who had rendered eminent service to the party, he came within the classification of those against whom, in accordance with Lenin's commandment, there could be no question of application of the death penalty. The question was, therefore, considered by the "Politburo," because the OGPU (naturally, at Stalin's wish) had demanded his execution.

The discussions in the Politburo were heated. Stalin was in favor of granting the OGPU's demand. His strongest argument was a reference to the growth of *terrorist sentiment among young people,* particularly in the Komsomol (Young Communist League). Reports of the OGPU were replete with stories of terroristic talk among *young workers and students.* Moreover, quite a number of terroristic acts against minor Soviet Officials and party officers had become known. Against such terrorists the party did not shrink from resorting to the "supreme penalty," even when it was a question of members of the Komsomol, Stalin maintaining that it was politically illogical and unjust to administer such severe punishment to those who performed terroristic acts while sparing those whose political propaganda had inspired these acts. He recommended that no undue attention be given to the small fry, but that the Politburo go straight to the root and cause of the matter. Riutin's program, Stalin said, was a direct justification of and an apology for the necessity for murdering him.

I can no longer recall the actual division of opinion in the Politburo when this question was being considered. I only know that Kirov[1] spoke with particular force against recourse to the death penalty. Moreover, he succeeded in winning over the Politburo to this view. Stalin was prudent enough not to push matters to an open conflict. Riutin's life was thus spared. He was sentenced to a long term in an "isolator" where a particularly severe regime was in vogue. It became

[1] Sergei M. Kirov, member of the Politburo, first secretary of the Communist Party for the Leningrad Province, and Stalin's apparent second-in-command until his assassination under mysterious circumstances in December 1934.—Ed.

clear to everybody, however, that the Politburo would be compelled again to take up the big questions which had arisen, in one form or another, out of this affair. . . .

Kirov played an important part in the Politburo. He was a 100 percent supporter of the "general line," and distinguished himself during its operation by great energy and inflexibility. This caused Stalin to value him highly. But there was always a certain independence in Kirov's attitude which annoyed Stalin. The story is told that Stalin had prevented Kirov from attending the meetings of the Politburo in Moscow for several months under the pretext that his presence in Leningrad was indispensable. However, Stalin could never make up his mind to take strong measures against Kirov. It would have been folly to add to the already large number of the dissatisfied an important party leader such as Kirov, especially since Kirov had succeeded in surrounding himself in Leningrad with reliable and devoted aids. A new conflict with the Leningrad party might have been more fatal now than in Zinoviev's day. In the winter of 1933–1934, Kirov had so strengthened his position that he could afford to follow his own line. He aimed not only at a "Western orientation" in foreign policy, but also at the conclusions which would follow logically from this new orientation as far as home policy was concerned.

The task, therefore, was not only that of creating a mighty army in preparation for the impending military conflict, a conflict which appeared inevitable, but also, politically speaking, of creating the proper psychologic frame of mind on the home front. There were two alternatives: to pursue the former policy of crushing all dissenters, with the administrative pressure ruthlessly tightened and the terror intensified, or to try "reconciliation with the people," to gain their voluntary cooperation in the political preparation of the country for the coming war. The most convinced and most prominent advocates of the *second alternative* were *Kirov* and *Gorki* [Maxim Gorki, the writer]. It would be worthwhile to describe in greater detail Gorki's influence in the life of the party, particularly as it is now possible to speak more openly since his death. But that is another matter, and would take us too far afield. Gorki had exercised a great and beneficent influence upon Stalin. But, despite all his influence, Gorki was *not a member* of the Politburo, and had no direct part in the making of its decisions. Kirov's part became, therefore, all the more important.

Kirov stood for the idea of *abolition of the terror,* both in general and inside the party. We do not desire to exaggerate the importance of his proposals. It must not be forgotten that when the First Five-Year Plan was being put into effect, Kirov was one of the heads of the party, that he was among those who inspired and carried through the notoriously ruthless measures against the peasants and the wiping out of the kulaks. The Kem and Murmansk coasts, with their prison camps, and so forth, were under his jurisdiction. Furthermore, he was in charge of the construction of the Baltic-White Sea Canal. This is enough to make it clear that Kirov could not be reproached with any undue tenderness in the manner in which he disposed of human lives. But this very fact added to his strength in the official circles in which he had to defend his point of view. That he had so large a share of responsibility in the horrors of the First Five-Year Plan made it possible for him to come forward as a leader and protagonist of the policy of moderating the terror during the Second Five-Year Plan. Kirov's line of thought ran as follows: The period of destruction, which was necessary to extirpate the small proprietor elements in the villages, was now at an end; the economic position of the collectives was consolidated and made secure for the future. This constituted a firm basis for future development, and as the economic situation continued to improve, the broad masses of the population would become more and more reconciled to the government; the number of "internal foes" would diminish. It was now the task of the party to rally those forces which would support it in the new phase of economic development, and thus to broaden the foundation upon which Soviet power was based. Kirov, therefore, strongly advocated reconciliation with those party elements who, during the period of the First Five-Year Plan, had gone over to the Opposition, but who might be induced to cooperate on the new basis, now that the "destructive" phase was over. . . .

. . . Early in the summer of 1933, when it became certain that the harvest would be good, Kamenev, Zinoviev and a number of other former members of the Opposition were once again readmitted as members of the party. They were even permitted to choose their spheres of work, and some of them actually received invitations to the party congress (February 1934).

At that congress Kirov appeared in triumph. Previously, his election in Leningrad had been celebrated as was no other. At district conferences in various parts of the city, all of which he toured on the same day, he had been received with wild cheers. "Long live our Mironich!" the delegates shouted; it had been an exceedingly impressive demonstration and it showed that the entire Leningrad proletariat was behind Kirov. At the party congress, too, Kirov received an extraordinarily enthusiastic reception. He was cheered, the entire assembly rising to its feet on hearing his report. During the recesses there was discussion as to who had had the more tumultuous reception, Kirov or Stalin. This very comparison shows how strong Kirov's influence had already become.

Not only was Kirov reelected to the Politburo, but he was also chosen a secretary of the Central Committee, making it necessary for him to move to Moscow within a short time to take over direction of a whole group of departments which had heretofore been under Postyshev and Kaganovich. This was to insure putting into effect the new line which Kirov had inspired. His removal to Moscow was delayed, however. The official reason given was that his presence in Leningrad was indispensable; a substitute was supposedly being sought in Leningrad, but until someone could be found fit to take his place, his transfer to Moscow had to be postponed. In spite of this, he took part in the work of the Politburo, and his influence there continued to grow. . . .

. . . [Kirov's assassination put an end to any chance for liberation within the party. Thereafter] the trend was in quite the opposite direction: not toward reconciliation inside the party, but toward intensification of the terror inside the party to its logical conclusion, to the stage of *physical extermination of all those whose party past might make them opponents of Stalin or aspirants to his power.* Today, I have not the slightest doubt that it was at that very period, between the murder of Kirov and the second Kamenev Trial, that Stalin made his decision and mapped out his plan of "reforms," an essential component part of which was the trial of the *sixteen* and *other trials yet to come.* If, before the murder of Kirov, Stalin still had some hesitation as to which road to choose, he had now made up his mind.

The determining reason for Stalin's decision was his realization, arrived at on the basis of reports and information reaching him, that *the mood of the majority of the old party workers was really one of bitterness and hostility toward him.*

The trials and investigations which followed the Kirov affair had demonstrated unmistakably that the party had not reconciled itself to Stalin's personal dictatorship; that, in spite of all their solemn declarations, the old Bolsheviks rejected Stalin in the depths of their hearts, that this attitude of hostility, instead of diminishing, was growing, and that the majority of those who cringed before him, protesting devotion, would betray him at the first change of the political atmosphere.

This was the basic fact that emerged for Stalin from the documents compiled in the course of the investigation of Nikolayev's act [the assassination of Kirov]. It must be conceded that Stalin was able to provide a reasonable basis for this deduction, and from it he fearlessly drew his ultimate conclusions. As Stalin perceived it, the reasons for the hostility toward him lay in *the basic psychology of the old Bolsheviks.* Having grown up under the conditions of revolutionary struggle against the old regime, we had all been trained in the psychology of oppositionists, of irreconcilable nonconformists. Involuntarily, our minds work in a direction *critical* of the existing order; we seek everywhere its weak sides. In short, we are all critics, destructionists—not builders. This was all to the good—in the past; but now, when we must occupy ourselves with constructive building, it is all hopelessly bad. It is impossible to build anything enduring with such human materials, composed of sceptics and critics. What must be considered now, first and foremost, is the necessity of enduring Soviet construction, particularly because Soviet Russia is facing tremendous perturbations, such as will arise inevitably with the coming of war. It was thus that Stalin reasoned.

The conclusion he drew from all this was certainly daring: if the old Bolsheviks, the group constituting today the ruling caste in the country, are unfit to perform this function, it is necessary to remove them from their posts, to create a new ruling caste. Kirov's plans presupposed reconciliation with the nonparty intelligentsia and enlistment of nonparty workers and peasants in the tasks of social and political life, as a means of widening the social basis of the Soviet regime and promoting its cooperation with the democratic elements of the population. Under Stalin's plan these very same proposals acquired quite a different significance; they were to facilitate a complete revision of the personnel of the ruling caste by expelling from its midst all those infected with the spirit of criticism, and the substitution of a new ruling caste, governed by a new psychology aiming at positive construction. . . .

All of us old Bolsheviks who have any sort of prominent revolutionary past are now hiding in our lairs, trembling. For has it not been demonstrated theoretically that under present circumstances we are an undesirable element? It is sufficient for any one to have crossed the path of a person implicated in an investigation for his fate to be sealed. No one will dare defend us. At the same time, all sorts of benefits and alleviations are being heaped upon the general population. The purpose of this is deliberate: let the memory of our crucifixion be inextricably bound in the minds of the people with the improvements they have received from Stalin.

Nikita S. Khrushchev
THE CULT OF PERSONALITY

The ultimate step of the Stalin Revolution, climaxing the Soviet dictator's accumulation of personal power, was the Great Purge of 1936–1938. Its magnitude was officially revealed along with an attempt to explain its motives by Nikita Khrushchev (1898–1971) in his celebrated "Secret Speech" to the Twentieth Congress of the CPSU in 1956, shortly after he had succeeded to Stalin's position as party leader.

When we analyze the practice of Stalin in regard to the direction of the party and of the country, when we pause to consider everything which Stalin perpetrated, we must be convinced that Lenin's

Excerpts reprinted from the translated text issued by the United States Department of State, June 4, 1956.

fears were justified. The negative characteristics of Stalin, which, in Lenin's time, were only incipient, transformed themselves during the last years into a grave abuse of power by Stalin, which caused untold harm to our party.

We have to consider seriously and analyze correctly this matter in order that we may preclude any possibility of a repetition in any form whatever of what took place during the life of Stalin, who absolutely did not tolerate collegiality in leadership and in work, and who practiced brutal violence, not only toward everything which opposed him, but also toward that which seemed to his capricious and despotic character, contrary to his concepts.

Stalin acted not through persuasion, explanation, and patient cooperation with people, but by imposing his concepts and demanding absolute submission to his opinion. Whoever opposed this concept or tried to prove his viewpoint, and the correctness of his position, was doomed to removal from the leading collective and to subsequent moral and physical annihilation. This was especially true during the period following the Seventeenth Party Congress, when many prominent party leaders and rank-and-file party workers, honest and dedicated to the cause of Communism, fell victim to Stalin's despotism.

We must affirm that the party had fought a serious fight against the Trotskyites, rightists and bourgeois nationalists, and that it disarmed ideologically all the enemies of Leninism. This ideological fight was carried on successfully, as a result of which the party became strengthened and tempered. Here Stalin played a positive role.

The party led a great political ideological struggle against those in its own ranks who proposed anti-Leninist theses, who represented a political line hostile to the party and to the cause of socialism. This was a stubborn and a difficult fight but a necessary one, because the political line of both the Trotskyite-Zinovievite bloc and of the Bukharinites led actually toward the restoration of capitalism and capitulation to the world bourgeoisie. Let us consider for a moment what would have happened if in 1928–1929 the political line of right deviation had prevailed among us, or orientation toward "cotton-dress industrialization," or toward the kulak, etc. We would not now have a powerful heavy industry, we would not have the kolkhozes,

we would find ourselves disarmed and weak in a capitalist encirclement.

It was for this reason that the party led an inexorable ideological
fight and explained to all party members and to the nonparty masses
the harm and the danger of the anti-Leninist proposals of the Trotskyite Opposition and the rightist opportunists. And this great work
of explaining the party line bore fruit; both the Trotskyites and the
rightist opportunists were politically isolated; the overwhelming party
majority supported the Leninist line and the party was able to awaken
and organize the working masses to apply the Leninist party line and
to build socialism.

Worth noting is the fact that even during the progress of the
furious ideological fight against the Trotskyites, the Zinovievites,
the Bukharinites and others, extreme repressive measures were not
used against them. The fight was on ideological grounds. But some
years later when socialism in our country was fundamentally con-
structed, when the exploiting classes were generally liquidated, when
the Soviet social structure had radically changed, when the social
basis for political movements and groups hostile to the party had
violently contracted, when the ideological opponents of the party
were long since defeated politically—then the repression directed
against them began.

It was precisely during this period (1935–1937–1938) that the practice of mass repression through the government apparatus was born,
first against the enemies of Leninism—Trotskyites, Zinovievites,
Bukharinites, long since politically defeated by the party, and subsequently also against many honest Communists, against those party
cadres who had borne the heavy load of the Civil War and the first
and most difficult years of industrialization and collectivization, who
actively fought against the Trotskyites and the rightists for the
Leninist party line.

Stalin originated the concept "enemy of the people." This term
automatically rendered it unnecessary that the ideological errors of
a man or men engaged in a controversy be proven; this term made
possible the usage of the most cruel repression, violating all norms
of revolutionary legality, against anyone who in any way disagreed
with Stalin, against those who were only suspected of hostile intent,

against those who had bad reputations. This concept, "enemy of the people," actually eliminated the possibility of any kind of ideological fight or the making of one's views known on this or that issue, even those of a practical character. In the main, and in actuality, the only proof of guilt used, against all norms of current legal science, was the "confession" of the accused himself; and, as subsequent probing proved, confessions were acquired through physical pressures against the accused.

This led to glaring violations of revolutionary legality, and to the fact that many entirely innocent persons, who in the past had defended the party line, became victims.

We must assert that in regard to those persons who in their time had opposed the party line, there were often no sufficiently serious reasons for their physical annihilation. The formula, "enemy of the people," was specifically introduced for the purpose of physically annihilating such individuals.

It is a fact that many persons, who were later annihilated as enemies of the party and people, had worked with Lenin during his life. Some of these persons had made errors during Lenin's life, but, despite this, Lenin benefited by their work, he corrected them and he did everything possible to retain them in the ranks of the party; he induced them to follow him. . . .

Lenin used severe methods only in the most necessary cases, when the exploiting classes were still in existence and were vigorously opposing the revolution, when the struggle for survival was decidedly assuming the sharpest forms, even including a civil war.

Stalin, on the other hand, used extreme methods and mass repressions at a time when the revolution was already victorious, when the Soviet state was strengthened, when the exploiting classes were already liquidated and socialist relations were rooted solidly in all phases of national economy, when our party was politically consolidated and had strengthened itself both numerically and ideologically. It is clear that here Stalin showed in a whole series of cases his intolerance, his brutality and his abuse of power. Instead of proving his political correctness and mobilizing the masses, he often chose the path of repression and physical annihilation, not only against actual enemies, but also against individuals who had not committed any crimes against the party and the Soviet government.

Here we see no wisdom but only a demonstration of the brutal force which had once so alarmed V. I. Lenin.

Lately, especially after the unmasking of the Beria[1] gang, the Central Committee has looked into a series of matters fabricated by this gang. This revealed a very ugly picture of brutal willfulness connected with the incorrect behavior of Stalin. As facts prove, Stalin, using his unlimited power, allowed himself many abuses, acting in the name of the Central Committee, not asking for the opinion of the committee members nor even of the members of the Central Committee's Political Bureau; often he did not inform them about his personal decisions concerning very important party and government matters. . . .

In practice Stalin ignored the norms of party life and trampled on the Leninist principle of collective party leadership.

Stalin's willfulness vis-à-vis the party and its Central Committee became fully evident after the Seventeenth Party Congress which took place in 1934.

Having at its disposal numerous data showing brutal willfulness toward party cadres, the Central Committee has created a Party Commission under the control of the Central Committee Presidium; it was charged with investigating what made possible the mass repressions against the majority of the Central Committee members and candidates elected at the Seventeenth Congress of the All-Union Communist Party (Bolsheviks).

The commission has become acquainted with a large quantity of materials in the NKVD archives and with other documents and has established many facts pertaining to the fabrication of cases against Communists, to false accusations, to glaring abuses of socialist legality—which resulted in the death of innocent people. It became apparent that many party, Soviet and economic activists who were branded in 1937–1938 as "enemies" were actually never enemies, spies, wreckers, and so forth, but were always honest Communists; they were only so stigmatized, and often, no longer able to bear barbaric tortures, they charged themselves (at the order of the investigative judges–falsifiers) with all kinds of grave and unlikely

[1] Head of the secret police, 1938–1953; executed after Stalin's death.—Ed.

crimes. The commission has presented to the Central Committee Presidium lengthy and documented materials pertaining to mass repressions against the delegates to the Seventeenth Party Congress and against members of the Central Committee elected at that Congress. These materials have been studied by the Presidium of the Central Committee.

It was determined that of the 139 members and candidates of the party's Central Committee who were elected at the Seventeenth Congress, 98 persons, that is, 70 percent, were arrested and shot (mostly in 1937–1938). (*Indignation in the hall.*)

What was the composition of the delegates to the Seventeenth Congress? It is known that 80 percent of the voting participants of the Seventeenth Congress joined the party during the years of conspiracy before the revolution and during the Civil War; this means before 1921. By social origin the basic mass of the delegates to the congress were workers (60 percent of the voting members).

For this reason, it was inconceivable that a congress so composed would have elected a Central Committee, a majority of which would prove to be enemies of the party. The only reason why 70 percent of the Central Committee members and candidates elected at the Seventeenth Congress were branded as enemies of the party and of the people was that honest Communists were slandered, accusations against them were fabricated, and revolutionary legality was gravely undermined.

The same fate met not only the Central Committee members but also the majority of the delegates to the Seventeenth Party Congress. Of 1,966 delegates with either voting or advisory rights, 1,108 persons were arrested on charges of antirevolutionary crimes, that is, decidedly more than a majority. This very fact shows how absurd, wild and contrary to common sense where the charges of counterrevolutionary crimes made out, as we now see, against a majority of participants at the Seventeenth Party Congress. (*Indignation in the hall.*)

We should recall that the Seventeenth Party Congress is historically known as the Congress of Victors. Delegates to the congress were active participants in the building of our socialist state; many of them suffered and fought for party interests during the prerevolutionary years in the conspiracy and at the Civil War fronts; they fought their enemies valiantly and often nervelessly looked into the face of death. How then can we believe that such people could prove to be "two-faced" and had joined the camps of the enemies of socialism during the era after the political liquidation of Zinovievites, Trotskyites and rightists and after the great accomplishments of socialist construction?

This was the result of the abuse of power by Stalin, who began to use mass terror against the party cadres.

What is the reason that mass repressions against activists increased more and more after the Seventeenth Party Congress? It was because at that time Stalin had so elevated himself above the party and above the nation that he ceased to consider either the Central Committee or the party. While he still reckoned with the opinion of the collective before the Seventeenth Congress, after the complete political liquidation of the Trotskyites, Zinovievites and Bukharinites, when as a result of that fight and socialist victories the party achieved unity, Stalin ceased to an ever greater degree to consider the members of the party's Central Committee and even the members of the Political Bureau. Stalin thought that now he could decide all things alone and all he needed were statisticians; he treated all others in such a way that they could only listen to and praise him.

After the criminal murder of S. M. Kirov, mass repressions and brutal acts of violation of socialist legality began. On the evening of December 1, 1934, on Stalin's initiative (without the approval of the Political Bureau—which was passed two days later, casually) the secretary of the Presidium of the Central Executive Committee, Yenukidze, signed the following directive.

   I. *Investigative agencies are directed to speed up the cases of those accused of the preparation or execution of acts of terror.*
  II. *Judicial organs are directed not to hold up the execution of death sentences pertaining to crimes of this category in order to consider the possibility of pardon, because the Presidium of the Central Executive Committee [of the] USSR does not consider as possible the re ceiving of petitions of this sort.*
 III. *The organs of the Commissariat of Internal Affairs [NKVD] are directed to execute death sentences against criminals of the above-mentioned category immediately after the passage of sentences.*

This directive became the basis for mass acts of abuse against socialist legality. During many of the fabricated court cases the accused were charged with "the preparation" of terroristic acts; this deprived them of any possibility that their cases might be reexamined, even when they stated before the court that their "confessions" were secured by force, and when, in a convincing manner, they disproved the accusations against them.

It must be asserted that to this day the circumstances surrounding Kirov's murder hide many things which are inexplicable and mysterious and demand a most careful examination. There are reasons for the suspicion that the killer of Kirov, Nikolayev, was assisted by someone from among the people whose duty it was to protect the person of Kirov. A month and a half before the killing, Nikolayev was arrested on the grounds of suspicious behavior, but he was released and not even searched. It is an unusually suspicious circumstance that when the Chekist[2] assigned to protect Kirov was being brought for an interrogation, on December 2, 1934, he was killed in a car "accident" in which no other occupants of the car were harmed. After the murder of Kirov, top functionaries of the Leningrad NKVD were given very light sentences, but in 1937 they were shot. We can assume that they were shot in order to cover the traces of the organizers of Kirov's killing. (*Movement in the hall.*)

Mass repressions grew tremendously from the end of 1936 after a telegram from Stalin and Zhdanov,[3] dated from Sochi on September 25, 1936, was addressed to Kaganovich, Molotov and other members of the Political Bureau. The content of the telegram was as follows:

> *We deem it absolutely necessary and urgent that Comrade Yezhov be nominated to the post of people's commissar for internal affairs. Yagoda has definitely proved himself to be incapable of unmasking the Trotskyite-Zinovievite block. The OGPU is four years behind in this matter. This is noted by all party workers and by the majority of the representatives of the NKVD.*

Strictly speaking we should stress that Stalin did not meet with and therefore could not know the opinion of party workers.

This Stalinist formulation that the "NKVD is four years behind" in applying mass repression and that there is a necessity for "catch-

2 "Chekist"—familiar term for a member of the secret police, from "Cheka," the name of the secret police, 1917–1922.—Ed.
3 Kirov's successor as head of the party in Leningrad.—Ed.

ing up" with the neglected work directly pushed the NKVD workers on the path of mass arrests and executions.

We should state that this formulation was also forced on the February-March plenary session of the Central Committee of the All-Union Communist Party (Bolsheviks) in 1937. The plenary resolution approved it on the basis of Yezhov's report, "Lessons flowing from the harmful activity, diversion and espionage of the Japanese-German-Trotskyite agents," stating:

The plenum of the Central Committee of the All-Union Communist Party (Bolsheviks) considers that all facts revealed during the investigation into the matter of an anti-Soviet Trotskyite center and of its followers in the provinces show that the People's Commissariat of Internal Affairs has fallen behind at least four years in the attempt to unmask these most inexorable enemies of the people.

The mass repressions at this time were made under the slogan of a fight against the Trotskyites. Did the Trotskyites at this time actually constitute such a danger to our party and to the Soviet state? We should recall that in 1927 on the eve of the Fifteenth Party Congress only some 4,000 votes were cast for the Trotskyite-Zinovievite Opposition, while there were 724,000 for the party line. During the ten years which passed between the Fifteenth Party Congress and the February-March Central Committee plenum Trotskyism was completely disarmed; many former Trotskyites had changed their former views and worked in the various sectors building socialism. It is clear that in the situation of socialist victory there was no basis for mass terror in the country.

Stalin's report at the February-March Central Committee plenum in 1937, "Deficiencies of party work and methods for the liquidation of the Trotskyites and of other two-facers," contained an attempt at theoretical justification of the mass terror policy under the pretext that as we march forward toward socialism, class war must allegedly sharpen. Stalin asserted that both history and Lenin taught him this.

Actually Lenin taught that the application of revolutionary violence is necessitated by the resistance of the exploiting classes, and this referred to the era when the exploiting classes existed and were powerful. As soon as the nation's political situation had improved, when in January 1920 the Red Army took Rostov and thus won a most important victory over Denikin, Lenin instructed Dzerzhinsky [the head of the Cheka] to stop mass terror and to abolish the death penalty. Lenin justified this important political move of the Soviet state in the following manner in his report at the session of the All-Union Central Executive Committee on February 2, 1920:

> *We were forced to use terror because of the terror practiced by the Entente, when strong world powers threw their hordes against us, not avoiding any type of combat. We would not have lasted two days had we not answered these attempts of officers and White Guardists in a merciless fashion; this meant the use of terror, but this was forced upon us by the terrorist methods of the Entente.*
>
> *But as soon as we attained a decisive victory, even before the end of the war, immediately after taking Rostov, we gave up the use of the death penalty and thus proved that we intend to execute our own program in the manner that we promised. We say that the application of violence flows out of the decision to smother the exploiters, the big landowners and the capitalists; as soon as this was accomplished we gave up the use of all extraordinary methods. We have proved this in practice.*

Stalin deviated from these clear and plain precepts of Lenin. Stalin put the party and the NKVD up to the use of mass terror when the exploiting classes had been liquidated in our country and when there were no serious reasons for the use of extraordinary mass terror.

This terror was actually directed not at the remnants of the defeated exploiting classes but against the honest workers of the party and of the Soviet state; against them were made lying, slanderous and absurd accusations concerning "two-facedness," "espionage," "sabotage," preparation of fictitious "plots," and so forth.

At the February-March Central Committee plenum in 1937 many members actually questioned the rightness of the established course regarding mass repressions under the pretext of combating "two-facedness."

Comrade Postyshev[4] most ably expressed these doubts. He said:

> *I have philosophized that the severe years of fighting have passed; party members who have lost their backbones have broken down or have joined the camp of the enemy; healthy elements have fought for the party. These were the years of industrialization and collectivization. I never*

---

4 At the time, second secretary for the Ukraine; later purged.—Ed.

thought it possible that after this severe era had passed Karpov and people like him would find themselves in the camp of the enemy. (Karpov was a worker in the Ukrainian Central Committee whom Postyshev knew well.) And now, according to the testimony, it appears that Karpov was recruited in 1934 by the Trotskyites. I personally do not believe that in 1934 an honest party member who had trod the long road of unrelenting fight against enemies, for the party and for socialism, would now be in the camp of the enemies. I do not believe it . . . I cannot imagine how it would be possible to travel with the party during the difficult years and then, in 1934, join the Trotskyites. It is an odd thing. . . .

(Movement in the hall.)

Using Stalin's formulation, namely that the closer we are to socialism, the more enemies we will have, and using the resolution of the February-March Central Committee plenum passed on the basis of Yezhov's report—the provocateurs who had infiltrated the state security organs together with conscienceless careerists began to protect with the party name the mass terror against party cadres, cadres of the Soviet state and the ordinary Soviet citizens. It should suffice to say that the number of arrests based on charges of counterrevolutionary crimes had grown ten times between 1936 and 1937.

It is known that brutal willfulness was practiced against leading party workers. The Party Statute, approved at the Seventeenth Party Congress, was based on Leninist principles expressed at the Tenth Party Congress. It stated that in order to apply an extreme method such as exclusion from the party against a Central Committee member, against a Central Committee candidate, and against a member of the Party Control Commission, "it is necessary to call a Central Committee plenum and to invite to the plenum all Central Committee candidate members and all members of the Party Control Commission"; only if two thirds of the members of such a general assembly of responsible party leaders find it necessary, only then can a Central Committee member or candidate be expelled.

The majority of the Central Committee members and candidates elected at the Seventeenth Congress and arrested in 1937–1938 were expelled from the party illegally through the brutal abuse of the Party Statute, because the question of their expulsion was never studied at the Central Committee plenum.

Now when the cases of some of these so-called "spies" and "saboteurs" were examined it was found that all their cases were fabricated. Confessions of guilt of many arrested and charged with enemy activity were gained with the help of cruel and inhuman tortures.

At the same time Stalin, as we have been informed by members of the Political Bureau of that time, did not show them the statements of many accused political activists when they retracted their confessions before the military tribunal and asked for an objective examination of their cases. There were many such declarations, and Stalin doubtlessly knew of them.

The Central Committee considers it absolutely necessary to inform the congress of many such fabricated "cases" against the members of the party's Central Committee elected at the Seventeenth Party Congress.

IV INTERPRETATIONS AND PERSPECTIVES

James H. Billington
THE LEGACY OF RUSSIAN HISTORY

From the standpoint of the historian of Russian culture there is much that is familiar in the method and spirit of Stalin's rule, harking back more to the tone of old Muscovy than to the westernizing currents of the immediate prerevolutionary and postrevolutionary eras. James Billington (b. 1929) of Princeton University in his monumental account of the development of the Russian mind, The Icon and the Axe, *sets Stalin squarely in the old tradition.*

For the historian of culture, Lenin's brief rule was still something of a chaotic interregnum; and it is the age of blood and iron under Stalin that marks the real watershed. Once his dictatorial power was securely established in the late twenties, Stalin systematically imposed on Russia a new monolithic culture that represented the antithesis of the varied, cosmopolitan, and experimental culture that had continued on into the twenties from prerevolutionary days. During the quarter of a century that stretched from the beginning of his First Five-Year Plan in 1928 to his death in 1953, Stalin sought to convert all creative thinkers into "engineers of the human soul." They were to be cheerleaders along his assembly lines—deliberately kept uncertain of what cheer was required of them and denied that last refuge of human integrity in most earlier tyrannies: the freedom to be silent. . . .

The qualities that Stalin professed to admire in Lenin—"hatred for snivelling intellectuals, confidence in one's own strength, confidence in victory"—were those which he attempted to instill in himself. To these were added the compulsive chauvinism of the provincial parvenu, the scholastic dogmatism of the half-educated seminarian, and a preoccupation with organizational intrigue already noticeable during his revolutionary apprenticeship in the world's largest oil fields in Baku.

Stalin's only god was Lenin; yet in Stalin's depiction the god acquires a bestial if not satanic form. Stalin compared Lenin's arguments to "a mighty tentacle which twines all around you and holds you as a vice"; Lenin was said to have been obsessively concerned that the enemy "has been beaten but by no means crushed" and to have rebuked his friends "bitingly through clenched teeth: 'Don't whine, comrades. . . .'"

Stalin's formula for authoritarian rule was experimental and eclectic. It might be described as Bolshevism with teeth or Leninism minus Lenin's broad Russian nature and ranging mind. Lenin, for all his preoccupation with power and organization, had remained, in part, a child of the Volga. He had a revolutionary mission thrust upon him and took his revolutionary name from one of the great rivers of the Russian interior: the Lena.

Stalin, by contrast, was an outsider from the hills, devoid of all personal magnetism, who properly derived his revolutionary name from *stal'*, the Russian word for "steel." His closest comrade—and the man he picked to succeed him as formal head of state throughout the 1930s went even further—shed his family name of Scriabin, so rich in cultural association, for Molotov, a name derived from the Russian word for "hammer." No figure better illustrates the unfeeling bluntness and technological preoccupations of the new Soviet culture than this expressionless bureaucratic hammer of the Stalin era, who was generally known as "stone bottom" (from "the stone backside of the hammer"—*kamenny zad molotova*).

Yet for all the grotesqueness, gigantomania, and Caucasian intrigue of the Stalin era, it may in some way have had roots in Russian culture deeper than those of the brief age of Lenin. Lenin benefited from the St. Petersburg tradition of the radical intelligentsia, studied briefly in St. Petersburg, began his revolution there, and was to give his name to the city. When Lenin moved the capital from St. Petersburg and entered the Moscow Kremlin for the first time on March 12, 1918, he was uncharacteristically agitated, remarking to his secretary and companion that "worker-peasant power should be completely consolidated here." Little did he imagine how permanent the change of capital was to prove and how extensive the consolidation of power in the Kremlin. The year of Lenin's death brought a flood to the former capital, newly rebaptized as Leningrad. It was an omen perhaps of the traditionalist flood that was about to sweep the revolutionary spirit out of the Leninist party. With Stalin in the Kremlin, Moscow at last wreaked its revenge on St. Petersburg, seeking to wipe out the restless reformism and critical cosmopolitanism which this "window to the West" had always symbolized.

Stalin had many roots in the Russian past. His addiction to mass armies overbalanced with artillery follows a long tradition leading back to Ivan the Terrible; his xenophobic and disciplinarian conception of education is reminiscent of Magnitsky, Nicholas I, and Pobedonostsev; his passion for material innovation and war-supporting technology echoes Peter the Great and a number of nineteenth-century Russian industrialists. But Stalinism in the full sense of the word seems to have its deepest roots in two earlier periods of Russian history: the nihilistic 1860s and the pre-Petrine era.

First of all, Stalinism appears as a conscious throwback to the militant materialism of the 1860s. Insofar as there was a positive content to Stalinist culture, it was rooted in the ascetic dedication to progress of the materialistic sixties rather than the idealistic spirit of the populist age. Stalin and some of his close associates—Molotov, Khrushchev, and Mikoyan—were like Chernyshevsky and so many other men of the sixties largely educated by priests, and had merely changed catechisms in midstream. Stalin's belief in physiological and environmental determinism—evidenced in his canonization of Pavlov and Lysenko—reflects the polemic prejudices of Pisarev more than the complex theories of Engels, let alone the thoughts of practicing scientists. His suspicion of all artistic activity without immediate social utility reflects the crude aesthetic theory of the sixties more than that of Marx.

All of the enforced artistic styles of the Stalin era—the photographic posters, the symphonies of socialism, the propagandistic novels, and the staccato civic poetry—appear as distorted vulgarizations of the predominant styles of the 1860s: the realism of the "wanderers," the programmatic music of the "mighty handful," the novels of social criticism, and the poems of Nekrasov. This artificial resurrection of long-absent styles brought a forced end to the innovations in form so characteristic of art in the silver age. Whole areas of expression were blighted: lyric poetry, satirical prose, experimental theater, and modern painting and music.

Art was, henceforth, to be subject not just to party censorship but to the mysterious requirements of "socialist realism." This doctrine called for two mutually exclusive qualities: revolutionary enthusiasm and objective depiction of reality. It was, in fact, a formula for keeping writers in a state of continuing uncertainty as to what was required of them: an invaluable device for humiliating the intellectuals by encouraging the debilitating phenomena of anticipatory self-censorship. It seems appropriate that the phrase was first used by a leading figure in the secret police rather than a literary personality. Publicly pronounced in 1934 at the First Congress of the Union of Writers by Andrew Zhdanov, Stalin's aide-de-camp on the cultural front, the doctrine was given a measure of respectability by the presence of Maxim Gorky as presiding figurehead at the congress. Gorky was one of the few figures of stature who could be held up as an exemplar of the new doctrine. He had a simple background, genuine socialist convictions, and a natural realistic style developed in a series of epic novels and short stories about Russian society of the late imperial period.

Socialist realism no less than the revolution itself was to "dispose of its children." Gorky died under still-mysterious circumstances two years later in the midst of the terror which swept away imaginative storytellers like Pil'niak and Babel, lyric poets like Mandel'shtam, theatrical innovators like Meierhold, as well as the inclination toward experimentalism in such gifted young artists as Shostakovich. . . .

The peculiarities of Stalinist architecture lead us into a world very different from anything imagined by Lenin, let alone the materialists of the 1860s. The mammoth mosaics in the Moscow subway, the unnecessary spires and fantastic frills of civic buildings, the leaden chandeliers and dark foyers of reception chambers—all send the historical imagination back to the somber world of Ivan the Terrible. Indeed, the culture of the Stalin era seems more closely linked with ancient Muscovy than with even the rawest stages of St. Petersburg-based radicalism. One can, to be sure, find a certain bias in favor of bigness in the earlier period of rapid industrial development in the 1890s—evidenced in the preponderance of large factory complexes and in the building of the Trans-Siberian railway. There are also hints of classical Oriental despotism in the spectacle of giant canals and ostentatious public buildings thrown up by forced labor. Plans for a canal strikingly similar to Stalin's famous White Sea Canal of the early thirties had been mooted late in the Muscovite era at the court of Alexis Mikhailovich. If this, the first major forced labor project of the Soviet era, had in some ways been anticipated in the Muscovite era, the site chosen in the twenties for the first of the new prison camp complexes of the USSR was one of the enduring symbols of Old Muscovy: the Solovetsk monastery. Ivan IV had been the first to use this bleak island monastery near the Arctic Circle as a prison for ideological opponents, and the Soviet government—by evacuating the monks—was able to accommodate large numbers.

Quietly heroic testimony to some survival of Old Russian culture into the twenties is provided in the works published with the apparent consent of camp authorities by intellectuals incarcerated on the archipelago. In the monthly journal *Solovetsk Islands,* "an organ of the directorate of the Solovetsk Camps of ordinary designation OGPU," we read during the twenties of new discoveries of flora, fauna, and historical remains; of the founding of new museums; of 234 theatrical performances in a single year; and of a nineteen-kilometer ski race between inmates, Red Army guards, and the camp directorate. One article writes with obvious sympathy about Artemius, the first prisoner in Solovetsk under Ivan IV, as "a great seeker of truth and an agitator for freedom of thought."

The camps of the Stalin era seemed at times to contain more scholars than the universities; but the relative freedom of Solovetsk in the early days was not to be maintained in the thirties; and only the terrible northern cold was to remain a constant feature of Stalin's concentration-camp empire. It seems eerily appropriate that the last publications to appear from Solovetsk (in 1934–1935, long after the monthly journal had ceased to appear) tell of discovering prehistoric relics on the archipelago and exploring the vast, uncharted labyrinths that had long fascinated visitors to the monastery.

At the very time when the emaciated prisoners of Solovetsk were plunging down to chart its frozen catacombs, thousands of laborers under various forms of compulsion were plunging even deeper beneath Moscow itself to build the greatest of all monuments of the Stalin era: the Moscow subway. From all over the empire party officials flocked to the capital like the faceless priests of some prehistoric religion to place ornate stalactites and stalagmites from the local republics into this giant communal labyrinth. The cult of the underground party also began in earnest at this time. Traditional idealistic leaders of foreign Communist parties began to be replaced by serpentine Stalinists: a cold-blooded species capable of fast, lizard-like movements in dark places and sudden chameleon-like changes of color.

Silenced prisoners in Solovetsk and authoritarian power in the Moscow Kremlin present a picture strangely reminiscent of ancient Muscovy. In some ways, the Stalin era calls to mind the compulsive Byzantine ritualism of those pre-Petrine times which had remained "contemporary" for so many Russians throughout the Romanov era. Icons, incense, and ringing bells were replaced by lithographs of Lenin, cheap perfume, and humming machines. The omnipresent prayers and calls to worship of Orthodoxy were replaced by the inescapable loudspeaker or radio with its hypnotic statistics and invocations to labor. The liturgy or "common work" of believers was replaced by the communal construction of scientific atheists. The role once played by the sending of priests and missionaries along with colonizing soldiers into the heathen interior of Russia was now assumed by "soldiers of the cultural army," who departed from mass rallies for "cultural relay races" into the countryside to see who could win the most converts for communism and collectivization in the shortest possible time.

Something like the role of the holy fools and flagellants of Muscovy was played by frenzied "heroes of socialist labor" ascetically dedicated to "overfulfilling their norms." Just as Ivan the Terrible canonized his favorite holy fool and built a cathedral later named for him, so Stalin canonized and built a national movement around Nicholas Stakhanov, a coal miner who in a fit of heroic masochism cut out 102 tons of coal (fourteen times his quota) in one shift. "Voluntary subscriptions to the state loan" replaced earlier tithes as a token of devotion to the new church; the "shock quarter" of the year replaced Lent as the periodic time of self-denial in the name of a higher cause. Like the zealous Old Believers, who sought to storm the gates of heaven by outdoing the Orthodox in their fanatical adherence to the letter of the old liturgy, the Stakhanovites sought to hasten the millennium by their "storming" (*shturmovshchina*) of production quotas. These were looked at in the way the Old Believers looked at sacred texts: as something not to be tampered with by bureaucratic innovators or scoffed at by Western sceptics, as a program of salvation if acted upon with urgency.

The Third Rome had been succeeded by a new Third International; and the ideal cultural expression in the latter as in the former was the believer's cry of hallelujah in response to the revealed word from Moscow. The term *alliluishchik* ("hallelujah singer") was in fact widely used in the Stalin era. Russia, which had overthrown a discredited monarchy, suddenly fell back on the most primitive aspect of the original tsarist mystique: the idea that the *batiushka,* the father-deliverer in the Kremlin, would rescue his suffering children from malevolent local officials and lead them into the promised land.

Thus, Stalin was able to succeed Lenin as supreme dictator not only because he was a deft intriguer and organizer but also because he was closer than his rivals to the crude mentality of the average Russian. Unlike most other Bolshevik leaders—many of whom were of Jewish, Polish, or Baltic origin—Stalin had been educated only in the catechistic theology of Orthodoxy. At Lenin's funeral, when the other Bolshevik leaders were speaking in the involved rhetoric and glowing generalities of the intellectual community, Stalin spoke in terms more familiar to the masses with his litany-like exhortations:

> Departing from us, Comrade Lenin adjured us to hold high and keep pure the great title of member of the party. We swear to thee, Comrade Lenin, that we will fulfill thy bequest with honor! . . .
> Departing from us, Comrade Lenin adjured us to guard the unity of our party like the apple of our eye. We swear to thee, Comrade Lenin, that this obligation too, we will fulfill with honor!

The seminarian was clearly in a better position than the cosmopolitan to create a national religion of Leninism. He felt no sense of embarrassment as Lenin's embalmed body was laid out for public veneration with hands folded in the manner of the saints in the monastery of the caves of Kiev. The incongruous mausoleum in Red Square, which paid tribute to Lenin and the new order by exemplifying the purely proletarian "constructivist" style of architecture, was forced to pay a deeper tribute to an older order represented by the crypt beneath and the Kremlin walls above it. Stalin transformed the simple building into a shrine for pilgrims and the site of his own periodic epiphanies on festal days. He chose the traditional, theological way of immortalizing Lenin in contrast to the Promethean effort by the revolutionary intellectuals to discover after Lenin's death the material forces behind his genius through "cyto-architectonic" research (involving imported German scientists, innumerable microphotographs of his brain, and the projected comparative study of minute cranial slices from other leading thinkers).

For the rest of his life Stalin claimed to be nothing more than the rock on which Lenin had built his church. His theoretical writings were always presented as updated thoughts on "problems of Leninism." In the name of Lenin's theory of the past Stalin felt free to contradict both Lenin and himself and, of course, to suppress Lenin's final uncomplimentary assessment of Stalin.

Along with the forms of theological discourse went the new content of Great Russian patriotism. Stalin rehabilitated a whole host of Russian national heroes in the thirties and introduced ever sharper differentiations in pay and privilege to goad on production. The ingeniously Marxist and almost nameless sociological histories of Pokrovsky, which had dominated Soviet historical writing until his death in 1932, were "unmasked" two years later as a deviation from "true Marxism," which henceforth glorified such unproletarian figures as Peter the Great and General Suvorov. The fiercely proletarian novels of the period of the First Five-Year Plan, such as *Cement* and *How the Steel Was Tempered,* were replaced by a new wave of chauvinistic novels and films glorifying Russian warriors of the past.

By the late thirties, Stalin had produced a curious new mass culture that could be described by inverting his classic phrase "nationalist in form, socialist in content." The *forms* of Russian life were now clearly socialist: all agriculture had been collectivized and all of Russia's expanding means of production brought under state ownership and central planning. But socialization throughout the Stalin era brought few material benefits to the consumer, or spiritual benefits to those concerned with greater equality or increased freedom. The *content* of the new ersatz culture was retrogressively nationalistic. Under a patina of constitutions and legal procedures lay the dead hand of Nicholas I's official nationalism and some of the macabre touches of Ivan the Terrible. Stalin's proudly announced "wave of the future" looks, on closer analysis, more like backwash from the past: ghostly voices suddenly returning like the legendary chimes from the submerged city of Kitezh on Midsummer Eve—only to jangle on uncontrolled and out of tune. . . .

Perhaps the best synoptic view of Russian culture under Stalin is provided by the development of the cinema, an art medium with little history prior to the Soviet period. The innumerable movie theaters large and small that sprang up all over the USSR in the twenties and thirties were the new regime's equivalent to the churches of an earlier age. Within the theaters, the prescribed rituals of the new order—its chronicles of success and promises of bliss—were systematically and regularly presented to the silent masses, whose main image of a world beyond that of immediate physical necessity was now derived from a screen of moving pictures rather than a screen of stationary icons. Like Soviet industry, the cinema produced in the age of Stalin a great quantity of films, including some of real quality. Yet despite the many new techniques and skilled artists involved, the Stalinist cinema represents a regressive chapter in the history of Russian culture. At best, it offered little more than a pretentious extension of the most chauvinistic aspects of prerevolutionary culture; at worst it was a technological monstrosity seeking to cannibalize one of the world's most promising theatrical traditions.

Hopes were high when idealistic young revolutionaries first wandered into the deserted studios of the infant Russian film industry during the revolutionary period. Here was an art medium closely linked to the liberating force of technology, uniquely suitable for spreading the good news of a new social order to all people. Here also was a relatively untouched world of artistic possibility: a cultural *tabula rasa.* For, since the first public movie theater had appeared in 1903, the Russian film industry had assumed no very distinctive character. It was an imitative, commercially oriented medium largely involved in producing never-never land sentimentality and melodramatic happy endings.

Placed under the commissariat of education by a Leninist decree of August 1919, and faced with the emigration of almost all its artists and technicians, the Soviet film industry became a major center for on-the-job training in the arts and an arena for florid experimentation. During the relatively relaxed period of the early twenties a variety of new styles appeared, and a vigorous discussion ensued about the nature of cinematic art and its relation to the new social order. The remarkable "movie eye" (*kinoko*) group flourished briefly, with its fanatical dedication to documentary accuracy and precise chronology; a former architect and sculptor, Leo Kuleshov, pioneered in the use of open-air scenes, untrained actors, and monumental compositions; and scattered efforts were made to break down the flow of pictures into expressionistic or abstract forms.

But as in all fields of Soviet culture, the rise of Stalin to absolute power in the late twenties led to the adoption of a propagandistic official style that brought an end to creative experiment. The new style was perhaps the best example of that blend of revolutionary message and realistic form that came to be called socialist realism. At the same time, the subject matter of the cinema in the thirties and forties illustrates the increasing drift toward chauvinistic traditionalism in Stalinist Russia.

There were many influences behind the new Soviet film style. In a sense it was a return to the old tradition of the illustrated chronicle (*litsevaia letopis'*) with which the heroic history of the Church Victorious had been popularized in the late Muscovy. It was also a continuation and vulgarization of the traditions of heroic historical painting and mammoth exhibitions that had been developed in the nineteenth century. To these traditions was added the dream of a new type of revolutionary mystery play originated during the exciting days of War Communism. Open-air mass theatrical pageants were improvised as thousands took part in a cycle which attempted to reenact seven major popular revolutions in Russian history; eighty thousand took part in Maiakovsky's *Mystery-Bouffe,* and more than one hundred thousand in the ritual reenactment of the storming of the Winter Palace. Michelet said that the French Revolution really began not with the storming of the Bastille on July 14, 1789, but with the symbolic reenactment of the event a year later. In like manner, one could say that the Russian Revolution—as a symbol of liberation— was born not in the turbulent events of November, 1917, but in these subsequent scenes of pictorial pageantry and mythic recreation.

Rudolf Schlesinger

THE LOGIC OF THE REVOLUTION

Rudolf Schlesinger *(1909–1969) was a German-English scholar of Marxist persuasion who wrote extensively on Soviet doctrine and social policies. In* The Spirit of Post-War Russia *he sketched a history of how Soviet thinking and aims had evolved since the revolution. He took the unusual view that the Stalin Revolution was a breakaway from the original Marxist plan, but that it was nevertheless necessary and desirable to bring the Russian Revolution to complete fruition.*

The Russia of the NEP, that the British Trade Unionist Delegation visited in 1925 . . . , made a strong impression not only on them, but on progressive minds in the West in general. For it was still very near to the average Western progressive mentality. Its economics were run along easily comprehensible lines, with a larger number of factories in public ownership than any Western socialist dared to dream of for another generation. This country, the most backward in Europe only ten years previously, now had the most progressive labor legislation. Even if there were some unemployment —and of course there was if the state itself had to close down its factories when working uneconomically—the treatment of the unemployed was more liberal than in any other country. There were the most powerful trade unions in the world, with an acknowledged share in the government of state-owned factories, but also with the right to strike occasionally (especially, of course, in the privately-owned factories). No judge or policeman interfered with such strikes. Last but not least there was quite a remarkable amount of freedom even of public political discussion. It is true, with a few recognized exceptions, this was restricted to the factions of the one ruling party, and the opinions discussed had to be expressed in a certain political jargon. But it does not much matter what a thing is called. Eager prophets might foretell the transformation of these factions into several parties representing, within a virtually parliamentary regime, the interests of the various strata of the population. Certain ideological limits were set for the members of the ruling party but, apart

From Rudolf Schlesinger, *The Spirit of Post-War Russia* (London: Dennis Dobson, Ltd., 1947), pp. 13–19. Reprinted by permission of the publisher.

from this, the Russia of the NEP was anything but a totalitarian state. Anyone who sincerely believed that the tsar and the landlords had been dealt with according to their deserts, and that the church should deal only with spiritual affairs, enjoyed a quite remarkable freedom of expression.

Had the revolution been able to stop short at this point the Bolsheviks would have achieved, with due modifications for twentieth-century conditions such as the nationalization of the big factories, banks, and so forth, what the Jacobins had attempted. Backward Russia would have become the most advanced democratic country in the sense of the French Revolution and of the Chartist Movement.[1] In due course out of the well-to-do farmers, and successful merchants, a new middle class would have developed. The enthusiasts for the new state of affairs, like Bukharin, might hope that this class would "automatically," by the progress of cooperation, "grow into socialism." The more sceptical might call the same process a transformation of the Soviet Republic into an "ordinary" liberal though doubtless a very progressive state with the most advanced social legislation, the most progressive schools and by far the most advanced nationality policies in the world. Doubtless it would have been worth the millions of victims fallen in the great struggle. Russia, even so, would have entered the ranks of the leading nations of the world. He who dreamed of the former socialist ideals might rest assured that the workers of the West as well as the colonial slaves of the East would have received a clear lesson that revolution does pay. Russia would have done her part—provided only she could stay where she was. But she could not.

Without capitalists, but with the most progressive labor legislation in the world, the state-owned factories worked better than they had done in private hands. Within a few years they reached and surpassed the prewar level. But how, under these conditions of labor, could sufficient profits be made to build new factories at more than a very modest pace? The well-to-do peasants were highly satisfied with the freedom of trade. But they took it to mean that they were allowed to retain the bulk of the harvest until late in spring and then to use the shortness of supply as an instrument of pressure to

[1] The Chartist Movement: British democratic movement of the 1830s and 1840s.—Ed.

extort economic and political concessions. The "tax in natura"[2] prevented the worst. But year by year spring was announced by a political crisis within the ruling party, caused essentially by the problem of what concessions to grant the kulaks (well-to-do farmers). And the richer they grew, the more they asked. In the spring of 1928 things came very near to a strike of supply. The state had to answer by measures that left nothing of the principle of free trade but the name. What would the peasants do in the case of war?

And war would come—maybe war against a united capitalist world. So the Russians thought, as anyone who was in their country then will admit, at least since 1927 when the Tory government followed Locarno with the rupture of Anglo-Russian diplomatic relations. This conviction of the responsible leaders of Russian policy decided the whole pace of subsequent events. I am, consciously, speaking merely of the pace. In no case could revolutionary Russia have allowed herself to be starved, or brought under political pressure, by the kulaks. And even the most modest aspirations for her future reconstruction needed a greater degree of industrialization than could be obtained without greater efforts. But a different pace in Soviet industrialization and collectivization, if it had been possible without risking the defeat of the revolution, would have meant the whole difference between some additional economic exertion and the enormous price in human suffering and spiritual sacrifice that the Russian Revolution was to pay for its survival. Had external peace been secured, the grain stocks accumulated as a war reserve together with the normal activities of the tax-collector should have sufficed to bring the kulak to reason. In due course home-built or imported agricultural machines would have made it possible for the cooperative to throw him out of the market by "peaceful" competition. And had it been possible freely to import foreign machines and to concentrate on building the factories necessary for a peaceful economic development, industrialization would hardly have cost the country more than the postponement of some otherwise desirable wage-increases or social reforms. There would then have been no danger of dissent growing within the party to such a degree that the "outs" accused the "ins" of betraying the revolution, and that the

[2] "Tax in natura": The "tax in kind," a limited tax on the peasants which replaced the unlimited "requisitioning" of food in 1921.—Ed.

"ins" believed (and had moreover good reason to believe) that such propaganda by the "outs" might bring about the downfall of the revolutionary regime. I doubt very much whether there is much chance of finding *in Moscow* the individuals responsible (in so far as individuals have some responsibility for great historical events) for the fact that tens of thousands of kulaks were to die in the northern forests, that the freedom of the churches was to be reduced to mere worship while all religious propaganda was forbidden, and that dissent within the party on essentials of politics was to be regarded as a kind of treason. Whoever in Berlin, since 1918, was responsible for a policy that demanded Western capitalist support for defeating the German revolution, based on the promise that bourgeois Germany would form a bulwark of Western civilization against the Bolshevist danger, whoever in London, in the spring of 1927, was responsible for the Arcos[3] raid, inevitably succeeded in convincing the Russians that they had, at any price, to prepare for war. You can, of course, accuse them of having partly been frightened by a nightmare, for neither Baldwin nor Chamberlain brought Britain into war against the USSR. Nevertheless they made it possible for someone else to wage war against the USSR as well as against Britain. In view of recent events one can hardly deny the full justification of every sacrifice that enabled the USSR, by industrialization and agricultural collectivization, to be prepared for the ordeal.

Full preparedness for an approaching war once given as a condition for the survival of revolutionary Russia, events had to take their course: what in fact was a second revolution (as the Russians now acknowledge) had become inevitable. If grain was to be collected by force from the kulak he was bound to sabotage production. The state, therefore, was bound not only to arrest the kulak, but to replace him, since the country could not exist without grain. The kulak was to be replaced by agricultural cooperatives which would, at first, be supported only by the poor peasants who immediately gained by the expropriation of the kulak. For the experiment had to be made before there was anything like a sufficient amount of agricultural machinery to make these cooperatives, the kolkhozes, a convincing success from the point of view of the average peasant.

---

[3] "Arcos": The Anglo-Russian Trading Co., a Soviet agency in London, raided by the police in 1927 on suspicion of espionage.—Ed.

Lacking conviction that collectivization meant prosperity for him, the peasant, when induced to join the kolkhozes would, in most cases, previously slaughter his cattle. There would be shortage of food and rationing in the towns. The state would have to build a considerable number of factories which, by the very nature of armament production, were bound to devour a large part of the national income without at any time refunding the labor involved in their construction in the shape of goods increasing the national wealth. Another large group of factories in the heavy industries would make that contribution, by producing useful goods for peacetime industries, only many years after their construction had devoured billions of rubles. Imports of foreign machinery would be necessary. These imports would not only have to replace the valuable consumption goods which could otherwise have been imported—to pay for them it would even be necessary to export some of the butter which the urban population needed. Certainly, during the first years, less rather than more food would be available. But millions of people would enter industry to build new factories, some under inconceivably hard conditions. These new millions of workers would have to share with the millions already employed in industry a rather limited supply of goods suitable for individual consumption.

In compensation for all their exertions the state could, in the beginning, give its citizens little but the conviction that they were building the material foundations of a new and better society. The state, therefore, had to oppose by every means those who denied the possibility of building, in contemporary Russia, such a society. The latter were bound, by their very convictions, to oppose with all available means what, in their eyes, must seem to be a senseless exploitation of the people by leaders who had betrayed the revolution. What was growing in the Russia of the late twenties and early thirties was bound to appear, in the eyes of the opponents, to be merely a kind of state-capitalism which every class-conscious worker was bound to oppose by the usual methods of a radical labor movement. But a state which, in its very struggle for survival, was bound daily to do in a hundred places things that, under normal conditions, would undoubtedly justify the workers in calling a strike, was bound to consider as enemies of the revolution people who spoke of "state-capitalism" and, thus, were likely to organize strikes against socialist reconstruction. From the point of view of the Opposition, Stalin's state was counterrevolutionary; it was a specially dangerous kind of counterrevolution because it was able to deceive the workers by revolutionary phraseology. Against such an adversary any method of struggle, including the preparation of armed force, seemed justified from the Trotskyist point of view. There are certain fundamental Communist views on the tactics to be applied once a reactionary state is confronted with external war. Karl Liebknecht[4] had taught that it is in each socialist's own country that he has to look for the enemy. For the Trotskyist the enemy was in Russia.

Thus all the tragedy of the later purges was made inevitable by the developments of 1929–1933. Millions, many more than had participated in the battles of the Civil War, paid the heaviest sacrifices for what they believed the future of their people in "peaceful" work in icy steppes or in the everyday struggle with the dark inheritance of the Russian village. But in the same fateful years thousands of people who had shared in the first struggle despairingly doubted whether it had been worthwhile to fight for such a future.

Much later on, when all was over, Stalin wrote a very characteristic passage, expressing something that, during those years, everyone had known, but hardly anyone had dared to express openly. The collectivization of agriculture had been "a profound revolution . . . equivalent in its consequences to the revolution of October 1917. The distinguishing feature of this revolution is that it was accomplished *from above,* on the initiative of the state, and directly *supported from below"*—by the peasants participating in the antikulak and collectivization movements.

It is somewhat surprising that none, so far as I can remember, of the many writers on Russian problems has appreciated the whole importance in the evolution of Soviet ideology of this acknowledgement. "Revolution from above" had, hitherto, not been exactly popular with Marxist opinion, including opinion in Russia. There is, of course, an enormous difference between a "revolution from above" initiated by a state intent on securing and developing the achievements of the "revolution from below" which had created it only ten years before and, on the other hand, that "revolution from above" by

[4] Karl Liebknecht: Leader of the left wing of the German socialists at the time of World War I.—Ed.

which Bismarck took the wind out of the sails of the 1848 "revolutionaries from below." And it is the latter instance that forms the
basis of most Marxian opinion on "revolution from above." But the
left-wing everywhere is in the habit of glorifying the revolutionary
initiative of the masses as distinct from state authority. During the
great crisis, the Russians themselves were no exception to this rule,
as anyone who has seen a film or read a Soviet book on the events
of the First Five-Year Plan will confirm. The heroes are the workers
of the factory who answer the cautious and hesitant plans of old-
fashioned specialists with "counterplans" and succeed against all
the handicaps imposed by red tape in realizing these plans; or the
poor young peasants who against all the prejudices of their neigh-
bors, including the local or district organs of the party, succeed in
building a flourishing kolkhoz. The leaders of party and state are
kept rather in the background, directing the revolutionary efforts
from below as Lenin had, from his hiding place, directed the exertions of the 1917 revolutionaries. Without undue violence to the facts
one can, in either case, stress one side or the other of the picture—
the role of the leaders or the role of the masses. When speaking,
in 1938, of the 1928–1933 revolution Stalin preferred to stress not
only the role of the leaders, as the Bolsheviks had always done, but
also particularly the fact that they had acted as leaders of the state;
all achievements of the revolution now at last firmly established were
due to the state. Evidently the latter was not, as Lenin had thought
all his life, the mere ephemeral instrument of the victorious working
classes, destined to "wither away" and to make room for a free community based on personal freedom and voluntary subordination to
the will of the majority. Utopia had, in 1938, fallen back before reality.
The revolution was accomplished.

Just as during the first great crisis of the revolution, in the period
of "War Communism," so also during the second, the rapid industrialization of the country and collectivization of agriculture, there
were people who attempted to make a revolutionary program out of
the necessities of the hour. The leftist saw that the old specialists
and the right wingers of the party could not imagine Russia as a
first-class industrial country and deemed it impossible to build huge
modern factories out of almost nothing. The leftist had to fight such
an attitude; therefore, to him, the giant scale of an economic project

seemed in itself, independent of its economic merits, an achievement for socialism. To build more and still more new giant factories
came to be regarded as an essential element of future progress, as
opposed to the capitalist countries where, during the great depres-
sion, harvests were being plowed in and factory-plants were being
destroyed.

In the young and poor kolkhozes, enthusiasm had to replace
economic rewards for increased exertions, and even in industry the
stimulating effects of piece-work were problematic when the only
part of the national income accessible to the worker was the minimum granted on the ration-books. The most secure way of dis-
tributing extra food among the people doing heavy work, without
risking the goods going on the black market to the highest bidder,
was to organize canteens providing cheap meals in the factories.
And the necessary condition for drawing young peasant women into
industrial work or even into work in the kolkhoz was to organize
crèches for their infants. All these things found sufficient justification
in the facts of everyday life. But Soviet ideology during the First
Five-Year Plan tended to build out of such natural facts of actual
organization a conception of the coming socialist society without
any private interests and private life at all. If possible even the
pullets in the kolkhoz had to be collectivized. Any personal care of
the parents for their children was regarded as very nearly a reactionary prejudice. The community had to fill not only a very important
part—as any Soviet people would agree—but nearly the whole, or at
the least the central place in any citizen's mind, and the interest of
the community had to replace such inferior stimuli as private interest. In fact, the Dnieper aggregate, Magnitogorsk and Kusnetsk
arose, out of the steppes, and 200,000 kolkhozes were organized,
out of a semiilliterate peasantry, without the people who accomplished these things expecting any other reward than the consciousness of having helped to build a better life for the community. Such
inspiration, in war as well as in revolution, is the great strength of
the Soviet peoples. But could they be expected to build an efficient
national economy for everyday purposes on such lines?

The responsible leaders of the Soviet state did not believe in
ideologies as a sufficient basis for permanent social organization,
nor in the permanent efficiency of mere enthusiasm as a stimulus for

the average man and woman. One could not proceed indefinitely in the spirit of the First Five-Year Plan. Besides, would it be worthwhile? The threat of war had stood behind the plan, and this specter now put on flesh and blood. Whilst the new factories arose out of the steppes, in Germany Hitler drew nearer to the conquest of power. Half-finished giants would be of little use in the hour of supreme danger, especially if they lacked the necessary workers. You can, by the force of enthusiasm, get a minority to work overtime even in a snowstorm to get a new factory built according to the plan. In a country like Russia such a minority may number some millions, and you will get your factories built. But you cannot by mere enthusiasm induce the average worker, freshly arrived from his village, to put forth the continuous effort essential in acquiring industrial skill, and not only to fulfill the plan, but to maintain, too, the quality of output. So one had somehow to stop the pace of "assault." What was needed was a normal economy and a normal society where work, generally speaking, was not building new factories but producing goods, and the reward for work was the power to buy a part of these goods in proportion to one's exertions.

Already in June 1931 Stalin had spoken of the necessity of working with, and duly rewarding, the old specialists who had formerly been considered as brakes on enthusiastic reconstruction, and also of increasing the average worker's interest in, and personal responsibility for, his work. After 1930 the agricultural artel was accepted as the most suitable type of agricultural collectivization. As distinct from the agricultural commune, which originally had been encouraged as the highest type of collectivization, the artel leaves to its members a certain private economy, and even the right to sell the products of his private husbandry in the markets. In 1932, at last, the new tractor-building factories began to work. Now, collective agriculture could get a real technical advantage over the old methods easily understood by the average peasant. On 1 December 1934, it became possible to abolish the rationing of bread. During 1935 the free market was restored for almost all goods, on a price-level averaging between the prices the state had asked for the guaranteed ration-minimum, and those the customer had paid to the peasants for additional goods on the kolkhoz market. Now increased wages or salaries meant proportionally increased purchasing power. The Stak-

hanovite movement was initiated. Now the workers were encouraged
not only to make temporary exertions and occasional proposals for
rationalization, but to achieve a permanent increase of skill and of
output, in quantity as well as in quality.

Boris N. Ponomaryov
FULFILLING THE LENINIST PLAN

*In 1956, at the time Khrushchev began his downgrading of Stalin, Soviet
historical writing was sharply criticized for having succumbed to the "cult
of personality," that is, the glorification of Stalin. The old 1938 official history
of the Communist Party of the Soviet Union, which Stalin had closely super-
vised, was dropped from circulation. A committee of Soviet scholars under
the chairmanship of Boris N. Ponomaryov (b. 1905), member of the Secretariat of the Communist Party, was appointed to prepare a new text. The
new work duly appeared in 1959 and was translated into English in 1960.
Stalin's name was systematically removed from any favorable connection,
while credit for achievements which the authors regarded as positive went
simply to "the party." Surprisingly enough, the actual text—particularly
concerning the collectivization of agriculture—was otherwise scarcely altered
from the 1938 version.*

The development of socialist construction and vast, long-term capital
investments required a higher level of economic planning. Large-
scale socialist industry, which had grown and gained strength, now
played the dominant role in the economy. The party had accumulated
considerable experience in planning, and was now [in 1927] in a
position to advance from annual targets to long-term plans for a
number of years. This was a major victory for the Leninist economic
policy of the party.

In his last articles, devoted to the plan for building socialism,
Lenin wrote that for the first time in history the Soviet state had the
opportunity "of ascertaining the period necessary for bringing about

From Boris N. Ponomaryov et al., *History of the Communist Party of the Soviet
Union* (Moscow: Foreign Languages Publishing House, 1960), pp. 421–422, 424,
426–428, 435, 441–442, 446–449, 459–460, 474–476.

radical social changes; we now see clearly *what* can be done in five years, and what requires much more time" (*Collected Works,* Vol. 33, pp. 441–442).

The Fifteenth Congress adopted directives for the First Five-Year Plan of development of the national economy.

The basic economic tasks of this plan were, as the congress pointed out, steadily to expand large-scale socialist industry, to use it for bringing about a rapid growth of all branches of the national economy and an increase of the share of its socialist sector, and to squeeze out the capitalist elements more vigorously, with a view to launching a socialist offensive against the remnants of capitalism along the whole economic front.

The adoption of directives for the First Five-Year Plan signified a new and higher stage of planning in the Soviet national economy, in the battle to build socialism. These directives specified the schedules and rates of the great social transformations to take place in the Soviet Union. . . .

In pursuance of the Fifteenth Congress decisions, the party with renewed force went ahead with socialist industrialization and preparations for the mass collectivization of agriculture based on Lenin's plan for building socialism in the USSR.

The socialist reconstruction of the national economy evoked the stubborn resistance of the capitalist elements inside the country and greatly alarmed the world bourgeoisie. The imperialists and the landlords, the big industrialists and bankers who had fled the Soviet country saw in the Nepmen and the kulaks their mainstay in the bitter struggle to frustrate the building of socialism in the USSR. . . .

The frenzied resistance of the kulaks to the measures taken by the Soviet government in the countryside encouraged concealed enemy groups in their struggle to restore capitalism in the country. At the beginning of 1928 a big saboteur organization consisting of bourgeois specialists was discovered in the Shakhty and in other areas of the Donets coalfield (the "Shakhty case"). For several years a group of these specialists and camouflaged Whites had engaged secretly in subversive work aimed at destroying the coal industry in the Donets coalfield, carrying out assignments of the former owners of the mines—Russian and foreign capitalists—and of foreign intelligence services. The saboteurs caused explosions in the mines and flooded them, damaged costly new equipment, set fire to power stations and deliberately misspent the people's money earmarked for capital construction. Members of this subversive organization purchased abroad equipment for the mines and power stations that was obviously outmoded and useless. Especially dangerous were the wreckers' attempts to worsen the conditions of the miners. They deliberately disorganized the supply of food and consumer goods to the miners and their families, cheated the workers in paying wages, held up housing programs and infringed safety rules in the mines, which endangered the lives of the miners. The underlying purpose was to cause discontent among the workers and turn them against the party and the Soviet government.

The wreckers also aimed at undermining the defense of the country and clearing the way to intervention by the imperialist powers. Nearly 300 one-time big capitalists and nobles were among the saboteurs exposed in the "Shakhty case." . . .

The difficulties encountered in socialist reconstruction, and the inevitable sharpening of the class struggle as a result of the socialist offensive, gave rise to vacillations among the petty bourgeois strata of the population. There were echoes of this also in the party. A group of right-wing defeatists took shape. As early as 1925 Bukharin had proclaimed the slogan "Enrich yourselves!" In practice this slogan signified a policy of support for the kulak farms in the countryside. But when the party was engaged in combating the Trotskyists and Zinovievites as the main danger, the right wingers, carefully concealing their differences with the party, had been lying low, making a show of fighting against the Trotskyists. But when the party launched its decisive offensive against the kulaks, the leaders of the right wingers—Bukharin, Rykov and Tomsky—openly came out against the policy of socialist industrialization and the collectivization of agriculture.

While admitting in words that it was possible to build socialism in the USSR, the Right opportunists in fact resisted the policy of the all-out expansion of heavy industry. They opposed rapid rates of industrialization.

The right wingers opposed the all-out socialist offensive along the whole front and the liquidation of the capitalist elements in the national economy. They opposed the offensive against the kulaks. At a time when the capitalist elements were waging a fierce struggle against the construction of socialism, the right wingers propounded the "theory" that the class struggle in the country was subsiding and that the kulaks could peacefully grow into socialism. They refused to admit that the broad highway to socialism in the countryside was, as Lenin taught, the producer cooperation in its highest form—the collective farm. Lenin's cooperative plan could not be put into effect unless the kulaks were eliminated as a class. The right wingers held that the countryside could be directed along socialist lines only through the marketing and purchasing cooperatives. They suggested giving "free rein" to spontaneous development of the market and removing all restrictions on kulak farming. Abandoning Lenin's concept of the class struggle and the dictatorship of the proletariat, the right wingers would have the party and state organizations make direct concessions to the capitalist elements.

Thus, in practice, they denied that socialism could be built in the USSR. In the party they spread the *ideology of defeatism* in the face of difficulties, and sought an *agreement* with the kulak and capitalist elements in town and country. Their stand ultimately meant the restoration of capitalism. The Central Committee rallied the party and the working class for a decisive struggle against the right-wing defeatists, now the main danger in the party, the mouthpiece of the anti-Soviet forces in the country and a weapon of the capitalist encirclement. . . .

Industrialization was carried out with a truly Bolshevik élan, such as the world had never seen before. The working class provided splendid examples of labor valor. The scale and the rate of construction in the USSR astonished the world. Enemies asserted that the targets planned by the party would never be reached and foretold the failure of the Soviet plans. The working people in all countries were gladdened by the successes of the Soviet Union.

The vast scale of industrialization and the heroism displayed by the working class exerted a strong influence on the masses of the working peasantry. They saw that the party and the government, overcoming difficulties, were building factories to make tractors and new farm machines. Numerous peasant delegations visited the new factories and construction sites, attended workers' meetings and were inspired by their enthusiasm. Upon returning to their villages the advanced representatives of the working peasantry took the initiative in setting up new collective farms. The organized workers of industrial enterprises and building sites assumed patronage over rural areas, and sent numerous workers' teams to the countryside.

That was how the mass movement for joining the collective farms was prepared and began, a movement which grew into solid collectivization. The peasantry turned to the socialist path of development, to the collective-farm path. The middle peasants followed the poor peasants into the collective farms. . . .

While the whole capitalist world was in the grip of the economic crisis, the USSR was steadily proceeding with socialist construction. The average annual increase of its industrial output in the first two years of the Five-Year Plan was about 20 percent.

Along with the rapid growth of industry, the mass collective-farm movement was under way in the country. By the beginning of 1930 the five-year program of collective-farm development had, in the main, been fulfilled. A number of regions became regions of *solid collectivization,* when the peasants of whole villages, districts and areas joined the collective farms. In 124 districts more than 70 percent of all the peasant farms were collectivized. The largest number of districts of solid collectivization were in the Volga region, the North Caucasus and the steppe part of Ukraine.

The transition to solid collectivization signified a *radical turn* of the bulk of the peasantry toward socialism. Prior to the mass collective-farm movement there were 24.5 million individual peasant farms in the USSR, of which about 8.5 million belonged to poor peasants, 15 million to middle peasants and more than one million to kulaks. The poor and middle peasants together constituted the most numerous laboring class in the USSR. Though petty peasant commodity economy was not of a capitalist nature, it was essentially of the same type, since it based itself on private property in the means of production and engendered kulak capitalists from its midst. When joining the collective farms, the peasants socialized the basic means of production. The working peasantry was abandoning the old path of development which spontaneously engendered capitalism and led to the enslavement of the poor and middle peasants by the kulaks; it was taking a new, socialist path, free of kulak bondage and capitalist exploitation. A socialist, collective-farm system was being established in the countryside. . . .

The development of the socialist sector of the national economy, the new alignment of class forces in the country and the possession by the state of its own grain-producing base—the collective and state farms—enabled the party to proceed at the end of 1929 from the policy of restricting and squeezing out the kulaks to the policy of eliminating them as a class on the basis of solid collectivization. The essence of this policy was to *deprive the kulak class of the means of production essential for its existence and development,* namely, the free use of land, the instruments of production, the renting of land and the right to hire labor. This policy was legislatively embodied in a number of decisions adopted by the higher organs of the Soviet state. In districts of solid collectivization the laws on the renting of land and the hiring of labor on individual peasant farms were repealed.

Solid collectivization meant that all the land in the area of a particular village passed into the hands of a collective farm. All kulak plots in this land were transferred to the collective farm. Thus the kulaks were deprived not only of the right to rent any land, but also of those plots of land which had been used by them previously. The nationalization of the land accomplished as a result of the October Revolution made possible such surveying and demarcation of the lands as benefited the collective farms. Lenin pointed out that the nationalization of the land gave "the proletarian state the maximum opportunity of passing to socialism in agriculture" (*Collected Works,* Vol. 28, p. 291). The collective farms did not have to make any redemption payments to the peasants for their plots of land, or to recompense them for the lands which were passing into collective use. Thus the absence of private property in land in the USSR facilitated the socialist reconstruction of the countryside and the struggle against the kulaks.

The collectivization of agriculture proceeded in bitter class struggle with the kulaks, in conditions of a hostile capitalist encirclement. The kulaks carried on malicious propaganda against the collective-farm movement, spread all kinds of provocative rumors, set fire to collective-farm buildings, poisoned the livestock, damaged tractors and other machines, assassinated rural Communists, chairmen of

collective farms, rural newspaper correspondents and village activists. They did everything in their power to prevent the peasants
from joining the collective farms and to frustrate collectivization.
The entry of the majority of the peasantry into the collective farms
on a mass scale was therefore accompanied by a decisive struggle
against the kulaks. The peasants demanded the complete expropriation of the kulaks and their expulsion from the villages.

Supporting in every way the struggle of the poor and middle
peasants against the kulaks, the Soviet government lifted the ban
on expropriation of the kulaks. Local organs of Soviet power in the
districts of solid collectivization were granted the right to evict the
most malicious kulaks to districts far removed from their places
of residence and to confiscate all their means of production (cattle,
machines and other farm property), transferring them to the possession of collective farms. The kulaks were completely expropriated.
This was the only way to deal with the kulaks. These measures fully
met the interests of socialist construction, and ensured the success
of the collective-farm movement and the consolidation of the
collective farms.

Thus, at the very beginning of the mass building of collective
farms the Central Committee of the party, proceeding from Lenin's
teachings on cooperation, gave the party, the working class and the
working peasantry a concrete plan of struggle for the victory of the
collective-farm system. . . .

January and February 1930 were months of headlong growth of
the collective farms. The movement for solid collectivization embraced ever new regions of the country. During this period about 10
million peasant households joined the collective farms.

But along with real progress in collectivization, there were also
unhealthy signs. There turned out to be certain distortions of party
policy in collectivization, distortions which caused discontent among
the middle peasants.

Above all, the Leninist voluntary principle of forming collective
farms was being violated. Not infrequently patient organizing and
explanatory work was being replaced by mere injunctions and
coercion against the middle peasants. Voluntary entry into collective
farms was being replaced by compulsion, on pain of being "dekulakised," disfranchised, and so on. In some districts as many as

15 percent of the peasants were "dekulakised" and from 15 to 20 percent disfranchised.

The party's directive concerning the agricultural artel as the chief form of the collective-farm movement was also being violated. In a number of places attempts were made to skip the artel form and pass straight to the commune by collectivizing small livestock, poultry, and so forth. . . .

The enemies of Soviet power, and above all the kulaks, tried to take advantage of these mistakes and excesses committed by party organizations. Former Whites, Socialist-Revolutionaries and other hidden anti-Soviet elements raised their heads again. The enemy acted with craft and cunning. Every device was used—from provocation to brutal assassination of Communists and active nonparty people in the villages. The class enemies instigated the peasants to slaughter their animals before entering the collective farms, spreading the rumor that all the livestock would be taken away anyhow. Giving way to this provocation of the kulaks, many peasants slaughtered their cows, pigs, sheep and poultry. In the economic year 1929–1930 the number of head of cattle in the country decreased by 14.6 million, pigs by one-third, sheep and goats by more than a quarter. Almost all this livestock was slaughtered mainly in February and March 1930. As a result of these hostile actions of the kulaks and their toadies, animal husbandry in the USSR suffered a heavy loss from which it could not recover for a long time. . . .

In conditions of the colossal construction during the years of the First Five-Year Plan the country had to put up with many privations and hardships. It was still a poor country. There was a shortage of clothing, footwear, and many other articles of primary necessity. At the construction sites the workers lived in tents and temporary wooden barracks. Foodstuffs and many manufactured goods were strictly rationed. All these difficulties were shouldered primarily by the working class. But the workers realized that, in conditions of a hostile capitalist encirclement, there was no other way of transforming their country into a mighty industrial power. They understood that industry could be built up only at the cost of sacrifice and the most rigorous economy. Stinting themselves in everything, and tightening their belts, the workers displayed unprecedented labor heroism. The working class and all the working people were firmly convinced of the victory of socialism in the USSR, of the correctness of the policy of the party; and they advanced unswervingly toward their goal. The unity, high degree of organization and selflessness of the working class exerted a tremendous moral influence on the poor and middle peasants who were developing the collective-farm movement. Particularly great was the labor enthusiasm of the youth. In response to the appeal of the party, tens of thousands of young people were sent by the Young Communist League organizations to work in still undeveloped localities, and to construction sites in the Urals, Kuznetsk coalfield, Donets coalfield, Far East and Central Asia.

Mobilizing the creative activity of the working class for the fulfillment of the Five-Year Plan in four years, the Central Committee of the party in September, 1930, addressed an appeal to the workers calling on them to organize socialist emulation for successful fulfillment of the targets of the third year of the Five-Year Plan. There was not a single enterprise where the workers did not respond to this appeal of the party. The socialist emulation movement developed with still greater force throughout the country. The atmosphere of the factories changed, and with it their habitual tenor of life. Workers at kindred construction sites, factories and plants began to exchange their labor experience, while production reviews and competitions for the best shop and workers' team were organized in the individual factories. New indices of the work of advanced workers' teams and shock workers appeared on the boards of honor in factories and at construction sites. The number of heroes of labor steadily grew. . . .

At the beginning of 1933 the glad news spread throughout the country that the First Five-Year Plan had been fulfilled ahead of time —in four years and three months. In January, 1933, a joint plenary meeting of the Central Committee and Central Control Commission of the party reviewed the results of the Five-Year Plan. It noted the following major results:

The USSR had been converted from an agrarian into an *industrial* country. The socialist system had completely eliminated the capitalist elements in industry and had become the sole economic system. In 1932 the volume of output of large-scale industry exceeded the prewar level more than threefold, and that of 1928 more than twofold. Its proportion of the total output of the national economy had risen to 70 percent. The USSR had created its own advanced technical basis which had made possible the reconstruction of all branches of the national economy. During the First Five-Year Plan period 1,500 new industrial enterprises had been put into operation. A number of new industries had been built up, such as an up-to-date iron and steel industry, a tractor industry, an automobile industry, a chemical industry, and an aircraft industry. A new coal and metallurgical base had been created in the east, the Urals-Kuzbas base. The output of electric power had increased by more than 150 percent. The economic independence of the country had been strengthened: the USSR had now begun to produce most necessary industrial equipment at its own enterprises. The Soviet Union had strengthened its defense capacity.

In agriculture, as a result of the determined swing of the poor and middle peasants toward socialism, the collective and state farms had become the predominant force. A collective-farm system, large-scale socialist farming, had been created in the countryside. From a country of petty peasant farming the USSR had become a country where agriculture was run on the largest scale in the world. A leap from an old qualitative state to a new qualitative state had taken place in agriculture. The elimination of the kulaks as a class had been carried out on the basis of solid collectivization. The machine-and-tractor stations, equipped with tractors and the most up-to-date agricultural machinery, had become important levers in reorganizing agriculture along socialist lines. The agricultural artel had become the principal form of the collective-farm movement.

The progress of socialism in all spheres of the national economy had brought about a *radical improvement in the material conditions of the working people.* Unemployment in the towns, this scourge of the working class of all capitalist countries, had been completely abolished in the USSR. The collective-farm system had put an end to kulak bondage and to impoverishment of the working peasantry. The poor peasants and the lower stratum of the middle peasants had been raised to a level of material security in the collective farms. The growth of the national income and the improvement of the material conditions of the working people had been accompanied by a marked rise of their cultural level and the rapid growth of a new, Soviet intelligentsia.

The foundations of socialism had been laid in the Soviet Union. As in the towns, the socialist form of economy had firmly established itself in the countryside, too. The question: "Who will beat whom?", posed by Lenin, had been settled in favor of socialism. Radical changes had taken place in the class structure of Soviet society. The capitalist elements in the country had, in the main, been eliminated. The social basis of the dictatorship of the proletariat had been extended and consolidated. The collective-farm peasantry had become the firm *mainstay* of Soviet power. This was already a *new* class, building a new life on the basis of collective ownership of the means of production. The alliance of the working class and peasantry had undergone a change in aspect, and had acquired a new content. Lenin's wise policy of an alliance between the working class and the poor peasants, on the one hand, and the middle peasants, on the other, had helped to draw the bulk of the peasantry into socialist construction and had ensured victory over the capitalist elements. The alliance of the working class and collective-farm peasantry was being established on a *new basis—the community* of their interests in the building-consolidation and development of socialism in town and country.

This was an epoch-making victory of the working class, working peasantry and intelligentsia of the USSR, won under the leadership of the Communist party.

The results of the First Five-Year Plan were of tremendous international significance.

The Soviet Union had demonstrated to the whole world the superiority of the planned socialist system of economy over the capitalist system, strengthened its economic might and independence and become an important factor in international affairs.

The fulfillment of the Five-Year Plan exerted a revolutionizing influence on the working masses of the capitalist countries. The alignment of class forces markedly changed in favor of socialism. The results of the Five-Year Plan raised the revolutionary spirit of the working class all over the world and strengthened its confidence in ultimate victory.

Even the enemies of the Soviet Union had to admit the success of the Five-Year Plan. The predictions of the world bourgeoisie and its agents about its inevitable failure had proved false. The working class and the working peasantry of the USSR had proved that they could manage without landlords, capitalists and kulaks, that they could create a new and better socialist system, which knew no crises and unemployment and ensured a continuous improvement in their material and cultural well-being.

Leon Trotsky
SOVIET BONAPARTISM

Leon Trotsky (1879–1940), one-time second-in-command to Lenin, defeated by Stalin in the controversies of the 1920s, is the great tragic figure of the Russian Revolution. He was expelled from the Communist Party in 1927 and deported from Russia in 1929. He finally settled in Mexico, where, in 1940, he was assassinated by a Soviet agent. During the years of exile Trotsky published a steady stream of articles and books, attacking Stalin's rule in Russia as a bureaucratic and "Bonapartist" perversion of the Russian Revolution analogous to the rule of Napoleon Bonaparte in France.

Owing to the insignificance of the Russian bourgeoisie, the democratic tasks of backward Russia—such as liquidation of the monarchy and the semifeudal slavery of the peasants—could be achieved only through a dictatorship of the proletariat. The proletariat, however, having seized the power at the head of the peasant masses, could not stop at the achievement of these democratic tasks. The bourgeois revolution was directly bound up with the first stages of a socialist revolution. That fact was not accidental. The history of recent decades very clearly shows that, in the conditions of capitalist decline, backward countries are unable to attain that level which the old centers of capitalism have attained. Having

From Leon Trotsky, *The Revolution Betrayed: What Is the Soviet Union and Where Is It Going?*, translated by Max Eastman (Garden City, N.Y.: Doubleday, Doran and Co., 1937), pp. 5–8, 19–20, 45–47, 54–56, 275–279. Reprinted by permission of Pioneer Publishers of New York.

themselves arrived in a blind alley, the highly civilized nations block the road to those in process of civilization. Russia took the road of proletarian revolution, not because her economy was the first to become ripe for a socialist change, but because she could not develop further on a capitalist basis. Socialization of the means of production had become a necessary condition for bringing the country out of barbarism. That is the *law of combined development* for backward countries. Entering upon the socialist revolution as "the weakest link in the capitalist chain" (Lenin), the former empire of the tsars is even now, in the nineteenth year after the revolution, still confronted with the task of "catching up with and outstripping" —consequently in the first place *catching up with*—Europe and America. She has, that is, to solve those problems of technique and productivity which were long ago solved by capitalism in the advanced countries.

Could it indeed be otherwise? The overthrow of the old ruling classes did not achieve, but only completely revealed, the task: to rise from barbarism to culture. At the same time, by concentrating the means of production in the hands of the state, the revolution made it possible to apply new and incomparably more effective industrial methods. Only thanks to a planned directive was it possible in so brief a span to restore what had been destroyed by the imperialist and civil wars, to create gigantic new enterprises, to introduce new kinds of production and establish new branches of industry.

The extraordinary tardiness in the development of the international revolution, upon whose prompt aid the leaders of the Bolshevik party had counted, created immense difficulties for the Soviet Union, but also revealed its inner powers and resources. However, a correct appraisal of the results achieved—their grandeur as well as their inadequacy—is possible only with the help of an international scale of measurement. . . .

. . . During the last three years the production of iron has doubled. The production of steel and the rolling mills has increased almost 2½ times. The output of oil, coal and iron has increased from 3 to 3½ times the prewar figure. In 1920, when the first plan of electrification was drawn up, there were ten district power stations in the country with a total power production of 253,000 kilowatts. In 1935,

FIGURE 6. The vanquished among the ruins—Trotsky, in exile, visiting Pompei (*Bettmann Archive, Inc.*).

there were already ninety-five of these stations with a total power of 4,345,000 kilowatts. In 1925, the Soviet Union stood eleventh in the production of electroenergy; in 1935, it was second only to Germany and the United States. In the production of coal, the Soviet Union has moved forward from tenth to fourth place. In steel, from sixth to third place. In the production of tractors, to the first place in the world. This also is true of the production of sugar.

Gigantic achievements in industry, enormously promising beginnings in agriculture, an extraordinary growth of the old industrial cities and a building of new ones, a rapid increase of the number of workers, a rise in cultural level and cultural demands—such are the indubitable results of the October Revolution, in which the prophets of the old world tried to see the grave of human civilization. With the bourgeois economists we have no longer anything to quarrel over. Socialism has demonstrated its right to victory, not on the pages of *Das Kapital,* but in an industrial arena comprising a sixth part of the earth's surface—not in the language of dialectics, but in the language of steel, cement and electricity. Even if the Soviet Union, as a result of internal difficulties, external blows and the mistakes of its leadership, were to collapse—which we firmly hope will not happen—there would remain as an earnest of the future this indestructible fact, that thanks solely to a proletarian revolution a backward country has achieved in less than ten years successes unexampled in history. . . .

. . . The national income per person in the Soviet Union is considerably less than in the West. And since capital investment consumes about 25 to 30 percent,—incomparably more than anywhere else—the total amount consumed by the popular mass cannot but be considerably lower than in the advanced capitalist countries.

To be sure, in the Soviet Union there are no possessing classes, whose extravagance is balanced by an underconsumption of the popular mass. However the weight of this corrective is not so great as might appear at first glance. The fundamental evil of the capitalist system is not the extravagance of the possessing classes, however disgusting that may be in itself, but the fact that in order to guarantee its right to extravagance the bourgeoisie maintains its private ownership of the means of production, thus condemning the economic system to anarchy and decay. In the matter of luxuries the bourgeoisie, of course, has a monopoly of consumption. But in things of prime necessity, the toiling masses constitute the overwhelming majority of consumers. We shall see later, moreover, that although the Soviet Union has no possessing classes in the proper sense of the word, still she has very privileged commanding strata of the population, who appropriate the lion's share in the sphere of consumption. And so if there is a lower per capita production of things of prime necessity in the Soviet Union than in the advanced capitalist countries, that does mean that the standard of living of the Soviet masses still falls below the capitalist level.

The historic responsibility for this situation lies, of course, upon Russia's black and heavy past, her heritage of darkness and poverty.

There was no other way out upon the road of progress except through the overthrow of capitalism. To convince yourself of this, it is only necessary to cast a glance at the Baltic countries and Poland, once the most advanced parts of the tsar's empire, and now hardly emerging from the morass. The undying service of the Soviet regime lies in its intense and successful struggle with Russia's thousand-year-old backwardness. But a correct estimate of what has been attained is the first condition for further progress.

The Soviet regime is passing through a *preparatory* stage, importing, borrowing and appropriating the technical and cultural conquests of the West. The comparative coefficients of production and consumption testify that this preparatory stage is far from finished. Even under the improbable condition of a continuing complete capitalist standstill, it must still occupy a whole historic period. . . .

The material premise of communism should be so high a development of the economic powers of man that productive labor, having ceased to be a burden, will not require any goad, and the distribution of life's goods, existing in continual abundance, will not demand—as it does not now in any well-off family or "decent" boardinghouse—any control except that of education, habit and social opinion. Speaking frankly, I think it would be pretty dull-witted to consider such a really modest perspective "utopian."

Capitalism prepared the conditions and forces for a social revolution: technique, science and the proletariat. The communist structure cannot, however, immediately replace the bourgeois society. The material and cultural inheritance from the past is wholly inadequate for that. In its first steps the workers' state cannot yet permit everyone to work "according to his abilities"—that is, as much as he can and wishes to—nor can it reward everyone "according to his needs," regardless of the work he does. In order to increase the productive forces, it is necessary to resort to the customary norms of wage payment—that is, to the distribution of life's goods in proportion to the quantity and quality of individual labor.

Marx named this first stage of the new society "the lowest stage of communism," in distinction from the highest, where together with the last phantoms of want material inequality will disappear. In this sense socialism and communism are frequently contrasted as the lower and higher stages of the new society. "We have not yet, of course, *complete* communism," reads the present official Soviet doctrine, "but we have already achieved socialism—that is, the *lowest* stage of communism." In proof of this, they adduce the dominance of the state trusts in industry, the collective farms in agriculture, the state and cooperative enterprises in commerce. At first glance this gives a complete correspondence with the a priori—and therefore hypothetical—scheme of Marx. But it is exactly for the Marxist that this question is not exhausted by a consideration of forms of property regardless of the achieved productivity of labor. By the lowest stage of communism Marx meant, at any rate, a society which from the very beginning stands higher in its economic development than the most advanced capitalism. Theoretically such a conception is flawless, for taken *on a world scale* communism, even in its first incipient stage, means a higher level of development than that of bourgeois society. Moreover, Marx expected that the Frenchman would begin the social revolution, the German continue it, the Englishman finish it; and as to the Russian, Marx left him far in the rear. But this conceptual order was upset by the facts. Whoever tries now mechanically to apply the universal historic conception of Marx to the particular case of the Soviet Union at the given stage of its development, will be entangled at once in hopeless contradictions.

Russia was not the strongest, but the weakest link in the chain of capitalism. The present Soviet Union does not stand above the world level of economy, but is only trying to catch up to the capitalist countries. If Marx called that society which was to be formed upon the basis of a socialization of the productive forces of the most advanced capitalism of its epoch, the lowest stage of communism, then this designation obviously does not apply to the Soviet Union, which is still today considerably poorer in technique, culture and the good things of life than the capitalist countries. It would be truer, therefore, to name the present Soviet regime in all its contradictoriness, not a socialist regime, but a *preparatory* regime *transitional* from capitalism to socialism. . . .

. . . Experience revealed what theory was unable clearly to foresee. If for the defense of socialized property against bourgeois counterrevolution a "state of armed workers" was fully adequate, it was a very different matter to regulate inequalities in the sphere of consumption. Those deprived of property are not inclined to create and defend it. The majority cannot concern itself with the privileges of the minority. For the defense of "bourgeois law" the workers' state was compelled to create a "bourgeois" type of instrument— that is, the same old gendarme, although in a new uniform.

We have thus taken the first step toward understanding the fundamental contradiction between Bolshevik program and Soviet reality. If the state does not die away, but grows more and more despotic, if the plenipotentiaries of the working class become bureaucratized, and the bureaucracy rises above the new society, this is not for some secondary reasons like the psychological relics of the past, and so forth, but is a result of the iron necessity to give birth to and support a privileged minority so long as it is impossible to guarantee genuine equality.

The tendencies of bureaucratism, which strangles the workers' movement in capitalist countries, would everywhere show themselves even after a proletarian revolution. But it is perfectly obvious that the poorer the society which issues from a revolution, the sterner and more naked would be the expression of this "law," the more crude would be the forms assumed by bureaucratism, and the more dangerous would it become for socialist development. The Soviet state is prevented not only from dying away, but even from freeing itself of the bureaucratic parasite, not by the "relics" of former ruling classes, as declares the naked police doctrine of Stalin, for these relics are powerless in themselves. It is prevented by immeasurably mightier factors, such as material want, cultural backwardness and the resulting dominance of "bourgeois law" in what most immediately and sharply touches every human being, the business of insuring his personal existence. . . .

While the growth of industry and the bringing of agriculture into the sphere of state planning vastly complicates the tasks of leadership, bringing to the front the problem of *quality,* bureaucratism destroys the creative initiative and the feeling of responsibility without which there is not, and cannot be, qualitative progress. The ulcers of bureaucratism are perhaps not so obvious in the big industries, but they are devouring, together with the cooperatives, the light and food-producing industries, the collective farms, the small local industries—that is, all those branches of economy which stand nearest to the people.

The progressive role of the Soviet bureaucracy coincides with the period devoted to introducing into the Soviet Union the most important elements of capitalist technique. The rough work of borrowing, imitating, transplanting and grafting, was accomplished on the bases laid down by the revolution. There was, thus far, no question of any new word in the sphere of technique, science or art. It is possible to build gigantic factories according to a ready-made Western pattern by bureaucratic command—although, to be sure, at triple the normal cost. But the farther you go, the more the economy runs into the problem of quality, which slips out of the hands of a bureaucracy like a shadow. The Soviet products are as though branded with the gray label of indifference. Under a nationalized economy, *quality* demands a democracy of producers and consumers, freedom of criticism and initiative—conditions incompatible with a totalitarian regime of fear, lies and flattery.

Behind the question of quality stands a more complicated and grandiose problem which may be comprised in the concept of *independent, technical* and *cultural creation.* The ancient philosopher said that strife is the father of all things. No new values can be created where a free conflict of ideas is impossible. To be sure, a revolutionary dictatorship means by its very essence strict limitations of freedom. But for that very reason epochs of revolution have never been directly favorable to cultural creation: they have only cleared the arena for it. The dictatorship of the proletariat opens a wider scope to human genius the more it ceases to be a dictatorship. The socialist culture will flourish only in proportion to the dying away of the state. In that simple and unshakable historic law is contained the death sentence of the present political regime in the Soviet Union. Soviet democracy is not the demand of an abstract policy, still less an abstract moral. It has become a life-and-death need of the country.

If the new state had no other interests than the interests of society, the dying away of the function of compulsion would gradually acquire a painless character. But the state is not pure spirit. Specific functions have created specific organs. The bureaucracy taken as a whole is concerned not so much with its function as with the tribute which this function brings in. The commanding caste tries to strengthen and perpetuate the organs of compulsion. To make sure of its power and income, it spares nothing and nobody. The more the course of development goes against it, the more ruthless it becomes toward the advanced elements of the population. Like the Catholic Church it has put forward the dogma of infallibility in the period of its decline, but it has raised it to a height of which the Roman pope never dreamed.

The increasingly insistent deification of Stalin is, with all its elements of caricature, a necessary element of the regime. The bureaucracy has need of an inviolable super-arbiter, a first consul if not an emperor, and it raises upon its shoulders him who best responds to its claim for lordship. That "strength of character" of the leader which so enraptures the literary dilettantes of the West, is in reality the sum total of the collective pressure of a caste which will stop at nothing in defense of its position. Each one of them at his post is thinking: *l'état—c'est moi.* In Stalin each one easily finds himself. But Stalin also finds in each one a small part of his own spirit. Stalin is the personification of the bureaucracy. That is the substance of his political personality.

Caesarism, or its bourgeois form, Bonapartism, enters the scene in those moments of history when the sharp struggle of two camps raises the state power, so to speak, above the nation, and guarantees it, in appearance, a complete independence of classes—in reality, only the freedom necessary for a defense of the privileged. The Stalin regime, rising above a politically atomized society, resting upon a police and officers' corps, and allowing of no control whatever, is obviously a variation of Bonapartism—a Bonapartism of a new type not before seen in history.

Caesarism arose upon the basis of a slave society shaken by inward strife. Bonapartism is one of the political weapons of the capitalist regime in its critical period. Stalinism is a variety of the same system, but upon the basis of a workers' state torn by the antagonism between an organized and armed soviet aristocracy and the unarmed toiling masses.

As history testifies, Bonapartism gets along admirably with a universal, and even a secret, ballot. The democratic ritual of Bonapartism is the *plebiscite.* From time to time, the question is presented to the citizens: *for* or *against* the leader? And the voter feels the barrel of a revolver between his shoulders. Since the time of Napoleon III, who now seems a provincial dilettante, this technique has received an extraordinary development. The new Soviet constitution which establishes *Bonapartism on a plebiscite basis* is the veritable crown of the system.

In the last analysis, Soviet Bonapartism owes its birth to the belatedness of the world revolution. But in the capitalist countries the same cause gave rise to fascism. We thus arrive at the conclusion, unexpected at first glance, but in reality inevitable, that the crushing of Soviet democracy by an all-powerful bureaucracy and the extermination of bourgeois democracy by fascism were produced by one and the same cause: the dilatoriness of the world proletariat in solving the problems set for it by history. Stalinism and fascism, in spite of a deep difference in social foundations, are symmetrical phenomena. In many of their features they show a deadly similarity. A victorious revolutionary movement in Europe would immediately shake not only fascism, but Soviet Bonapartism. In turning its back to the international revolution, the Stalinist bureaucracy was, from its own point of view, right. It was merely obeying the voice of self-preservation.

Carl J. Friedrich and Zbigniew K. Brzezinski

THE MODEL OF TOTALITARIANISM

In the broader perspective of the twentieth-century world the regime fashioned by Stalin invites comparison with other revolutionary dictatorships whether of the Left or of the Right. The concept of "totalitarianism" as the common denominator of these systems, and as the essence of Stalinism, has nowhere been more vigorously argued than in the work of the political

Reprinted by permission of the publishers from Carl J. Friedrich and Zbigniew K. Brzezinski, *Totalitarian Dictatorship and Autocracy,* rev. ed. (Cambridge, Mass.: Harvard University Press, 1965), pp. 17–18, 21–22, 31–37, 219–222, 369, 372–374. Copyright © 1956, 1965 by the President and Fellows of Harvard College.

scientists Carl Friedrich (b. 1901) of Harvard and Zbigniew Brzezinski (b. 1928) of Columbia University, Totalitarian Dictatorship and Autocracy.

It is our contention . . . that totalitarian dictatorship is historically an innovation and *sui generis.* It is also our conclusion from all the facts available to us that Fascist and Communist totalitarian dictatorships are basically alike, or at any rate more nearly like each other than like any other system of government, including earlier forms of autocracy. These two theses are closely linked and must be examined together. . . . What is really the specific difference, the innovation of the totalitarian regimes, is the organization and methods developed and employed with the aid of modern technical devices in an effort to resuscitate such total control in the service of an ideologically motivated movement, dedicated to the total destruction and reconstruction of a mass society. It seems therefore highly desirable to use the term "totalism" to distinguish the much more general phenomenon just sketched, as has recently been proposed by a careful analyst of the methods of Chinese thought control.

Totalitarian dictatorship then emerges as a system of rule for realizing totalist intentions under modern political and technical conditions, as a novel type of autocracy. The declared intention of creating a "new man," according to numerous reports, has had significant results where the regime has lasted long enough, as in Russia. In the view of one leading authority, "the most appealing traits of the Russians—their naturalness and candor—have suffered most." He considers this a "profound and apparently permanent transformation," and an "astonishing" one. In short, the effort at total control, while not achieving such control, has highly significant human effects.

The Fascist and Communist systems evolved in response to a series of grave crises—they are forms of crisis government. Even so, there is no reason to conclude that the existing totalitarian systems will disappear as a result of internal evolution, though there can be no doubt that they are undergoing continuous changes. The two totalitarian governments that have perished thus far have done so as the result of wars with outside powers, but this does not mean that the Soviet Union, Communist China, or any of the others necessarily will become involved in war. We do not presuppose that totalitarian societies are fixed and static entities but, on the contrary, that they have undergone and continue to undergo a steady evolution, presumably involving both growth and deterioration. . . .

The basic features or traits that we suggest as generally recognized to be common to totalitarian dictatorships are six in number. The "syndrome," or pattern of interrelated traits, of the totalitarian dictatorship consists of an ideology, a single party typically led by one man, a terroristic police, a communications monopoly, a weapons monopoly, and a centrally directed economy. Of these, the last two are also found in constitutional systems: socialist Britain had a centrally directed economy, and all modern states possess a weapons monopoly. Whether these latter suggest a "trend" toward totalitarianism is a question that will be discussed in our last chapter. These six basic features, which we think constitute the distinctive pattern or model of totalitarian dictatorship, form a cluster of traits, intertwined and mutually supporting each other, as is usual in "organic" systems. They should therefore not be considered in isolation or be made the focal point of comparisons, such as "Caesar developed a terroristic secret police, therefore he was the first totalitarian dictator," or "the Catholic Church has practiced ideological thought control, therefore . . ."

The totalitarian dictatorships all possess the following:

1. An elaborate ideology, consisting of an official body of doctrine covering all vital aspects of man's existence to which everyone living in that society is supposed to adhere, at least passively; this ideology is characteristically focused and projected toward a perfect final state of mankind—that is to say, it contains a chiliastic claim, based upon a radical rejection of the existing society with conquest of the world for the new one.

2. A single mass party typically led by one man, the "dictator," and consisting of a relatively small percentage of the total population (up to 10 percent) of men and women, a hard core of them passionately and unquestioningly dedicated to the ideology and prepared to assist in every way in promoting its general acceptance, such a party being hierarchically, oligar-

chically organized and typically either superior to, or completely intertwined with, the governmental bureaucracy.

3. A system of terror, whether physical or psychic, effected through party and secret-police control, supporting but also supervising the party for its leaders, and characteristically directed not only against demonstrable "enemies" of the regime, but against more or less arbitrarily selected classes of the population; the terror whether of the secret police or of party-directed social pressure systematically exploits modern science, and more especially scientific psychology.

4. A technologically conditioned, near-complete monopoly of control, in the hands of the party and of the government, of all means of effective mass communication, such as the press, radio, and motion pictures.

5. A similarly technologically conditioned, near-complete monopoly of the effective use of all weapons of armed combat.

6. A central control and direction of the entire economy through the bureaucratic coordination of formerly independent corporate entities, typically including most other associations and group activities. . . .

*   *   *

The idea of totalitarian dictatorship suggests that a dictator who possesses "absolute power" is placed at the head. Although this notion is pretty generally assumed to be correct and is the basis of much political discussion and policy, there have been all along sharp challenges to it; it has been variously argued that the party rather than the dictator in the Soviet Union wields the ultimate power, or that a smaller party organ, like the Politburo, has the final say. Similarly, it has been claimed that the power of Hitler or Mussolini was merely derivative, that "big business" or "the generals" were actually in charge, and that Hitler and his entourage were merely the tools of some such group. While the dictatorships of Mussolini, Hitler, and Stalin were still intact, there existed no scientifically reliable way of resolving this question, since the testimony of one observer stood flatly opposed to that of another. We are now in a more fortunate position. The documentary evidence clearly shows that Stalin, Hitler, and Mussolini were the actual rulers of their countries. Their views were decisive and the power they wielded was "absolute" in a degree perhaps more complete than ever before. And yet this documentary material likewise shows these men to have stood in a curious relationship of interdependence with their parties—a problem we shall return to further on. As for Stalin, the famous revelations of Khrushchev sought to distinguish between his personal autocracy and the leadership of the Communist Party. Even before, the large body of material which skillful research in a number of centers had developed suggested that Stalin's position, particularly after the great purges of the thirties, was decisive. A number of participants in foreign-policy conferences with Soviet leaders had already noted that only Stalin was able to undertake immediately, and without consultation, far-reaching commitments. Furthermore, the personal relationships among Soviet leaders, to the extent that they were apparent at such meetings, also indicated clearly that Stalin's will could not be questioned. A similar situation seems now to have developed in Communist China. Although our sources are quite inadequate, various indications suggest that Mao Tse-tung has achieved a personal predominance comparable to that of Stalin and Hitler. His position is enhanced by the long years during which he led the Communist Party in its struggle to survive. However, his style of leadership is different. Part of his power is based upon his capacity to inspire intellectual respect. The "thought of Mao" is a source of much of the personality cult surrounding his overweening position. It has served as a cloak by providing, in Mao's own words, the collective-leadership principle as the key to Chinese leadership.

The partisan political flavor of the argument over collective leadership and the cult of personality have obscured the basic process by which a collective leadership in any hierarchic and highly bureaucratized organization is apt to yield to the dominance and eventual rule of a single man. This monocratic tendency was noted by Max Weber and has been fairly generally recognized since. The skill and hypocrisy with which both Stalin and Khrushchev, not to mention Mao, proclaimed the "principle" of collective leadership, while each allowed the cult of their own person to go forward, can most readily be explained in terms of a desire to prevent the rise of any rivals who could always, like Kao by Mao, be accused of this "cult."

A very interesting and to some extent deviant case is presented by Fidel Castro. Basically inclined toward accepting the cult of personality and lacking any effective party organization, he found that he could not handle the Cuban situation, as it evolved toward totalitarianism. Hence a "union" with the Communist Party (PSP) had to be worked out, and Castro became its secretary general, thus providing himself with that minimum of organized support that is quintessential to the totalitarian dictator. The predominance of such leaders does not destroy the decisive importance of the party, which becomes manifest at a succession crisis. But it is nonetheless very real. Stalin's autocracy was in fact made the key point of attack in Khrushchev's speech at the Twentieth Party Congress, in which he developed his points condemning Stalin's cult of personality and attendant autocratic behavior. The argument has since been toned down somewhat.

It might be objected, however, that, had Stalin's position indeed been so predominant, the transition of power following his death would not have been quite so smooth. This objection is not valid, for the transition was not altogether smooth. Stalin's death led to the attempted Beria coup, which manifested itself first of all in seizures of power by the Beria elements at the republic levels. It was only through decisive action at the very top, and almost at the last moment, that the party Presidium succeeded in decapitating the conspiracy. The fact that the Soviet system continued to maintain itself after Stalin's death is significant; however, it points not to the lesser significance of Stalin but to the higher degree of institutionalization of the totalitarian system through an elaborate bureaucratic network, operated at the top by the political lieutenants of the leader. It is they who pull the levers while the dictator calls the signals. When the dictator is gone, they are the ones to whom falls the power.

"Party ideological unity is the spiritual basis of personal dictatorship," one experienced Communist has written. Ideological unity as such will be discussed later. However, it is necessary at this point in our analysis of the dictator to speak briefly of his ideological leadership. Unlike military dictators in the past, but like certain types of primitive chieftains, the totalitarian dictator is both ruler and high priest. He interprets authoritatively the doctrines upon which the movement rests. Stalin and Mao, Mussolini and Hitler, and even Tito and other lesser lights have claimed this paramount function, and their independence is both manifested and made effective in the degree of such hierocratic authority. It also embodies the dictator's ascendancy over his lieutenants. In a firmly knit totalitarian set-up, the dictator and his direct subordinates are united in ideological outlook; a breach in this unity signalizes that a particular lieutenant is no longer acceptable. "The continuance of ideological unity in the party is an unmistakable sign of the maintenance of personal dictatorship, or the dictatorship of a small number of oligarchs who temporarily work together or maintain a balance of power," Djilas has written, and at the same time pointed out that this enforced unity signifies the culmination of the totalitarian evolution. It provides the underpinning for the bureaucratization.

Bureaucracy has an inherent trend toward concentration of power at the top, that is to say, toward monocratic leadership, in Weber's familiar term. Totalitarian dictatorship provides striking evidence. Yet the bureaucratization does not exist at the outset, and hence the question of how the totalitarian dictator acquires his power must first be considered. Obviously he does not, like autocrats in the past, get it by blood descent, military conquest, and the like. Lenin, Mussolini, and Hitler first acquired their power through initiating and leading a movement and wielding its effective controls. By fashioning the movement's ideology, the leader provides it with the mainstay of its cohesion. It is in keeping with the "laws of politics" that such leaders become the dictators, once the government is seized. Having thus achieved absolute control of the "state," they then proceed to consolidate their power—a process in which they are aided and abetted by their immediate entourage, who expect to derive considerable benefits for themselves from the situation. There is nothing unusual about this process; it closely resembles that in a constitutional democracy, when the victor at the polls takes over the actual government. But under totalitarianism there now is no alternative; for the movement's ideological commitment is absolute, and its utopian thrust calls for the total marshaling of all available power resources. Hence the "structure of government" has no real significance because the power of decision is completely concentrated in a single leader. Any constitution is merely a disguise by which a "democratic" framework is being suggested, a kind of window dressing or facade for the totalitarian reality. Such groups in the Soviet Union and the several satellites as appear in the garb of "legislative bodies" are essentially there to acclaim the decisions made. Similarly, the judicial machinery, devoid of independence, is actually part and parcel of the administrative and bureaucratic hierarchy. The very shapelessness of the vast bureaucratic machinery is part of the technique of manipulating the absolute power that the dictator and his lieutenants have at their disposal. It is therefore necessary to say something more about these subleaders.

The significant role played in the totalitarian system by the political lieutenants of the dictator makes their coming and going a barometer of the system. These lieutenants wield the levers of control that hold the totalitarian dictatorship together and are instrumental in maintaining the dictator in power. There was a time when the crucial function of the subleaders tended to be ignored. The important role they played after Stalin's death changed all that. Sigmund Neumann's path-finding analysis has been amply borne out. He pointed to the four decisive elements that "make up the composite structure of the leader's henchmen." These were the bureaucratic, feudal, democratic, and militant.

The bureaucratic element, in the light of Neumann's analysis, is the outstanding feature of the totalitarian leadership elite. Modern totalitarianism, unlike the more traditional dictatorships, is a highly bureaucratized system of power. Without this complex bureaucracy the character of the system could not be maintained. The party organization in particular is a hierarchically structured political machine, and the efficient bureaucrat is indispensable to the dictator. In this respect the similarity between such men as Bormann and Malenkov is more than striking—they were both capable and efficient bureaucrats who held their positions by virtue not only of administrative ability but, and in totalitarianism this is more important, "because they were found worthy of the supreme leader's confidence."

The second characteristic of these lieutenants is their feudal type of leadership. It is perhaps not historically accurate to speak of the development of localized autocratic spheres of power as "feudal." But there can be little doubt that such was the implication of the "principle of leadership" (*Führerprinzip*) in Germany, as exemplified by the *Gauleiter* [district leader]. Comparable results can be observed in the conduct of *obkom* [provincial committee] secretaries. Such "feudal" vassals are not only territorially distributed; they also operate on the top levels, manipulating important levers of power such as the secret police. Himmler, Bocchini [Mussolini's police chief], and Beria were thus responsible for making sure that no internal challenge to the dictator's power arose, and the dictator at all times had to make certain that such posts were filled by men of unquestionable loyalty. In return, all of these lieutenants shared in the system of spoils, and every effort was made to develop in them a vested interest in the continued maintenance of the dictator's power.

The third feature of this leadership, called "democratic" by Neumann, might more properly be designated as "oligarchic." It is not subject to the democratic process of selection and election. The fact that these lieutenants "had better not play the boss within the circle of their associates" does not produce anything like the equality of opportunity characteristic of democratically organized groups. Rather, they display the typical propensities of oligarchic groups, with their intense personal rivalries, their highly developed sense of informal rank, and their esprit de corps toward outsiders. It is this feature of the group of subleaders which found expression in the sloganized principle of "collective leadership." It is risky to become too popular within such a group, as long as the sense of collective anonymity prevails; yet it is precisely behind this facade of anonymity that the emergent dictator, be it Stalin or Khrushchev, organizes his ascendancy toward predominance within and above the group. But even after such a position has been achieved by one, the rest of the group retains the oligarchic characteristics. It might be added, though it is a separate issue, that the jealousy of the dictator of any ascendant rival helps to maintain the oligarchic character of the group of lieutenants. He can fall back upon it as a safeguard against any challenge to his power and prestige.

The final element, growing out of the revolutionary character of

totalitarianism, is the militancy of the leadership. The political lieutenants must act as subleaders in the struggle for achieving the
totalitarian society. Each in his particular sphere, the totalitarian
lieutenant will attempt to break down all resistance to the ideological goals of the regime. He will lead the "battle of the grain," strive
for higher accomplishments in "socialist competition," or encourage
women to increase the number of their pregnancies. And it is
through his militancy, through such battles, be they local or national, that the political lieutenants are weaned, steeled, and promoted. In short, the lieutenants have the function of providing the
dictator with effective links to the vast apparatus of party and
government. They also share in manipulating patronage and thereby
in controlling political and administrative advancement. The resulting clienteles are likely to play a significant part in intraparty power
struggles. . . .

*   *   *

A totalitarian economy is centrally directed and controlled. In
order to execute such central direction and control, there must be a
plan. Since the economy has become one gigantic business enterprise, and yet an enterprise that does not get its incentives from the
desire to make a profit or from the consumers' needs and demands
as expressed in the price system, its managers must be told what
measuring rods to apply in determining what should be produced and
consequently how the scarce resources available for production
should be distributed among the various branches of productive
capacity. The slogan, "Guns rather than butter," is only a crude
indication of the vast range of decisions that have to be made. The
decisions involved in arriving at such a plan are the most basic ones
a totalitarian regime has to make. Hence the five-year plans of the
Soviet Union, the four-year plan of Hitler Germany, the two- and
five-year plans of the Soviet zone, and so on, are focal points of
political interest.

Characteristically, in a totalitarian dictatorship, the leader or
leaders at the top, men like Stalin, Hitler, or the party Presidium,
make the basic decision in terms of which the plan is organized.
This basic decision was, in the case of the Soviet Union, originally
that of industrializing the country; in the case of Nazi Germany,

that of eliminating unemployment and preparing for war; in the case of China, again industrialization but combined with "land reform"; and in the case of the Soviet zone of Germany right after the war, that of providing the large-scale reparations the Soviet Union demanded. These goals of planning are the most decisive issues to be settled in a totalitarian society. In the Soviet Union, more particularly, in recent years there has been extended discussion in the top hierarchy over the question of mass consumption and consumer-goods production, as against heavy machinery, basic raw materials, and preparation for war, including nuclear arms and space control. Any such basic decision provides the starting point for a system of priorities which can be utilized in allocating raw materials to the different sectors of the producing economy.

It is the absence of such a basic decision, and indeed the impossibility of securing it, that has led many to conclude that constitutional democracy is incompatible with planning or, to put it in another way, that any attempt to enter upon planning constitutes in effect the "road to serfdom." This is true if planning is understood in a total sense, and it is often so defined, especially by economists. Actually, the planning process in a democracy is very different; it is contingent upon the democratic process as a whole, whose outstanding characteristic is the continuous review of all decisions, including basic ones, by the people and their representatives. In autocratic systems, and more especially in totalitarian dictatorships, the purpose of the plan is determined by the autocratic leader or ruler(s). The plan implements their basic decision. It is carried forward by a bureaucracy that has the full backing of the terrorist and propagandist apparatus of the totalitarian dictatorship. Consequently, little if anything can be learned from the planning procedures of totalitarian societies when one comes to assess the planning process in democratic societies. But an understanding of the process, of course, is essential for an understanding of totalitarian dictatorship. The great advantage that a fixed goal or purpose possesses from a technical standpoint is counterbalanced by the disadvantage of not having the planning respond to the reactions of those affected by it. Which is the greater disadvantage only experience can tell.

A comparison of the planning experience in totalitarian dictatorship brings to light some very striking contrasts, as well as similarities. In the Soviet Union, a number of years passed before the central importance of planning was fully realized. Prior to the revolution, Russia had been far behind Western Europe in industrial development. Marx and Engels, believing that the Communist revolution would take place in an advanced industrial society, had not been at all concerned with the problem of planning industrialization. They had stressed control of the economy rather than industrialization and an increase in production; indeed, the revolution was to be the culminating point of capitalist development, after the means of production had, through trusts and vast monopolies, become concentrated in "fewer and fewer hands," and this shrinking group of exploiters would be confronted by an ever larger proletariat. All that the proletariat would have to do, consequently, would be to take over and run this gigantic productive apparatus. But in Russia, over 80 percent of the population lived on farms at the time of the revolution, and a similar situation prevailed in China at the time of the Communist seizure of power. This fact was so completely at variance with Marxist anticipations that novel approaches had to be developed.

This question preoccupied the Bolsheviks throughout the twenties and gave the post-Lenin struggles for power a marked theoretical flavor. A number of solutions were advocated, ranging from left-wing emphasis on immediate efforts to increase industrial output, even at high cost and considerable coercion (expounded most clearly by Preobrazhensky), to right-wing advocacy of adjustment to a temporary, transitional capitalist stage (as, for instance, voiced by Bukharin). The ensuing policy, based more on the requirements of the situation than on ideological dogma, was one of compromise and postponement of the radical solution.

Planning, accordingly, developed slowly and modestly. On February 22, 1921, the State Planning Commission (Gosplan) was set up. It was charged with the task of working out an over-all state economic plan and preparing the technical and managerial staffs and know-how necessary to its success. In fact, however, Gosplan's immediate tasks were more restricted and concentrated on developing the state plan for the electrification of Russia (Goelro), which had been prepared some time earlier and was to serve as the basis for further centralized planning. In addition, Gosplan assumed control over some sectors of the economy which were subject to crises and vital to economic survival, like the railroads. Thus, despite the very broad grant of planning and controlling power, Gosplan during the NEP period did not vitally influence the Russian economy. It concerned itself rather with collecting statistics, studying existing economic trends, and laying the groundwork for an over-all plan.

The big impetus to centralized state planning came with the political decision to launch a large-scale industrialization and agricultural collectivization program. The era of the five-year plans began in 1928. Since then Soviet economic life has been revolving around these broad, comprehensive schemes, developed in keeping with the policy decisions of the leadership by the planners of Gosplan. Indeed, the inauguration of the First Five-Year Plan can be described as the breakthrough of full-scale totalitarianism in Russia. Stalin's program, borrowed in many respects from the left-wing Opposition, notably Preobrazhensky, inevitably encountered resistance from the established peasantry and other groups. As resistance mounted, so did coercion. As pointed out earlier, the totalitarian regime matured in the struggle to put into practice what theory and ideology had preached. The launching of the plan, however, despite certain initial failures (camouflaged by scapegoat trials of engineers), fired to a great extent the imagination of the more youthful party members and raised the sagging morale of the whole party. Its results, therefore, were politically important. . . .

As we just noted and indicated at various points in our study, the totalitarian dictatorship emerges some time after the seizure of power by the leaders of the movement that had developed in support of the ideology. The typical sequence is therefore that of ideology, movement, party, government. The point of time when the totalitarian government emerges may be reasonably fixed and delimited. It is that point at which the leadership sees itself obliged to employ open and legally unadorned violence for maintaining itself, particularly against internal opposition due to ideological dissensions arising from within the movement's own ranks. In the Soviet Union, this point is marked by Stalin's liquidation of his erstwhile colleagues in the USSR's leadership and more particularly by his epochal struggle with Trotsky. In Nazi Germany, Hitler's bloody suppression of

Röhm and his followers represents this totalitarian breakthrough. In Mussolini's Italy, the Matteotti murder and its sequel are one turning point, the attack on Abyssinia another. In China, the totalitarian government seems to have emerged full-fledged because a kind of totalitarian government had been in existence for a considerable time prior to the Communists' establishment of control over all of China, namely, in those provinces they had controlled and developed in their war against the Japanese. But even here the true totalitarian maturation may be fixed at the point where there occurred the purge of competitors to Mao Tse-tung's absolute dictatorial control. . . .

We saw when discussing ideology that the radical change which a totalitarian ideology demands necessarily occasions adjustments and adaptations to reality and its situational needs when an attempt is made to "realize" such an ideology. The totalitarian revolutionaries are, in this respect, not in a different situation from other revolutionaries before them. In the French Revolution especially, the violent controversies over the ideological "meaning" of the revolution led to the terror. But since the ideology lacked that pseudo-scientific ingredient which has enabled the Communist and Fascist totalitarians to insist on the "mercilessness of the dialectics" (Stalin) and on "ice-cold reasoning" (Hitler), a totalitarian ideology did not develop. Whether its exponents are convinced or merely pretending, the totalitarian ideology requires that it be maintained even while it is being adapted to changing situations. It is at this point, when the inner contradictions of the totalitarian ideology become evident, that the totalitarian breakthrough occurs. For since there is no longer any possibility of maintaining the ideology on logical grounds, total violence must be deployed in order to do so. The mounting fierceness of the conflict between the Soviet Union and Communist China, in which tongue-lashing vituperation accompanies armed conflict at the border, appears to be a projection of this inherent "dialectic."

In the development of the party, which is closely related to this ideological evolution, an analogous process takes place. In the original movement, when the party fights for success against a hostile environment, all the leader's authority, or a very large part of it, springs from the genuine comradeship that unites the effective participants. After the seizure of power, this relationship continues to operate, but—owing to the new situation confronting the leadership with the vast tasks of a government that aspires to accomplish a total change and reconstruction of society—it becomes rapidly bureaucratized. Not only the government but the party is transformed into an increasingly formalized hierarchy. As is always the case, the *apparat* acquires its own weight and operates according to the inherent laws of large-scale bureaucracy. At the point of the totalitarian breakthrough, purges of former comrades reveal that it is no longer a matter of "belonging" to a movement, but one of submitting to autocratic decisions that determine a person's right to belong to the party.

Hand in hand with this development goes that of the secret police. In order to become the instrument of total terror that the police system is in a matured totalitarian system, it must acquire the requisite knowledge of its human material, the potential victims of its terroristic activity. Centers of possible opposition have to be identified, techniques of espionage and counterespionage have to be developed, courts and similar judicial procedures of a nontotalitarian past have to be subjected to effective control. Experience and observation show that the time required for these tasks varies. In the Soviet Union, the tsarist secret police provided a ready starting point, and hence the Soviets got under way in this field with the Cheka very quickly. The entrenched liberal tradition in Italy allowed the Fascists to organize the secret police effectively only in 1926, and it took another two years before it really took hold of the situation. The National Socialists, although anxious to clamp down at once, did not perfect their secret-police system until well after the blood purge of 1934, when Himmler first emerged as the key figure in the manipulation of this essential totalitarian tool.

It is at the point at which the totalitarian breakthrough occurs that the total planning of the economy imposes itself. For it is then that the social life of the society has become so largely disorganized that nothing short of central direction will do. In a sense, this total planning is the sign of the culmination of the process. In Soviet Russia, it is the year 1928, in Nazi Germany 1936, while in Italy it comes with the instituting of the corporative set-up in 1934 (it had been grandiloquently announced in 1930), though perhaps the Ethiopian war was even more decisive. It is not important in this connec-

tion to what the planning effort amounts; it will vary in inverse proportion to the economic autonomy of the country. The crucial point is
that this total planning imposes itself as the inescapable consequence of the totalitarian evolution in the economic field.

Roy A. Medvedev

THE SOCIAL BASIS OF STALINISM

*One of the most remarkable texts to come out of the Soviet Union in recent
years is the vast historical narrative and analysis by the philosopher Roy
Medvedev (b. 1925, twin brother of the biologist Zhores Medvedev),* Let
History Judge. *In this work, suppressed inside the USSR though it hardly
questions the premises of Communist rule, Medvedev brings a remarkable
degree of insight, objectivity, and archival knowledge to bear on the
problem of how and why Stalinism came to be.*

We have analyzed Stalin's motives, but there is a more important
problem than his motives: How did he manage to carry out his criminal plans? Why did the party allow so much bloodshed? Why was it
powerless to resist such enormous tyranny? What was inevitable in
this frightful tragedy, and what was accidental?

   Marx and Engels often referred to the possibility, or even the
inevitability, that a revolution would degenerate if it occurred in
objective historical conditions that did not correspond to its ideals.
Plekhanov also wrote about this several times in his arguments with
the populists. If the people, Plekhanov declared, approach power
when social conditions are not ripe, then "the revolution may result
in a political monstrosity, such as the ancient Chinese or Peruvian
empires, that is, in a tsarist despotism renovated with a communist
lining." Some of the people we have talked to see prophetic truth in
these words. They try to prove that it was inevitable, in the Soviet
Union of the twenties, for the likes of Stalin to come to power. "If

From *Let History Judge*, by Roy A. Medvedev, edited by David Joravsky and Georges
Haupt, trans. by Colleen Taylor. Copyright © 1971 by Alfred A. Knopf, Inc. Reprinted by permission of the publisher, and Macmillan London and Basingstoke.

Lenin had lived another ten or twenty years," the writer V. K——
told me, "he would certainly have been pushed out of the leadership
by the 'new' people, whose embodiment was Stalin." "The system
created after the October Revolution," said the economist I. P——,

> *was based on outright dictatorship, on force, to an excessive degree.*
> *Disregard of some elementary rules of democracy and lawful order in-*
> *evitably had to degenerate into Stalinist dictatorship. It was Stalin who*
> *fitted this system ideally, and he only developed its latent possibilities*
> *to the maximum degree. The whole trouble was that a socialist revolution*
> *in a country like Russia was premature. In a country that has not gone*
> *through a period of bourgeois democracy, where the people in its*
> *majority is illiterate and uncultivated, in such a country genuine socialism*
> *cannot be built without the support of other more developed socialist*
> *countries. By prematurely destroying all the old forms of social life, the*
> *Bolsheviks raised up and turned loose such forces as must inevitably*
> *have led to some form of Stalinism. Approximately the same thing is*
> *happening today in China and in Albania.*

This point of view, as applied to the Soviet Union, is one-sided
and incorrect. If the political and social system created after the
October Revolution inevitably engendered Stalinism, if history offered
no other possibilities of development, if everything was strictly determined, then the October Revolution must also have been determined
by the monstrous system of Russian autocracy. Thus we must conclude that the October and the February revolutions were not at all
premature or accidental events. In other words, to explain Stalinism
we have to return to earlier and earlier epochs of Russian history,
very likely to the Tartar yoke. But that would be wrong; it would be
a historical justification of Stalinism, not a condemnation.

I proceed from the assumption that different possibilities of development exist in almost every political system and situation. The
triumph of one of these possibilities depends not only on objective
factors and conditions, but also on many subjective ones, and some
of these factors are clearly accidental. . . .

To speak of various historical possibilities is to raise the question
of probability: which line of development was more likely, which
less? The question requires concrete investigation of all the objective and subjective circumstances in a given situation. Even a small

possibility of a given line of development does not constitute an impossibility.

From this point of view Stalinism was by no means inevitable, despite the defects in the political conception that the Bolsheviks brought to the October Revolution and despite the defects of the new Soviet regime. It also had many merits. The contest between various alternatives began under Lenin and was bound to grow more intense. But if he had not died in 1924, the victory of genuinely democratic and socialist tendencies would have been more probable than the victory of Stalinism.

Many foreign thinkers, including Communists, have studied this problem. After the Twentieth Congress, in March 1956, Palmiro Togliatti published his famous objection to a simple inversion of the cult of personality: blaming all evil on the superman who had formerly been praised for all good. Togliatti suggested that the system called Stalinist was to be explained by reference to the development of bureaucracy, deriving from prerevolutionary conditions and from the desperate need for centralized power during the Civil War. This context favored the rise of Stalin, a typical *apparatchik.*

Some Yugoslav thinkers have given much stronger expression to the view that the Stalinist system was foreordained. Veljko Korać, for example, follows a vivid characterization of the system—"a specific etatism and bureaucratic despotism, . . . the heartless destroying of men in the name of an ineffable mystique of the future, making politics and ideology absolute and the negation of human freedom" —with a declaration of its inevitability. He finds its causes in the occurrence of a socialist revolution without an adequate material base. The working class was too small, the culture of the masses too low. The poor peasants were an effective force for overthrowing the old order but not for self-disciplined participation in building the new. Political organization, power, compensated for the weakness of the material base.

Technical advance only enforced the ascendancy of this technobureau-cracy. . . . In the name of Marxism, Stalin distorted Marx's ideas into a closed system of dogmas making of himself the sole and absolute interpreter of those dogmas. . . . [The Stalinist system did] not come into being as a historical caprice or as the pressure of tradition of tsarist despotism. Instead it appears as a necessary accompaniment to the development of an undeveloped country which has undergone socialist revolution before industrial revolution.

Korać gives an accurate description of the historical and economic background, but he is wrong in his main argument. It is hard to agree that in an economically backward country, the socialist transformation of society and the industrial revolution must be accompanied by mass violence. Too many historical facts simply will not fit in this simplistic scheme. Were not the hundreds of thousands of officials destroyed in 1937–1938 the best promoters of industrialization? Why did the machine of state power, which they had created together with Stalin, have to fall on them?

The mass repression of the thirties cannot be attributed to any significant resistance to Stalin's arbitrary rule. The sad fact is that Stalin's drive for unlimited personal dictatorship encountered no significant resistance, even from the officials who were being struck down. The only forces opposed to Stalin were those which had been enemies of the proletarian dictatorship all along—world imperialism and the White Russian émigrés. Feeble resistance came from the remnants of the Socialist Revolutionary and Menshevik parties, which considered themselves the defenders of democratic socialism. The comparative ease of Stalin's usurpation of power cannot be explained by theories such as Korac's.

It was an historical accident that Stalin, the embodiment of all the worst elements in the Russian revolutionary movement, came to power after Lenin, the embodiment of all that was best. Nevertheless, the possibility of such an accident, and the factors that transformed the possibility into reality, demand close analysis. For the party must not only condemn Stalin's crimes; it must also eliminate the conditions that facilitated them.

We are also confronted with another question: How did Stalin manage to preserve not only power but also the respect and trust of the majority of Soviet people? It is an unavoidable fact that Stalin never relied on force alone. Throughout the period of his one-man rule he was popular. The longer this tyrant ruled the USSR, cold-bloodedly destroying millions of people, the greater seems to have been the dedication to him, even the love, of the majority of people.

These sentiments reached their peak in the last years of his life. When he died in March 1953, the grief of hundreds of millions, both in the Soviet Union and around the world, was quite sincere.

How can this unprecedented historical paradox be explained? We must look more closely at the conditions that facilitated Stalin's usurpation of power.

One condition that made it easy for Stalin to bend the party to his will was the hugely inflated cult of his personality. "For 1938," Ilya Ehrenburg writes in his memoirs,

> it is more correct simply to use the word "cult" in its original religious meaning. In the minds of millions Stalin was transformed into a mythical demigod; everyone trembled as they said his name, believed that he alone could save the Soviet Union from invasion and collapse.

The deification of Stalin justified in advance everything he did, everything connected with his name, including new crimes and abuses of power. All the achievements and virtues of socialism were embodied in him. The activism of other leaders was paralyzed. Not conscious discipline but blind faith in Stalin was required. Like every cult, this one tended to transform the Communist Party into an ecclesiastical organization, with a sharp distinction between ordinary people and leader-priests headed by their infallible pope. The gulf between the people and Stalin was not only deepened but idealized. The business of state in the Kremlin became as remote and incomprehensible for the unconsecrated as the affairs of the gods on Olympus.

The social consciousness of the people took on elements of religious psychology: illusions, autosuggestion, the inability to think critically, intolerance towards dissidents, and fanaticism. Perceptions of reality were distorted. It was difficult, for example, to believe the terrible crimes charged against the old Bolsheviks, but it was even more difficult to think that Stalin was engaged in a monstrous provocation to destroy his former friends and comrades. . . .

There was a two-way cause-and-effect relationship between the terror and the cult of Stalin's personality. Stalin's cult facilitated his usurpation of power and the destruction of inconvenient people, while his crimes, supported by the *apparat* and also by the deluded masses, extended and reinforced the cult of personality.

The cult of personality does not automatically lead to mass repression—much depends on the personality. Not every deified emperor or pharaoh was a cruel and bloodthirsty despot. But the most dangerous feature of the cult of a personality is that the leader's conduct depends not on laws or other rules but on his own arbitrary will. The party and state cannot endure such a situation, when the only guarantee of a citizen's rights, indeed of his very life, is the personal qualities of the leader.

It was fairly easy for Stalin to convince the Soviet people that he was fighting real enemies, destroying traitors. The dimensions of the fraud helped it to succeed. The charges were piled so high and repeated so often that deliberate deception seemed absolutely impossible. Goebbels said that the bigger the lie and the more often it is repeated, the easier it is for people to believe it. Stalin was a master of this cynical technique. . . .

Today some Communists call Stalin a counterrevolutionary, and consider the events of 1936–1938 a counterrevolutionary coup. This is an oversimplification. It is true that Stalin did more than slow down the development of socialist society. (The widespread cliché about this "slowing down" [*tormozhenie*] is also an oversimplification.) In many respects he and his accomplices turned the revolution backward, forcing the Soviet Union to diverge far from the principles of socialism proclaimed by the October Revolution. In these respects he can properly be called a counterrevolutionary. But he also continued to rely on the masses, which was the chief peculiarity of Stalin's actions and the ultimate determinant of his success.

Napoleon discarded revolutionary phraseology as he secured one-man rule. Stalin behaved differently, masking his usurpation of power in ultrarevolutionary phrases. Thus he secured the support of the people, without which even such a despot as Stalin could not have maintained himself. And he was obliged to refrain from complete subversion of socialist principles.

Of course Stalin's usurpation of power may be considered a coup d'état. But it was a very unusual coup. It was accomplished "from above," gradually, over the course of many years, with revolutionary slogans. It destroyed some of the gains of the revolution, but not all. . . .

The reconstruction of the Cheka-GPU went on for some years in the first half of the twenties. But it slowed down after the deaths of Lenin and Dzerzhinsky; indeed things started moving in an entirely different direction. The GPU gradually began to resume the functions that were appropriate only for a period of civil war. Under pressure from Stalin, a punitive organization reappeared, with the right to put people in jail and camps, to exile them to remote places, and later even to shoot them without any juridical procedure, simply as an administrative act.

V. R. Menzhinsky, the head of the GPU after Dzerzhinsky's death, was an old party official, but he lacked the influence and authority of his predecessor. He decried the tendency to make the GPU a private power base of a few individuals, but he was sick for long periods and rarely interfered in the day-to-day activity of the GPU. The real boss by the late twenties was his deputy, Yagoda, who was strongly influenced by Stalin. Those two introduced a new style of work, for example, in the seizure of valuables from Nepmen by massive use of violence and arbitrary force. The GPU was also assigned the job of transporting hundreds of thousands of kulak families to the eastern districts of the country. The families of "subkulaks" were also deported, which meant that hundreds of thousands of middle and even poor peasants were arbitrarily exiled. Collective farms were ravaged by the GPU during the grain-procurement campaigns of 1932 and 1933. It also administered the lawless repression of the intelligentsia in the late twenties and early thirties. At that time some GPU employees, with tacit support from above, were already creating false evidence, forcing prisoners to sign false interrogation records, inventing all kinds of plots and organizations, and beating and torturing prisoners. When one victim, M. P. Yakubovich, told his interrogator at the end of 1930 that such methods would have been impossible under Dzerzhinsky, the interrogator laughed: "You've found someone to remember! Dzerzhinsky—that's a bygone stage in our revolution."

This lawlessness was cloaked with various ideological arguments about the class struggle. But even if it was justified against members of hostile classes—and it was not—it still corrupted many employees of the punitive organs, developing the worst sides of their characters, training them to blind obedience and callousness toward the citizenry.

At the same time the GPU's influence and members grew; as early as 1926 Stalin signed a directive to increase its staff. For a while men of principle held on, but especially after 1934, when Menzhinsky died and Yagoda took his place, Stalin's unlimited control of the agency was assured.

After the murder of Kirov and especially after the first "open" political trial in 1936, a purge left adventurers and careerists in most of the leading positions within the NKVD. It is important to note that in 1937 the pay of NKVD employees was approximately quadrupled. Previously a relatively low pay scale had hindered recruitment; after 1937 the NKVD scale was higher than that of any other government agency. NKVD employees were also given the best apartments, rest homes, and hospitals. They were awarded medals and orders for success in their activities. And, in the latter half of the thirties, their numbers were so swollen as to become a whole army, with divisions and regiments, with hundreds of thousands of security workers and tens of thousands of officers. NKVD agencies were set up not only in every *oblast* center but in each city, even in each *raion* center. Special sections were organized in every large enterprise, in many middle-size ones, in railroad stations, in major organizations and educational institutions. Parks, theaters, libraries—almost all gathering places (even smoking rooms) came under constant observation by special NKVD operatives. An enormous network of informers and stool pigeons was created in almost every institution, including prisons and camps.

Dossiers were kept on tens of millions of people. In addition to the sections that kept tabs on Kadets[1] and monarchists, S-R's[2] and Mensheviks, and other counterrevolutionary parties, in the Fourth Administration (*upravlenie*) of the NKVD a section was created for the Communist Party. It maintained surveillance over all party organizations, including the Central Committee. All *raikom* [district committee], *gorkom* [city committee], and *obkom* [province committee] secretaries were confirmed in their posts only after the approval of

[1] Members of the moderate Constitutional Democratic Party, suppressed in 1918. —Ed.
[2] Members of the peasant-based Socialist Revolutionary Party, suppressed in 1918. —Ed.

the appropriate NKVD agencies. Special sections were also created to watch the Chekists themselves, and a special section to watch the special sections. The Chekists were trained to believe that Chekist discipline was higher than party discipline. "First of all," they were told, "you are a Chekist, and only then a Communist." Their training included learning the history of the trade, beginning with a very serious study of the Inquisition.

Stalin paid special attention to surveillance of his closest aides, the members of the Politburo. "The secret service of the sovereign," says an ancient Indian book, "must keep its eyes on all the high officials, directors of affairs, friends and relatives of the ruler, and likewise his rivals." Stalin watched every step of his closest aides, using the notorious law "On the protection of chiefs," enacted after Kirov's murder. While Stalin personally selected his own bodyguard and completely controlled it, the protection of other leaders was entrusted to the NKVD. They could not go anywhere without the knowledge of their guard, could not receive any visitor without a check by the guard, and so on.

Although the powers of the NKVD were unusually great in the early thirties, in the summer of 1936 the Central Committee passed a resolution, on Stalin's proposal, to grant the NKVD extraordinary powers for one year—to destroy completely the "enemies of the people." At the June plenum of the Central Committee in 1937 these powers were extended for an indefinite period. The result was a significant extension of the NKVD's juridical functions.

Before the repression began, a Special Assembly (*Osoboe Soveshchanie*) was set up in the NKVD. Then throughout the country an extensive system of *troiki,* or three-man boards, was created, subordinated to this Special Assembly. These illegal bodies, whose very existence violated the constitution of the USSR, independently examined political cases and passed sentences, completely ignoring the norms of jurisprudence. In this way the punitive organs were exempt from any control by the party and the soviets, the courts, and the procurator. Even when the NKVD investigators passed cases to the procurator's office or the courts, the latter obediently handed down verdicts prepared beforehand by the agency. In many *oblasti* procurators issued back-dated sanctions several months after an arrest, or even signed blank forms on which the NKVD subsequently entered any names they wanted. In reality, only one man had the right to control the activity of the punitive organs—Stalin himself.

Why did Stalin need this huge punitive *apparat,* the like of which history has never seen? No external danger justified its existence. It was directed primarily against "internal enemies," and it had to find these "enemies," if only to justify its own existence. Thus the ever-expanding punitive agencies, besides being a firm foundation of the Stalinist regime, became a source of never-ending repression. . . .

Anti-Communist literature includes many attempts to connect Stalin's cult and his totalitarian regime not only with peculiarities of Russian historical development—such explanations contain some truth—but also with peculiarities of the "Russian soul," and with the Russian school of eschatological thought that is supposed to be akin to Communist ideology. Such pseudoscholarly inventions must be firmly rejected. Nevertheless, it is mistaken to attribute the ideology and the practice of Stalinism only to the international position of the USSR or to Stalin's personal faults. It is necessary to analyze the social progresses that began after the revolution; the struggle between the proletariat and the bourgeoisie, and also the struggle between proletarian and petty-bourgeois, bureaucratic elements in the party.

Marxist sociology includes in the petty bourgeoisie not only peasants, artisans, small merchants, and the lower sections of office workers and professionals, but also déclassé elements at the bottom of society, a large group in Russia and many other backward capitalist countries. They are people who have lost or have never had even petty property; they have not grown accustomed to labor in capitalist industry, and live by occasional earnings. Despite great diversity, all these petty-bourgeois strata have certain features in common, including political instability and vacillation, a degree of anarchism, and small-proprietor individualism. Because of their political instability they may provide the reserves for revolution or for reaction, depending on circumstances. Unsettled and disoriented after World War I, they supported Fascist dictatorship in some European countries. The disintegration of the tsarist regime made such people revolutionary in Russia, and the Bolshevik Party drew many to its side. Several million proletarians were victorious only because they were supported by tens of millions of semiproletarian and petty-bourgeois elements.

It would be naive to think that these petty-bourgeois elements would be completely transformed by several years of revolutionary struggle. It would also be a mistake to idealize the proletariat, picturing it as purely virtuous. Not only in Russia but also in many industrially developed countries, a good part of the proletariat were infected with petty-bourgeois faults and moods. Thus petty-bourgeois elements penetrated workers' parties everywhere long before the October Revolution. That provided the social basis for the bureaucratic degeneration of party functionaries, especially at the peak of the hierarchy, in the parties of the Second International before World War I. The Bolshevik Party was not, of course, immune to this process.

Most professional revolutionaries, who formed the backbone of the party, derived from the intelligentsia, the lesser gentry, or the civil service. These origins did not prevent most of these people from merging heart and soul with the proletariat, directing it, and thus becoming proletarian revolutionaries in the full sense of the word. But by no means all the leaders of the party experienced a complete transformation. Besides, the revolution and the Civil War produced many new leaders who had not gone through the rigorous school of political and ideological struggle. The fact that many individuals who were not true proletarian revolutionaries became leaders of the party after Lenin's death was therefore not an accident or the result of insufficient wisdom. It was the natural result of a proletarian revolution in a petty-bourgeois country like Russia.

Lenin was well aware that one of the most difficult problems of the proletarian revolution was to safeguard the party cadres from bureaucratic degeneration. The transformation of the Bolshevik Party from an underground organization to a ruling party would greatly increase petty-bourgeois and careerist tendencies among old party members and also bring into the party a host of petty-bourgeois and careerist elements that had previously been outside. "A situation is gradually taking shape," said a resolution adopted in 1921 on Lenin's initiative, "in which one can 'rise in the world,' make a career for himself, get a bit of power, only by entering the service of the Soviet regime." In his last writings Lenin concentrated on this very problem: the interrelationships between petty-bourgeois and proletarian elements in the state, and the bureaucratization of the *apparat*. "We call ours," he wrote in 1922,

> an *apparat* that is in fact still thoroughly alien to us and constitutes a bourgeois and tsarist mishmash. . . . There is no doubt that the insignificant percent of Soviet and Sovietized workers will drown in this sea of chauvinistic Great Russian riffraff like a fly in milk.

It is only fair to note that degeneration of a part of the revolutionary cadres is the rule in every revolution, which attracts many people who are motivated by a desire for power or wealth. The French Revolution brought to the fore not only leaders like Marat but also careerists like Fouché, Talleyrand, Barras, and Tallien. The October Revolution did not escape the same fate. "Every revolution has its scum," Lenin said once. "Why should we be any exception?" Stalin combined the character traits and ideology of a proletarian revolutionary with those of a petty-bourgeois revolutionary inclined toward degeneration via careerism. But the problem did not lie in Stalin alone.

In the late twenties and early thirties, degeneration affected a significant part of the Leninist old guard. Great progress in socialist construction and great power turned their heads. The increasing centralization of power among the leaders was not matched by an increase of control from below. Communist conceit (*komchvanstvo*), susceptibility to adulation and flattery, began to develop among once modest revolutionaries. In their way of life many of them moved too far away from the people. Mikhail Razumov provides a typical example. A party member since 1912, secretary of the Tartar and then of the Irkutsk *obkom,* he turned into a magnate before the startled eyes of Evgeniya Ginzburg, who records the process in her memoirs. As late as 1930 he occupied one room in a communal apartment. A year later he was building a "Tartar Livadia," including a separate cottage for himself. In 1933, when Tartary was awarded the Order of Lenin for success in the *kolkhoz* movement, portraits of the "First Brigadier of Tartary" were carried through the city with singing. At an agricultural exhibition his portraits were done in mosaics of various crops, ranging from oats to lentils. Similar stories are told about Betal Kalmykov, the leader of the Kabardin-Balkar Bolsheviks; about E. P. Berzin, the head of Dalstroi; about Ya. S. Ganetsky and many old-guard Leninists.

There were various causes of such developments. It is easy to understand why Vyshinsky, a Menshevik turncoat, persecuted first his former Menshevik comrades and later his new comrades, the Bolsheviks. He was an unprincipled, cowardly politician, hungry for power. It is harder to understand why staunch Bolsheviks like Yaroslavsky or Kalinin broke and began to help Stalin. Personalities aside, the general rule is apparent. It was not the struggle with the autocracy, not jail or exile, that were the real tests for revolutionaries. Much harder was the test of power, at a time when the party acquired almost unlimited power.

In most cases bureaucratic degeneration did not reach the criminal extremes that it did in such individuals as Postyshev and Krylenko [commissioner of justice]. Usually "playing the magnate" was not accompanied by deeper moral and political degeneration. Razumov, Kalmykov, Berzin, and thousands of other such leaders retained their basic loyalty to the party. But they gradually acquired the habit of commanding, of administration by fiat, ignoring the opinion of the masses. Cut off from the people, they lost the ability to criticize Stalin's behavior and the cult of his personality; on the contrary, they became increasingly dependent on him. Their change in life style aroused dissatisfaction among workers and rank-and-file party members. One result was the relative ease with which Stalin subsequently destroyed such people, for he could picture their fall as a result of the people's struggle against corrupt bureaucrats. In the same way Mao Tse-tung calls for struggle against "people who are in power but are moving along the capitalist road." Stalin's demagogy is widely used in contemporary China.

The purge did not make the party more proletarian or bring its leaders closer to the people. To be sure, many young and subjectively honorable leaders appeared in the higher circles of the party at the end of the thirties. But in the conditions of the cult many of them became magnates even faster than their predecessors. The large number of unprincipled careerists who got into leading party posts did not need to degenerate, for they had never had such qualities as devotion to the people, a desire to serve the workers, and commitment to Marxist ideas. The old Leninist guard were an obstruction to these petty-bourgeois careerists, who therefore supported Stalin's crimes and later constituted the strongest bastion of support for his personal dictatorship. To be sure, the concrete circumstances of the Soviet system obliged these petty-bourgeois careerist elements to endorse Communism, if only in words. They learned to hide their true goals, their actual code of ethics, behind ostentatious revolutionism. Thus a whole stratum of "Soviet" philistines and "party" bourgeois took shape. They had some purely external features of socialist ideology and morality, and therefore differed from traditional bourgeois philistines only by their greater sanctimoniousness and hypocrisy. The influence of such petty-bourgeois elements was especially strong in the union republics where the proletarian nucleus was not as great and the revolution not as profound as in the basic regions of Russia.

It must also be recognized that the people who rose during the mass repression, who made careers out of persecutions and arrests, were hardly interested in democracy. Uncontrolled dictatorship suited these Stalinists, since they could retain their power only under such conditions. Timeserving and complete submission to those above was their defense against those beneath, the people. Thus the cult of personality was not only a religious and ideological phenomenon; it also had a well-defined class content. It was based on the petty-bourgeois, bureaucratic degeneration of some cadres and the extensive penetration of petty-bourgeois and careerist elements into the *apparat.* Stalin was not simply a dictator, he stood at the peak of a whole system of smaller dictators; he was the head bureaucrat over hundreds of thousands of smaller bureaucrats.

This is not to say that there was a complete transformation of the party between Lenin's lifetime, when the bureaucratic elements were held in check, and Stalin's time, when they won total ascendancy. Some observers hold to this view, though it is oversimplified to the point of extreme distortion.

The extremely complex social processes of the period after Lenin's death are still waiting for genuine scientific analysis. But certain trends are apparent. On the one hand, the working class, growing with exceptional speed, absorbed the déclassé urban bourgeoisie and petty bourgeoisie, and the millions of peasant migrants to the cities. In 1929–1935 new workers of these types were several times more numerous than the working class of the past. This rapid change in the composition of the working class was bound to affect its psychology and behavior, and also the composition of the party, facilitating the degeneration of some parts of the *apparat*. At the same time, an opposite process was taking place: the transformation of the semiproletarian masses by the propagation of Marxist-Leninist ideology and socialist morality. It was in those years that profound social processes prepared the way for an ultimate strengthening of socialist elements. Though many people acquired only the externals of socialist ideology and morality, many more internalized them. In 1922 Lenin could write that the party was still not sufficiently proletarian, the state *apparat* still a bourgeois mishmash. Ten years later the picture had substantially changed. The *apparat* was working much better, coping with more complex problems.

The socialist transformation proceeded in various ways at various levels. The spread of proletarian ideology and Communist morality was most intensive at the end of the twenties and the beginning of the thirties, and on the lower levels of society. During the mass repression that followed, all levels of the *apparat* suffered losses, but the lower suffered less than the upper. Thus, even during the years of the cult, genuinely proletarian Marxist-Leninist cadres and a basically Soviet atmosphere prevailed in most of the primary party organizations. Of course, they too were affected by the distortions connected with the cult. Many wrong and even criminal directives were carried out by primary party organizations. But there was far more sincere error and honest self-deception on these lower levels than there was higher up. Most of the directives sent down to them breathed the spirit of revolution, speaking about struggle with the enemies of socialism, concern for individuals, the need to advance the cause of Marxism-Leninism. The lower organizations, failing to see the gap between the words and deeds of Stalin and his associates, tried to adhere to political and moral norms that many people at the top did not consider binding on themselves.

On the middle levels of the party and the state, the situation was more complex. Many devoted Leninists rose to take the places vacated by repression, but too many replacements were unprincipled careerists and bureaucrats. At the top levels there was a reverse process: Leninist elements were replaced by people whom we today call Stalinists. Even at the top, however, there was some variety. One group, the Stalinist guard, were cruel, unprincipled men, ready to destroy anything that blocked their way to power. Some used physical methods directly, a type that Stalin preferred for the top leadership of the punitive agencies. Others were criminals of a new type, who did their bloody deeds at a desk, jailing, torturing, and shooting by pen and telephone. But these people were incapable of managing a big, complex governmental organism. Therefore Stalin had to bring into the leadership people of another type. They were comparatively young leaders who supported Stalin in almost everything but were not informed of many of his crimes. Though they shared certain characteristic faults of Stalin's entourage, they also wanted to serve the people. They lacked sufficient political experience to analyze and rectify the tragic events of the Stalinist period, and some of them perished toward the end of it. But others survived, and after Stalin's death gave varying degrees of support to the struggle against the cult.

Petty-bourgeois elements and degenerated cadres were not the only source of Stalin's strength. In the proletarian core of the party there were conservative tendencies that facilitated the rise and extended hegemony of Stalinism. The proletariat is the most advanced class of bourgeois society, but it would be a mistake to idealize it. In it, as in every class, there are people who are incapable of thinking. Such individuals are not attracted by the creative approach that is the essence of Marxism-Leninism. On the contrary, they prefer dogmatism, which frees them from the need to think. Instead of studying ever-changing reality, they use a few fixed rules. Although a revolution represents the victory of the new ideas over old dogmas, in time a revolution becomes overgrown with its own dogmas. In tsarist Russia such a tendency was more likely than usual, for a great many revolutionaries lacked education. In such a situation Stalin's ability to make extreme simplifications of complex ideas was not the least factor in his rise. Many party cadres knew Leninism only in its schematic Stalinist exposition, unaware that Stalin was vulgarizing Marxism-Leninism, transforming it from a developing, creative doctrine into a peculiar religion. Thus it would be wrong to attribute every mistake of former revolutionaries to petty bourgeois degeneration. Many of their errors were due not to a change in their earlier views but to an incapacity for change, in other words, to dogmatism.

Many dedicated revolutionaries, indifferent to personal advantage, were nevertheless incapable of carrying the revolution forward when a new stage required new methods. More and more their thought revealed the doctrinaire rigidity, the sectarian ossification, that Thomas Mann had in mind when he spoke of "revolutionary conservatism." Many leaders who excelled in the period of civil war were not effective at building a new society. Accustomed to resolving most conflicts by force of arms, they were incapable of complex educational work, which had to be the chief method in the new period. Instead of learning, some Communists even began to boast of their lack of education. "We never finished *gimnazii* [secondary schools], but we are governing *gubernii* [provinces]," a well-known Bolshevik declared at the end of the twenties, and his audience applauded. When such people ran into difficulties, they often turned into simple executors of orders from above, valuing blind discipline most of all. The closed mind, the refusal to think independently, was the epistemological basis of the cult of personality. It was not only degenerates and careerists who supported the cult; there were also sincere believers, genuinely convinced that everything they did was necessary for the revolution. They believed in the political trials of 1936–1938, they believed that the class struggle was intensifying, they believed in the necessity of repression. They became participants—and many of them subsequently became victims.

Suggestions for Further Reading

The quantity of literature on Soviet Russia and Communism now available in English is staggering. No attempt will be made here to cover it all, but only to suggest to the interested reader some of the most important works dealing with Soviet Russia in general or with particular topics that are especially relevant to the subject of the Stalin Revolution.

The books represented in this selection of readings, all fundamental sources for understanding Soviet Russia and its crucial development in the 1930s, are not repeated in the following list.

For a general view of Soviet history as a whole, there are numerous good texts. Particular mention may be made of Donald Treadgold, *Twentieth Century Russia,* 3rd ed. (Chicago, 1972); Basil Dmytryshyn, *USSR: A Concise History,* 2d ed. (New York, 1971), which includes a useful documentary appendix; and the interesting Menshevik interpretation by Raphael Abramovich, *The Soviet Revolution* (New York, 1962). A comprehensive history centering on the Communist Party as an institution is Leonard Schapiro, *The Communist Party of the Soviet Union,* rev. ed. (New York, 1970). Julian Steinberg, ed., *Verdict of Three Decades* (New York, 1950), is a useful collection of critical articles on various stages of Soviet history. The best official Soviet history, long out of print, is N. N. Popov, *Outline History of the Communist Party of the Soviet Union,* 2 vols. (New York, 1934). A selection of key statements by the Soviet leaders is contained in Robert V. Daniels, ed., *A Documentary History of Communism* (New York, 1960). For a general discussion of Communism in Russia and internationally see Robert V. Daniels, *The Nature of Communism* (New York, 1962).

The best study of the Russian historical and economic background as it relates to the Stalin Revolution is Sir John Maynard, *Russia in Flux* (New York, 1948). Various pertinent historical articles are contained in Ernest J. Simmons, ed., *Continuity and Change in Russian and Soviet Thought* (Cambridge, Mass., 1955) and in Cyril Black, ed., *The Transformation of Russian Society* (Cambridge, Mass., 1960). The more immediate background of Russia from 1917 to 1929 has been studied exhaustively by E. H. Carr in his *History of Soviet Russia,* 9 vols. in 11 parts to date (New York, 1951–). Stalin's personal background up to the revolution is recounted in Bertram D. Wolfe, *Three Who Made a Revolution* (New York, 1948) and in Edward Ellis Smith, *The Young Stalin* (New York, 1967). Trotsky's *Stalin: An Appraisal of the Man and his Influence* (New York, 1946) was compiled from notes left by the author when he was killed. The official edition of Stalin's *Collected Works* is available in translation, 13 vols. (Moscow, 1952–1955). T. H. Rigby, *Stalin* (Englewood Cliffs, N.J., 1966) brings together selections of Stalin's writing and comments on him by various contemporaries and historians.

The political events of the 1920s and 1930s are dealt with in detail in Boris Souvarine, *Stalin: A Critical Survey of Bolshevism* (London and New York, 1939) and in Bertram Wolfe, *Khrushchev and Stalin's Ghost* (New York, 1957). (The latter includes the full text of Khrushchev's 1956 secret speech and the text of Bukharin's controversial article of 1928, "Notes of an Economist.") The official hopes were stated by the then commissar of finance, G. F. Grinko (later purged), in *The Five-Year Plan of the Soviet Union* (New York, 1930), while the claims of progress were recorded in collected speeches of the top Soviet leaders—J. V. Stalin et al., *From the First to the Second Five-Year Plan* (New York, 1934), and *Socialism Victorious* (New York, 1935). An inside view of Soviet politics during the Stalin Revolution is afforded by the one-time Communist party official Abdurakhman Avtorkhanov, in *Stalin and the Soviet Communist Party* (New York, 1959).

There are many journalistic and autobiographical accounts of the Stalin Revolution. Representative books by correspondents are Walter Duranty, *Duranty Reports Russia* (New York and London, 1934); William Henry Chamberlin, *Russia's Iron Age* (Boston, 1937); Maurice Hindus, *Humanity Uprooted* (New York, 1930); and Hindus, *Red Bread* (New York, 1931). John Scott's *Behind the Urals* (Boston, 1943) is the account of an American who worked in the Soviet steel industry. Victor Kravchenko, *I Chose Freedom* (New York, 1946), is the personal account (apparently somewhat fictionalized) of a Soviet engineer who later defected to the West.

The background of socialist and Communist theory is ably presented in Carl Landauer, *European Socialism,* 2 vols. (Berkeley, California, 1959) and in John Plamenatz, *German Marxism and Russian Communism* (London and New York, 1954). A recent official interpretation of Marxism-Leninism is expounded in O. V. Kuusinen et al., *Fundamentals of Marxism-Leninism* (Moscow, 1961). Stalin's ideology is investigated in Robert C. Tucker, *The Soviet Political Mind* (New York, 1963). Certain theoretical implications of the Stalin Revolution are pursued in Robert V. Daniels, "Towards a Definition of Soviet Socialism," *New Politics* 1, no. 4 (1962): 111–118.

The development of the Soviet government before, during, and after the Stalin Revolution is treated in many texts, one of the best of which is Merle Fainsod, *How Russia Is Ruled* (Cambridge, Mass., 1953). W. W. Kulski, *The Soviet Regime,* 3rd ed. rev. and con. (Syracuse, 1954) is good on the political, economic, and legal institutions which emerged from the Stalin Revolution, and their impact on the Soviet citizen. A lengthy and favorable analysis of the Soviet system is contained in Sidney and Beatrice Webb, *Soviet Communism: A New Civilization?* 2 vols. (London, 1935). Soviet totalitarianism is analyzed in the symposium *Totalitarianism* edited by Carl J. Friedrich (Cambridge, Mass., 1954) and in the volume of the "Problems in European Civilization" series edited by Paul T. Mason, *Totalitarianism: Temporary Madness or Permanent Danger* (Boston, 1967). The events of the Great Purge are recounted in Zbigniew Brzezinski, *The Permanent Purge* (Cambridge, Mass., 1956) and in Robert Conquest, *The Great Terror* (New York, 1968). A broad comparative study is Samuel P. Huntington, ed., *Authoritarian Politics in Modern Society: The Dynamics of Established One-Party Systems* (New York, 1970).

The economic side of the Stalin Revolution and of Soviet Russia generally has been subjected to more careful analysis than any other aspect of these events. The principles of the Soviet economy are ably explained in Robert W. Campbell, *Soviet Economic Power,* rev. ed. (Cambridge, Mass., 1966), while the main economic institutions and problems are described in Marshall Goldman, *The Economy: Myth and Reality* (Englewood Cliffs, N.J., 1968). Alec Nove, *An Economic History of the USSR* (London, Allen Lane, 1969) is a good survey of the development of the Soviet economy; more specialized analyses are Naum Jasny, *Soviet Industrialization* (New York, 1961) and Abram Bergson, *The Real National Income of Soviet Russia since 1928* (Cambridge, Mass., 1961). The organization and problems of industry are treated in Joseph S. Berliner, *Factory and Manager in* the USSR (Cambridge, Mass., 1957), and in David Granick, *The Red Executive* (Garden City, New York, 1961). Arvid Brodersen, *The Soviet Worker* (New York, 1963) and Solomon Schwartz, *Labor in the Soviet Union* (New York, 1952), cover the history of labor conditions and organization. The collectivization of Soviet agriculture is appraised in Naum Jasny, *The Socialized Agriculture of the USSR* (Stanford, Calif., 1949) and Moshe Lewin, *Russian Peasants and Soviet Power* (Evanston, Ill., 1968). Ellsworth Raymond, *Soviet Economic Progress: Because of or in Spite of the Government?* (New York, 1957), is a useful collection of readings representing various judgments.

Two important books on the social policies of Stalin's government are Nicholas Timasheff, *The Great Retreat* (New York, 1946), and Max Eastman, *Stalin's Russia and the Crisis in Socialism* (New York, 1940). See also Robert V. Daniels, "Soviet Thought in the 1930's," *Indiana Slavic Studies* 1 (1956): 97–135. Particular areas of social and cultural policy have been treated in a series of good works in addition to those represented in the present volume: on law, Harold Berman, *Justice in the USSR,* rev. ed. (Cambridge, Mass., 1963); on religion, John S. Curtiss, *The Russian Church and the Soviet State* (Boston, 1953); on national attitudes and the minorities, Frederick Barghoorn, *Soviet Russian Nationalism* (New York, 1956); on philosophy and Marxist doctrine, Gustavo Wetter, *Dialectical Materialism* (New York, 1958) and Klaus Mehnert, *Stalin vs. Marx* (London, 1952); on history writing, Konstantin F. Shteppa, *Russian Historians and the Soviet State* (New Brunswick, N.J., 1962); on literature, Gleb Struve, *Soviet Russian Literature 1917–1950* (Norman, Oklahoma, 1951). The overall social impact of Stalinism is assessed in Barrington Moore, *Soviet Politics—The Dilemma of Power* (Cambridge, Mass., 1950); Francis B. Randall, *Stalin's Russia: An Historical Reconsideration* (New York, 1965); and in Alex Inkeles, *Social Change in Soviet Russia* (Cambridge, Mass., 1968).

1 2 3 4 5 6 7 8 9 10